The Author

Douglas Skelton is undoubtedly one of Scotland's most knowledgeable writers on crime. He is the author of nine books, seven of them in the true-crime genre. *Frightener: The Glasgow Ice Cream Wars*, co-written with Lisa Brownlie, campaigned to clear Thomas 'TC' Campbell and Joseph Steele of horrific, multiple murders that they did not commit. His other Scottish best-sellers include *Blood on the Thistle* and *A Time to Kill*.

Skelton has written for a variety of newspapers, including the *Evening Times, Sunday Mail, Daily Express* and *Daily Mail*. He has also appeared on television documentaries and news programmes, commenting on Scottish crime.

D0300430

SCOTLAND'S MOST WANTED

Douglas Skelton

Fort Publishing Ltd

First published in 2006 by Fort Publishing Ltd, Old Belmont House,
12 Robsland Avenue, Ayr, KA7 2RW

© Douglas Skelton, 2006

All rights reserved. No part of this publication may be reproduced, stored
in a retrieval system, or transmitted, in any form or by any means,
electronic, mechanical, photocopying, recording or otherwise, without the
prior permission of the publishers and copyright holders.

Douglas Skelton has asserted his right under the Copyright, Designs and
Patents Act 1988 to be identified as the author of this work.

Cover illustration by Andy Bridge

Graphics by Mark Blackadder

Typeset by Senga Fairgrieve

Printed by Bell and Bain Ltd, Glasgow

ISBN 10: 0-9547431-9-9
ISBN 13: 978-0-9547431-9-2

CONTENTS

ACKNOWLEDGEMENTS

Thanks to a number of people who have helped me in one way or another.

> To John Carroll for pointing out some useful websites.
> To Alan Muir of the *Scottish Sun* for the information.
> To Stephen Wilkie for the invaluable help and advice.
> To Katie and Alex Allison for the digs during research missions.
> To Gary McLaughlin and Elizabeth McLaughlin for the internet and computer assistance.
> To Eddie Murphy and Luan Johnston for the support.
> To Karin Stewart for always taking an interest.
> To Barbara Butler for the lodgings when the car was under the weather.

And very special thanks to Katie and Chris Bell and Mark Sweeney for being the Seventh Cavalry.

Douglas Skelton
Ayrshire, July 2006

INTRODUCTION

In twenty years of writing about crime I have met many criminals with violent pasts. There was little to set them apart from the so-called law-abiding members of society. They loved their kids and their pets. They liked a laugh. Most were loyal to friends and family. I have also been in the company of men convicted of murder, some of whom were actually guilty. Again, in the main, there were no outward signs that this person had, for whatever reason, snuffed out a life. There was no slavering, no raving, no baying at the moon.

Only one ever gave me the chills. He was a man who had both robbed and killed, not to mention hacked and slashed, through most of his adult life. When I entered a small, bare room in one of Scotland's tougher penal establishments, perhaps it was my imagination, but I felt something else was in there with us. Something older than both of us. Something with which he seemed comfortable but which scared the hell out of me. Of all the criminals I have met – and there have been more than a few – he was the only one who frightened me. He was a dangerous man – and he probably still is, although I hear he is living a quiet life these days. But back then, there was a menace that was evident in his manner and his voice and, more importantly, his eyes. Although he in no way threatened me overtly, I still felt nervous. God knows how I would have felt had he taken a sudden dislike to me. I was never so glad to get out of a room in my life.

I don't know what it was I felt in that small, bare room. Some people call it evil and although I don't particularly hold with that – it's too easy an explanation – it is as good a label as any. We are surrounded by evil. It is in mankind's nature, for although humanity's capacity to do good is vast, its propensity for doing ill is infinite.

The very word evil has been cheapened through overuse by newspapers. But what is it, exactly? According to my *Oxford Dictionary* it is something that is bad, harmful or wicked. And, although the dictionary does not tell us this, it never dies. This is true in a fictional, comic-book sense, and also in real life. According to Shakespeare, who seemed to know a thing or two about it, the evil that men do lives on after them. We remember the dark things far longer than the light. To an extent that is how things should be, for it has also been said that those who do not learn from history are doomed to repeat it. But as philosopher G. W. F. Hegel wrote, 'What experience and history teach is this – that people and governments never have learned anything from history, or acted on principles deduced from it.' In the half-century since the horrors of the Nazi concentration camps were revealed, we have had ethnic cleansing in Cambodia, the Balkan States and in Rwanda. And they were evil on an epic scale. Every day, in every country of the globe, there are smaller evils being perpetrated. Theft, rape, murder are all as old as Man himself. History, said James Joyce, is a nightmare from which I am trying to wake.

Yes, we can nurture and love and give and sacrifice. But we can also kill and maim and steal and cheat. All of us are capable of committing some kind of crime. It is only a question of degree. While honest, God-fearing folk deplore the actions of thieves, many of them will also obtain a new carpet for their home on the insurance by purposely spilling a pot of paint. They did not hold a gun on someone and take their wallet, or break into their home, but they are guilty of theft nonetheless. Bought a pirate DVD recently? That's theft, just as surely as walking into a store and slipping a real one into your pocket. And if theft is wrong, if it is *bad*, then it is, by definition, evil. And that means it's in all of us. But that is the duality of being, the good and the bad, the ying and the yang, the dark and the light.

Most of the people in this book are guilty of far more then petty theft. And most of them you would walk past in the street without a second glance. Certainly, for many (not all) of the subjects herein there must be something different going on in the mind. I was once asked what makes someone capable of committing murder and, not being a psychologist or even a criminologist, I answered in the only way I could, glibly and simplistically. We all have circuit breakers in the brain that shut down when the stimulus gets too overpowering. When our rage or hurt or frustration gets too much for us, when we want to lash out, the breaker kicks in and we calm down, give in or walk away from a situation. But there are those who don't have those circuit breakers, or they are faulty either for psychological or physiological reasons. When they are over-stimulated there is no life-saving shut down and they act, or react, as their darkest thoughts dictate.

Some, when the anger has subsided and conscience takes over, are haunted by their deeds and feel the need to confess. For others, the conscience trip switch is also missing or faulty, and they go on to commit more mayhem.

There are others in this book who were, for whatever reason, forced into committing an evil act or have been touched by one. There are people who have done something dreadful through personal trauma, desperation, fear, political beliefs or when their senses were impaired.

The thread that links every one of the cases that follow is that they grabbed headlines, sometimes across the globe but most often just here in Scotland. Their stories have, literally, been torn from the pages of your daily newspaper. As such, I have tried to retain as much journalistic detachment as possible but much of what you will read is disturbing. I have been writing about crime and murder for almost twenty years and even I was repulsed by a few of the guilty people I was asked to write about. For in them, I thought I detected that same thing I sensed in that small, spare, prison room.

Let's see if you feel it, too. For something wicked this way comes . . . .

Dr Paul Agutter
Love and the middle classes

There are certain criminal cases that capture the imagination of the public. Cases that are front-page news from the outset and to which acres of newsprint are devoted. Such a case occurred in Edinburgh in the mid-1990s. This one had everything: sex, greed, incredible coincidences and, to cap it all, the perpetrator and his victims were from the educated middle classes. The characters and the plot reminded many people of the popular television series *Morse*, in which the eponymous detective solves unlikely crimes in the genteel groves of academe. This was one that Inspector Morse would have relished.

It all started with a vermouth and tonic before dinner, an aperitif that almost proved fatal for Edinburgh woman Elizabeth Sharwood-Smith. She came very close to being the first victim of a bizarre plot that could very easily have gone horribly wrong. For the tonic she bought from a city supermarket was laced with a deadly poison, and she and her son were struck down. As luck would have it, Mrs Sharwood-Smith's husband, Geoffrey, was a consultant anaesthetist at Edinburgh Royal Infirmary and he suspected a toxin almost immediately. His fears were supported by houseguests who had arrived that fateful Wednesday night in August 1994: one was a chemist with expertise in hallucinogens; the other a neuropathologist.

The symptoms – including vomiting, dry mouth, hallucinations, a pulse thundering along at 140 beats per minute and temporary blindness – suggested atropine, a potentially lethal substance derived from nightshade berries. However, a search of the family garden revealed no such plant. Everyone believed the poisoning was an accident so no-one at this stage thought to check the two-litre bottle of tonic water. That changed two days later when, feeling a great deal better, Mrs Sharwood-Smith and her son drank more from the bottle. They fell ill immediately; Mrs Sharwood-Smith was paralysed and her son began to hallucinate.

This time, her husband realised the tonic was the source of the toxin and later had the remains analysed. The bottle was found to contain enough atropine to kill fifteen people. Someone had placed the doctored bottle on the supermarket shelves, in what appeared to be a deliberate attempt to commit mass murder.

In the meantime, mother and son were treated in hospital and, thankfully, survived. The supermarket, meanwhile, removed every bottle of tonic from its shelves. The damage had been done, however, because eventually eight people were rushed to hospital suffering from similar symptoms. The matter was now in the hands of the police and the hunt to track down the tonic-water poisoner began.

Normally, such a situation was linked to the extortion of large retail chains. Seven years before, the same Edinburgh supermarket was the focus of attention of a mysterious individual who called himself 'The Raven'. Jars of coleslaw and bottles of fruit juice appeared on the shelves with a home-made label warning that the contents had been mixed with weedkiller or ground glass. The Raven demanded £100,000 to stop what he was doing or next time there might be no tip-off. But the company refused to pay and The Raven gave up.

But this time there was no warning and no demand for money. Someone had deliberately poisoned some of those bottles of tonic. But who? And why? If it is true that there are only two basic motives for murder, love and money, and if the lack of a cash demand ruled out the latter, then the former must be the case. The first step would be to look at the families of the victims, and a prime suspect was revealed almost immediately.

One of the other victims was 39-year-old Alexandra Agutter, whose husband was Dr Paul Agutter, 48, a lecturer in biochemistry at the city's Napier University. It was he who had poured his wife a gin and tonic in their home in Athelstaneford, East Lothian. He had not taken a drink as he was due to drive their gardener home that evening. When his wife took ill he phoned the family doctor but only reached an answering machine. He left a message but took no further action, which was strike one against him.

A locum picked up the message and visited the Agutter home. She promptly called for an ambulance to rush the sick woman to hospital. The tainted glass was partly full and a paramedic took it to have the contents analysed, noticing as he did so that Dr Agutter's composure began to crack; strike two. Later, it was discovered that the glass contained a higher concentration of atropine than any of the other doctored bottles, which meant the poison could have been tipped directly into it. Agutter appeared to be outraged that someone had poisoned his wife, telling police, 'To tell you the truth, if I get hold of the blighter, I would kill him on the spot.'

But he had a great deal of knowledge at his fingertips about atropine and its properties, knowledge he revealed when he visited Mrs Sharwood-Smith at her home a few days after she had swallowed the poisoned tonic water. 'He knew how much you could put in before you could taste it,' she said, 'because it would have a bitter taste.' However, as a biochemist, he would have had such knowledge and, indeed, he was in the habit of dealing with the substance as part of his work. During the visit Agutter played the concerned husband, an act that Geoffrey Sharwood-Smith found less than convincing. 'It was chilling, because I just wondered if it might be him that was responsible.' he later said.

Police did follow other leads. These included a vague suggestion that a Gulf War veteran with a chip on his shoulder had carried out the attack and also a bogus claim of responsibility by a man who had earlier threatened to kill police officers by lacing bottles of Lucozade with weedkiller. Supermarket employees were also interviewed and one of them recalled a man who appeared to be concealing bottles underneath a green coat on the same day that Mrs Sharwood-Smith bought her tonic water: Wednesday, 24 August. After The Raven episode, the supermarket chain had invested in closed-circuit television at the store and police, armed with this information, scrutinised the tapes. They spotted the suspect and noted that he appeared to be wearing a purple top. He also looked surprisingly familiar.

Dr Paul Agutter was arrested at his home. Police, armed with a warrant, found the coat, purple top, a carrier bag with the supermarket's logo and a till receipt for Wednesday, 24 August 1994.

Strike three and out.

But what was Agutter's motive? At his trial in January 1995, a picture of his twisted state of mind came sharply into focus. He and his wife enjoyed an open marriage, apparently enjoying affairs with each other's knowledge. However, despite the freedom to form other relationships Paul Agutter wanted out. He had fallen in love with a former student and wanted to marry her. But could this really have been the motive for attempting to murder his wife? Alexandra Agutter knew about the liaison and was not in the least concerned: 'I did not consider it any of my business.' Indeed she had even met her husband's lover, who she thought was 'a perfectly nice person'. And, as the couple had discussed the possibility of an amicable divorce a few years before, it is hardly likely that she would have stood in his way if he had genuinely wanted to part from her.

The truth is that Paul Agutter may have been driven by his parlous financial situation. Despite earning a relatively high salary, he found it impossible to maintain the family home and the relationship with his lover. In consequence, he had run up substantial debts and had taken on two crippling loans. Just ten days before he poisoned his wife's drink – and while in a fit of depression – he told his general practitioner that he had come to a financial settlement with her but was paying too much.

The murder plot he hatched was based on the smokescreen principle. He laced seven bottles of tonic with atropine to make it look as if his wife was just one of many victims of a mad poisoner. The judge, Lord Morison, took a dim view of the plan: 'This was an evil and cunningly devised crime which was not only devised to bring about the death of your wife but also caused great alarm, danger and injury to the public.' The problem for Agutter was that the plan was badly executed; despite his undoubted intellectual credentials he failed to think it through. If he had taken his wife's glass after she drunk the poison, then washed it and laced it with a smaller amount of atropine it would have looked for all the world as if they were the innocent victims of a plot. It would also have helped if he had treated his wife's sudden illness with a degree of urgency.

Agutter proclaimed his innocence throughout the trial but the jury found him guilty and he was sentenced to twelve years in jail. An intelligent, even imaginative, man he may have been, but now his life was in tatters. He had been disgraced, he had lost his lover (who quite understandably jilted him during the trial) and now he was off to prison. He was often described as a model prisoner, helping illiterate convicts learn to read and write, but after his release a former inmate provided a different view. According to a press report in 2002, Agutter plotted revenge on his former girlfriend, having been stung by her selling her story to a national newspaper in the wake of his conviction. He knew his fellow prisoner at Glenochil jail was about to be released and wanted him to plant drugs in her car. But the con had no intention of carrying out the plan, telling the *Sunday Mail*, 'Agutter wanted revenge, pure and simple. He could not accept she had dumped him and then sold the story of their affair. He went on and on about it.'

Perhaps surprisingly, Agutter's wife stood by him throughout the trial, refusing to believe that he had tried to kill her. However, the couple were eventually divorced. After seven years inside Paul Agutter was freed and he retreated to his parents' home in Derbyshire. He managed to get a post as a part-time tutor at Manchester University, a development that provoked some controversy in the press. Strangely perhaps, the post involved lecturing on ethics.

Alison Anders and Royston Allen

'She was a sweetheart'

It all started as a joke, a bit of fun. The kind of throwaway remark you might make at the end of a good night out. But her light-hearted suggestion in an Aberdeen pub was to lead Alison Anders into planning the biggest fraud in Scottish criminal history. If it came off she and her associates would have got away with no less than £23 million. If the plot failed she faced, at best, life on the run, or, at worst, a long jail term.

Alison Anders was a highly-intelligent woman who had attended Dartford, a top public school in Kent, and she had gone on to university where she took an honours degree in archaeology. In 1987, at the age of thirty-one, she was a senior accounts officer with Britoil in Aberdeen, earning an annual salary of £11,500 a year. The job involved supervising the payment of invoices worth millions of pounds every month. Many would have considered this a prime position: although the salary was relatively modest, even in the 1980s, she was working for a blue-chip company in a growth industry. There must have been opportunities for advancement for a confident, educated and attractive young woman. But she was impatient and no doubt a little bored by a job that failed to tax her considerable abilities.

Her keen intellect had enabled her to spot a loophole in Britoil's money-transfer system and she immediately informed her bosses about the potential weakness. Perhaps surprisingly they seemed indifferent to her discovery and failed to plug the gap. Anders realised that anyone with knowledge of the system and a bit of gumption could divert payments away from their legitimate destination and into an account of their choosing. This knowledge undoubtedly played tricks with her mind; it would be an easy way to escape from the tedium of the office routine in Aberdeen and into a new life of luxury in more exotic climes.

But she needed a sounding-board, a kindred spirit, someone who would be receptive to the plan that was evolving in her head. She found one in her new lover, 36-year-old Royston Allen, a married company-director and former American footballer. Allen, who was tall, balding and bespectacled, had been hired by Britoil as a sub-contractor and had met Anders while working in her office. One night the couple were out playing bridge in a local pub. Anders had performed badly and let down her partner, who was a top-class player. At the end of the night – perhaps as a ploy to deflect attention from her poor play – she jokingly said to him, 'I think I need some practice, perhaps on the beach in Rio in July.' She then told Allen about a multi-million payment Britoil was due to make for the lease of an oil rig.

The pair realised how easy it could be to send the money to an account created for the purpose, perhaps in a country where banking practices are protected by strict confidentiality, like Switzerland. So they discussed and honed their scheme over the green baize tables at the Westburn Bridge Club, of which Alison Anders was a committee member. But the catalyst for action came when Allen visited Abu Dhabi on business. While in that country he arranged a night out with a friend from his American football days, whose name was Ruddell. Also in the party were Ruddell's wife, Gillian, and a mysterious man called Omar. It proved to be a memorable night and, as the drink flowed, Allen told his friends about a £23 million payment Britoil was due to make. Jokes were made about how easy it would be to get their hands on the money.

The next day, Royston Allen claimed, he was asked by Omar to meet his boss, Hajdin, a wealthy businessman with powerful contacts in Abu Dhabi and many other places. With Hajdin's help a Swiss bank account was opened in the name of Temsco Code International – a non-existent company with 'headquarters' in Geneva – and arrangements were made for the money to be divided up. Everything was in place; it all now depended on Alison Anders.

And so, on 29 June 1988, Anders forged a document designed to divert £23,331,996 of Britoil funds to the Swiss bank account. The money had been earmarked by Britoil for the Lombard finance company of London to pay the lease on an oil rig in the Clyde Field but now it was to make Anders, Allen and their shadowy associates in the Middle East filthy rich. However, she had been just a bit too clever with the paperwork. Although she had effectively faked the signatures of two of her bosses there was a flaw in her plan: in a bid to speed up the process she had included explicit written instructions on how the payment was to be made. She had also attached a telex, supposedly from the fictional company, to beef up the authenticity of the transaction. The false paperwork was sent to a Glasgow branch of the Bank of Scotland, where an observant bank employee found it extremely puzzling, having never seen such an authorisation before. She referred it to her boss who agreed that the matter should be brought to the attention of Britoil.

Back in Aberdeen, Alison Anders knew nothing of the developments in Glasgow and had planned to celebrate her birthday on 30 June by taking a half-day before jetting off to the Middle East to join her lover and enjoy her ill-gotten gains. But on arriving at the office she was hit by a serious setback. Shell and Esso – partners in the lease of the rig – had queried the amount payable, and the upshot was that her boss decided the transaction was to be suspended. Anders knew the money had been diverted to Switzerland and realised it was only a matter of time before her larceny was discovered. Had she stopped to think, had she stayed in the office that day, then perhaps her agile mind would have found a way to salvage the situation. Instead she became a victim of that great curse of the criminal classes – panic.

She accepted the birthday gift of some Body Shop products from her co-workers and then hurriedly left the office. The whole scheme had gone wrong, how badly she did not yet know, but she was not about to wait and find out. Instead of flying to Amsterdam, her planned first stop on the way to the Middle East, she caught a train to Glasgow then hopped on a flight to Paris. From there she caught a second flight to Abu Dhabi, where she gave Royston Allen the bad news.

The passport she used during her globetrotting was not her own. Taking a leaf from the fictional assassin in Frederick Forsyth's thriller *The Day of the Jackal*, she had travelled to Dartford, where she had gone to school. She recalled a girl who had died of bone cancer and planned to find her grave to obtain the exact dates of birth and death. However, she could not remember the girl's name and instead found the grave of Ann Killick, who had died in an accident in 1971 aged eight years and ten months. Lifting the information from the gravestone, she first obtained a copy of the girl's death certificate and with the details of her full name, date and place of birth she then bought a copy of her birth certificate. She came back to Scotland and, at Glasgow passport office, handed over the birth certificate and an application form, complete with the forged signature of the vicar of the churchyard where the girl was buried. She also provided a letter from Britoil, urging staff to issue her with a passport without delay.

Anders was in Abu Dhabi before her employers discovered something was seriously wrong. The Bank of Scotland had contacted them regarding the transfer and no-one at Britoil had heard of the Swiss-based company. Suspicion quickly fell on Anders, who had been instructed to take the original documents to the bank. At the time, her bosses thought she was off sick, and she even phoned-in on 1 July to say she would be back the following Monday. In fact she was thousands of miles away. The police launched a major investigation and made an appeal on BBC Television's *Crimewatch*. It was all to no avail; the young fraudster was completely off the radar.

In fact she was on the run again, this time because she feared for her life. She had let down the mysterious and powerful Hajdin, a man not to be trifled with. Hajdin told Anders that he was $500,000 out of pocket, money he had used to bribe the bank manager of the Geneva bank to which the £23 million was to have been diverted. There were also hints that the Mafia had been in on the deal and had taken a dim view when it had collapsed. Now, Anders would later claim, Hajdin just wanted her out of Abu Dhabi, on pain of her life: 'He said the desert was a very big place in a very big country and I wasn't a very big person and it would be very easy for me to disappear. It was fairly explicit what he meant.'

So after a week with Royston Allen in Abu Dhabi, Anders used her fake passport to fly to Vancouver in Canada, then to the USA, where she planned to start a new life. She pitched up in Portland, in the west-coast state of Oregon. Penniless, but still using the alias of Ann Killick, she began to make a new life for herself, although without a valid visa or work permit it would not be easy. But, as always, she was resourceful. She found lodgings, sharing a flat with another woman, Corinda Bohus, who believed her new flatmate was touring the States following the death of her parents. 'She was a sweetheart,' Ms Bohus would later say. 'She was really nice and would have been a great American.' Her new American friends even threw a surprise birthday party on 26 October, the birth date not of Alison Anders, but of Ann Killick.

There was also time for romance. Alison/Ann met, and planned to marry, the owner of a bakers shop. Brad Smith met her when he was making deliveries to the florist with whom she had found work. However, her brief but thwarted life of crime haunted her. After a drinking session, she confessed all to flatmate Corinda Bohus, while fiancé Brad Smith had a sixth sense there was something wrong. Later, he said he felt she wanted to tell him about her past life but could not bring herself to do so. 'She would wake up suddenly in the middle of the night,' he told reporters. 'It was as if people were chasing her all the time, even when she was sleeping.'

The British police were, of course, pursuing her but the trail had grown cold. There was no trace of Alison Anders leaving the country and no-one yet knew of the Ann Killick alias. In the end, it was her habit of keeping in contact with her married lover that proved her undoing. By the time Anders was hiding out in Portland, Allen's marriage had completely broken down and his wife had become involved with his business partner. It seems that Allen would not give her a divorce and when she discovered that he was still in touch with Alison Anders she told the police, who subsequently found a note of her telephone number in Portland. Allen was bitter about being found out. 'Life's a bitch, but it's hell being married to one,' he was quoted as saying.

Brad Smith found out about his bride-to-be's past in a telephone call she made to him from the local FBI office. 'Brad, this is Ann,' she said. 'My real name is Alison and I have been picked up by the FBI. Will you bring some personal effects?' He said she phoned him every night from the detention centre where she rubbed shoulders with drug addicts and prostitutes. 'Just like being back at school,' she quipped. For his part, Smith was ready to forgive both her deception and her past and would later say that he still loved her and wanted to marry her. His reasoning was that Anders had been lured into crime against her better judgement, to please the man she loved: 'I feel there is a wonderful person hiding behind a troubled shell. I believe if she fell for someone she would do everything in her power for that person.'

In June 1989 she was back in Aberdeen having waived extradition. Halfway through the trial, in September of that year, she changed her plea to guilty. She asked her lawyer publicly to apologise for her crime, both to the court and to Britoil. 'What started off as a Walter Mitty-type fantasy,' said lawyer Jack Davidson, 'turned into reality and a personal nightmare.' His client, he said, had packed in more during one year of life than most people do in a lifetime. The planning of the crime, he argued, had been naïve and not the action of 'a sophisticated, would-be arch criminal'.

Royston Allen toughed it out through the seven-day trial. He had only become involved, he insisted, because Hajdin had threatened his family. His QC, Ian Hamilton, claimed that the fraud was designed as a one-off exercise that did not 'entail a great deal of criminality'. The lawyer said, 'My client was tempted, fell and is broken.' However, Allen's claims of coercion cut no ice with the court. The jury was informed that before such a defence could be considered there had to be a number of qualifications. First, there had to be an immediate danger of either death or, at least, of serious injury. There also had to be an inability to resist violence and the accused had to play an inferior part in the crime. Finally, the accused was required to disclose the plan and make restitution at the earliest possible opportunity. It was the Crown's contention that Royston Allen fulfilled none of these criteria.

Allen's case was also damaged by the evidence of Gillian Ruddell, a surprise witness who had come forward voluntarily to give evidence at the trial. She confirmed she had met Allen in Abu Dhabi and he had told her about the plot. Ruddell also said she was to have been paid £1 million for taking Anders to Singapore after the diversion of funds until the heat died down. Not surprisingly, the jury took only forty-seven minutes to find Royston Allen guilty. The judge, Lord Morton, told Anders, 'It is quite obvious that this was a crime which was planned with some determination, if not very much time, and was planned and motivated by a considerable amount of greed and ignoring all questions of honesty and trust.' To Allen, he said, 'You again are motivated by greed and no doubt you will regret in the future the effect of that on your family and on your own life.'

They were both sentenced to five years, although this was reduced on appeal to four. Press reports at the time suggested that their romance was over but, two years later, after Anders had been freed and Allen was being given weekend leave as part of Training for Freedom, it was reported that the pair were seeing each other again. On his release, they set up home in a tiny cottage in the north of Scotland. Once they dreamt of having millions but now they were broke and even when Scottish Television planned an hour-long drama on the case – part of the ITV *Crime Story* series – they were to receive nothing.

Lee Bell

A danger to women

Lindsay Armstrong had everything to live for. She was a bright, attractive 17-year-old with ambitions to become a lawyer after seeing some of the world. But on Tuesday, 16 July 2002, she took her own life. Alone in her bedroom, she swallowed an overdose of anti-depressants and then lay down to die. On her stereo she had placed her current favourite Queen CD. In the early hours of the morning her parents found her. As they desperately fought to revive her, Freddie Mercury's distinctive voice told them that nothing really matters.

Lindsay had given evidence only days before against a local teenager who had brutally attacked her. In September 2001, he had ambushed her as she made her way to her home in New Cumnock, Ayrshire, then dragged her to a local park. Lindsay, suffering from a congenital back problem for which she had been receiving treatment, tried to fight him off but he tore at her clothes and raped her. The attack was reported to the police and the youth was arrested.

Lindsay had come through one ordeal, the memory of which haunted her. She did not know that she would have to go through another, in its own way just as traumatic as the rape. Her attacker, who as a minor could not be named at the time, had denied the charges and in order to secure a conviction she would have to appear in court and give evidence. The new Sexual Offences (Procedure and Evidence) (Scotland) Bill to protect rape victims from intrusive questioning was not due to come into force until the beginning of 2003.

She had to tell the court what happened. For the young woman, it must have felt like being raped all over again as she was forced to go into the witness box and hold up the g-string that she had been wearing. According to her family, she was made to feel cheap and dirty, as if she were somehow to blame for the attack. They were angry that that the focus was on her underwear, despite the fact that she had been wearing jeans and a jacket over a top and boots. After her court appearance, she told her mum and dad that she had been made to feel like 'a tart who deserved to be raped'.

Lindsay Armstrong came through the court ordeal and saw her attacker found guilty. But one week before he was due to be sentenced, something inside her just gave up and she turned to the anti-depressants prescribed to help her cope with her harrowing experience. As the minister at her funeral said, 'Lindsay has found release from the burdens of this world. All her cares have ceased and all her torment and despair has ended. Death itself has passed.'

A few days later, her rapist was sentenced, his identity still protected by court order. He was dubbed a danger to women but only received four years, plus three years' supervision. His name would also be added to the Sex Offenders Register. He was sent to Kerelaw House, a secure school for young offenders in Stevenston, Ayrshire where, it was claimed, he would spend his time free time watching television and playing video games. Although the image of a holiday camp was inaccurate, the news still left a rancid taste in the public's mouth.

He was not named until the following year, when he turned sixteen. Lee Don Bell was known to Lindsay because he was a local ned. But he was not a friend. And her family was bitter that throughout the case the law had apparently been on his side. A meeting with the procurator fiscal in Ayrshire also turned sour when he asked the family some very difficult questions. He also warned them that Bell would serve only thirty-two months of his four-year sentence.

Bell actually served more than two-and-a-half years before he was released. The Armstrong family had been promised they would be informed before he got out but Bell had been at liberty for five days before someone from the procurator fiscal's office in Ayr phoned them. He had been released just in time for Christmas. 'On Christmas Day, we will be visiting Lindsay's grave while her rapist enjoys his freedom and Christmas dinner,' said mum Linda to the *Daily Record*, which had made their story its own over the years. 'I hope he chokes to death on his turkey.'

Bell's name was on the sex offender's register and he was under close supervision in the community but that didn't soothe the Armstrongs' feelings. 'They said he had moved away because there was nothing to keep him in Scotland. But I don't believe that for a minute. All his family live in Ayrshire and I am convinced he could still be here.'

Bell, though, had not come back to New Cumnock. His mother, who never believed he was guilty, had moved away. The *Daily Record* tracked the young man down in Newcastle. Now eighteen, the youth at first tried to pretend he was a cousin when confronted by a journalist then refused to answer when asked if he wanted to apologise to Lindsay's family. The Armstrong family applauded the newspaper's decision to put his picture on its front page. 'I want everyone to know what he did and for people to recognise him so that there can be no escape for him,' said Linda. 'Every woman should remember that face and stay well away from him.'

Lee Bell may have been unwilling to talk, but his sister was not so squeamish. A month later, the *Daily Record* again highlighted the case by quoting her as saying that Lindsay 'deserves to be where she is after what she has put my brother through'. She went on to say that 'Lee has nothing to apologise for. He's not done anything wrong.' Linda Armstrong dismissed the girl as a 'stupid wee lassie who should learn to keep her mouth shut because it just causes even more hurt and grief'. Meanwhile, the Armstrong family campaigned for further support for the victims of rape, even going as far as setting up a special twenty-four-hour helpline for victims in Ayrshire.

Then came another bombshell for the Armstrong family. In the spring of 2006 Linda Armstrong spotted Bell in a supermarket in Ayr. She was aghast at seeing him again and angry that no-one from the authorities had told her he was back in Ayrshire. 'I looked up and spotted Bell. I was at the checkout and he was at the bottom of an aisle. He was looking at me and when I saw his eyes I felt sick.' The sighting was a major story for the press: on 12 April 2006 *The Scottish Sun* carried a front-page headline that read: 'Beast is Back' and devoted two full pages inside the paper to the encounter. It seems that for some victims the torment can never end.

George Belmonte

They called him Catweazle

Thanks to his long white hair and beard, he was nicknamed Catweazle, but that was doing an injustice to the wizard from the popular children's television programme of the 1970s. George Belmonte may have looked like a kindly, if eccentric, old man but he was a habitual paedophile who was hounded from a variety of homes as soon as his past caught up with him.

Jersey-born Belmonte was raised in a children's home but began his life of child abuse at an early age. Like the notorious Moors murderer, Ian Brady, Belmonte enjoyed tape recording the anguished cries of his young victims. It is unclear exactly how many children he abused but he spent almost twenty years behind bars for a variety of sex offences. When life became too hot for him in London, he moved to Edinburgh where he married the first of his three wives. His third wife, a prison visitor, married him in 1988 in Peterhead prison without realising the full nature of his crimes. He also fathered six children.

Despite his years in prison, he never rehabilitated, never showed remorse. Quite the opposite, in fact, according to his ex-wife: she said that, towards the end of his life, he told her he was writing a book detailing the hundreds of children he had abused; he even expressed a wish to have sex with one more child before he died. He told her that the small villages around Dumfries – where he ended his days – provided many opportunities for a man like him to satisfy his desires. Poor parents in council estates were 'easy fodder', he said, and that in country areas it was easy to get at little children.

He had landed in Dumfries in 2001 after serving his final stretch for assaulting a boy of seven and a girl of twelve he had lured to a picnic. At first, social workers lodged him in a luxury mansion but each time he settled, his identity surfaced and angry locals ensured he was moved on. While such a reaction is understandable, a mob can often be blinded by its own fury. In this case, a perfectly innocent elderly man was mistaken by the vigilantes for their target and terrorised. Belmonte, meanwhile, was placed in a room in Dumfries's Royal Oak hotel but he even had to quit that.

In February 2005 he was admitted to hospital suffering from cancer. He died in March of that year, totally unrepentant. Speaking after his death, his third wife hinted that he may have been responsible for more than sex abuse of children. In an interview with the *Sunday Mail* she said, 'He'd ask me if I realised just how easy it was to get rid of a body, especially a little body of a child.'

She asked him if he had killed but he merely laughed and said 'Wait until you read my book.' We can only hope that is one volume that will never see the light of day.

John Bermingham

It runs in the family

The girl was only eleven when she was attacked. She was only twelve when she gave evidence against the perpetrator. She told how he seized her in Edinburgh's Fountainhill Road as she was walking home from a dance class, how he clamped one hand over her mouth, how he dragged her over a wall to a grassy area behind a library.

And there she was sexually assaulted. When it was over, he tossed her £20, as if she was a common prostitute. Don't tell the police, he told her; if you do I'll come after you.

The foul act lasted only a few minutes. The disturbing memory of it would last considerably longer.

An hour earlier, an 18-year-old nursing assistant had been jumped as she left the city's Cameron Toll shopping mall and headed for a bus stop. A man dressed in dark clothing came out of nowhere in Gilmerton Road, grabbed her arms and pulled her into bushes. Pinning her to the ground, a gloved hand over her mouth, he told her to keep quiet, that there was something he wanted her to do for him. The frightening thing was that, as he did this, people walked close by and asked what was going on. They were told the young woman had had too much to drink. But one passer-by didn't swallow the story and caused a scene. The attacker took fright and the girl seized the chance to get away. The man reached out to stop her, but all he caught was her scarf, which slid from her neck. The teenager kept running.

The twin attacks took place in November 2000. A huge manhunt was launched to catch the culprit. Police even appeared on *Crimewatch* appealing for information. There had been two sex attacks in one day. The likelihood was there would be more. This man, as they often say, had to be caught.

One year later, he was. The attacker had left a glove at the scene of the first attack and a semen sample at the second. This meant the detectives had DNA. All they needed was a match. It took a while, but finally a name was thrown up: Glaswegian John Bermingham, then living in the Muirhouse area of Edinburgh. He was a known crook – a serial housebreaker – but, puzzlingly, not a known sex offender, although he had been mentioned in connection with a sex attack in England. He became a target when an officer pointed out that he fitted the description they had of the attacker. He was, as one police officer pointed out, one of thousands of suspects processed during the inquiry but, when police tried to interview him, he was nowhere to be found. His wife also provided him with an alibi. Detectives became more suspicious when he was only one of three suspects who refused to provide a DNA sample.

The irony was that the national DNA database had already thrown out his name as a match to the sample taken from the assault on the 11-year-old. However, due to a processing error, the results were not properly analysed and detectives were unaware of this vital break in their case for a further five months. Then he was named as a suspect in another assault and a warrant was issued for his arrest.

Bermingham had fled south after the double attack. He had previously lived in London and, with his brother Duncan resident in Manchester, he knew his way around. However, in November 2001, he ventured back to Scotland again and was spotted driving a blue Ford Escort near Loch Lomond. When police tried to arrest him he led them on a thirty-mile high-speed chase through the countryside. All the while, Bermingham took swigs from a bottle of booze and made obscene gestures at his pursuers as a police helicopter buzzed overhead, filming everything. He bounced onto a pavement to avoid an attempt by police to burst his tyres but came a cropper at roadworks. He careered through traffic cones but continued to evade capture with a set of temporary traffic lights trailing from his car. By this time, police cars had managed to box him in and he was bundled from his car into custody.

He came to trial in June 2002. The red glove recovered from the scene of the first attack had been analysed and fibres from it matched samples found inside and around the pocket of a set of tracksuit trousers that belonged to Bermingham. DNA found inside the glove also matched Bermingham's while samples on the outside matched the victim. In addition, the DNA extracted from the semen sample from the second attack matched his. According to the boffins, the odds against the DNA being anyone other than Bermingham's were an amazing one billion to one.

Bermingham could not explain how his genetic fingerprint ended up in the sample. All he could suggest was that he was being fitted up by police officers. He denied he was responsible for the attacks, claiming he had been in Glasgow on that day trying to sell stolen antiques. He produced a ticket for the Glasgow underground, date-stamped 04NOV00.

The jury was unimpressed. At the end of the three-week trial, Bermingham was convicted of attempting to rape the 11-year-old girl and assault with intent to rape in the case of the 18-year-old. Other charges were dropped but he was also found guilty of driving danger-ously while under the influence of alcohol and possession of a knife. He was to serve a minimum of nine years of a twelve-year sentence in prison for the sex attacks and to be under extended supervision for the remaining three. He received an additional eighteen months for the driving offence and six months for possession of the knife.

As he languished in jail awaiting sentencing, Bermingham tried to kill himself. According to press reports, he slashed his wrists in Edinburgh's Saughton prison. An inmate who heard the man scream said he saw prison staff rush into his cell. When the witness peeked in, he saw blood on the floor and a nurse bandaging his arm. The witness said that he was shouting, 'What's the point? I'm going to get years anyway.'

How right he was. At the sentencing hearing in Glasgow in July, Lord Hamilton said that his crimes were 'appalling and despicable' and he felt it his duty to impose the lengthy jail sentence to protect the public from serious harm. Bermingham glared at him as he was led from the dock and said, 'I hope you're proud of yourself.' His wife, meanwhile, refused to believe he was guilty. 'He's done nothing wrong,' she insisted, 'He's innocent and I am staying with him.'

Although Bermingham was known as a housebreaker – and indeed confessed to as much – he was not a known sex offender. However, after the trial, some disturbing facts came to light. Police in Manchester had questioned him and his older brother Duncan in connection with a number of attacks on women. According to an unnamed Manchester police source quoted in the *Sunday Mail*, the names of both brothers came up whenever there was a sex crime in the city. In 1996, Duncan Bermingham was jailed for life for the murder of student Rachel

Thacker; he abducted her in his car, which she believed was a taxi, and then tried sexually to assault her. When she fought him off, he battered her with a breeze block, breaking every bone in her face. Then he set fire to her body and dumped her remains in a wheelie bin.

As if all this was not bad enough for his family, Bermingham's son William was convicted of attempting to rape a 17-year-old girl in Grangemouth. The 16-year-old boy was on a supervised day out from a young offenders institution when he sneaked away from his escort and attacked the girl. He was sentenced to five years in prison.

But John Bermingham's troubles were not over. In February 2004 he came off worst in an encounter with a twenty-two-stone fellow inmate in Peterhead prison. Convicted drug dealer Peter Docherty was said to have attacked Bermingham on a Sunday afternoon in the recreation area of A hall. The two slugged it out until a prison officer tried to get between them. The prison officer ended up with twelve stitches in his head. The battling convicts were finally separated but not before Docherty, nicknamed 'The Blob', inflicted a beating on Bermingham who, as an ex-boxer, is no powder puff. 'Docherty is a very big guy,' said an insider to the press. 'You would think that at twenty-two stone he would be unfit but if he throws his weight at someone they've got no chance.'

Paul Bints
King Con

We all, at one time or another, wish we were someone else. At best this could be ambition. At worst, it can be delusion. There are, however, individuals who have the ability to turn themselves almost at will into something they are not. America's Frank Abegnale – played by Leonardo De Caprio in the film *Catch Me If You Can* – was such a man. He spent five years dodging the authorities, posing as a doctor, a pilot, anything really that took his fancy. An earlier example from America is Ferdinand Waldo Demara (played by Tony Curtis in *The Great Impostor*) who also managed to pass himself off in a number of professions, including those of teacher, psychologist, surgeon and priest.

There are examples closer to home. In Scotland, Brandon Lee was a popular student at Bearsden Academy. The 17-year-old Canadian pupil wrote for the school magazine and appeared in school plays. In reality, he was 32-year-old Brian McKinnon, who had dropped out of studying for a medical degree and wanted a second chance at becoming a doctor, so he created his younger alter ego and went back to school for further qualifications. There was no criminality in his actions but when his lies were uncovered his story hit the headlines. There was even a film planned but so far unmade.

Paul Bints, though, was a different kettle of fish. He was a con man who tried to dupe people in order to line his pockets. The Northamptonshire hairdresser already had a twenty-year career as a grifter behind him before he came to the attention of Scottish courts. Over the years he had posed as lawyers, peers and bankers, tricking his victims out of cash and self-esteem. He also used his roguish charm to lure beautiful women into his bed.

His favourite pose was as a doctor – first attempted when he was only fourteen – and in the 1980s he preyed on hospitals across north-west England, dispensing drugs and tending patients, including sewing twelve stitches into a man's head and treating the teenage victim of a car crash. Her parents were relieved to hear the 'doctor' tell them she would be fine but the poor girl died within six hours.

He did not get away Scot-free. In those twenty years he was in court twenty times and was convicted of 115 offences. They called him King Con but clearly this was largely due to the quantity of scams rather than the quality.

By 2000 he was in Scotland and claiming to be the grandly-named Lachlan Campbell-Brierdan, a lawyer involved in the Lockerbie trial. His silver tongue managed to convince Virgin Trains to put him up at a five-star Edinburgh hotel after he loudly complained that his lap-top computer had been stolen on the journey north. It was while he was in Edinburgh that he met the beautiful Nicki Gonelli, a one-time Miss Edinburgh. He wooed the former beauty queen over five weeks, proposed with a £26,000 engagement ring and promised to marry her on the Caribbean island of St Lucia. Ms Gonelli even picked out a £2,000 wedding dress for the big day. But her plans for wedded bliss fell apart when Bints was arrested for stealing papers from the Court of Session and her love for him evaporated when he was later jailed for assaulting her.

On his release from Saughton prison in July 2001, Bints immediately went back to his old ways. In an Edinburgh bar, his eye fell on 25-year-old Andrea McLaren. Dressed in a designer suit, and using the name Richard Campbell-Breedem, he told the attractive nurse his father was the judge in the trial of Barry George, who had been accused of murdering television personality Jill Dando. He made many more outlandish claims: he was ex-army and had been injured by an IRA nail bomb; now he was a merchant banker who was currently involved in a multi-billion pound takeover of Vodafone, the mobile-phone company.

However, the first time this 'highly successful investment banker' took his new love on holiday, it wasn't to the Caribbean, New York or even Paris. It was to the Las Vegas of Lancashire, Blackpool, albeit to the best hotel in town.

Eventually though, Andrea McLaren, like many other bemused women before her, found out that the man she thought was a fine catch was nothing more than a shadow, a flash will o' the wisp. Her lover was arrested for the theft of the Aston Martin DB7 in which he had been driving her around. In four days he had travelled 900 miles and caused £15,000 worth of damage to the high-performance motor.

The story of how he got the car is typical of his chutzpah. Bints had made off with the £55,000 vehicle after posing as a Mr Blenheim, a nightclub and hotel owner. He tricked the boss of a Glasgow show-room into a test drive, palming a second set of keys before he set off. While he and his escort from the garage were in a pub, Bints/ Blenheim excused himself and, using the stolen set of keys, vanished with the car. In court, Bints claimed he was the victim of an insurance scam, saying that he had been hired to take the car and deliver it to London. The court was having none of it. In November 2001, he was sentenced to two years and nine months for this latest con. The sheriff, on passing sentence, refused pleas for psychiatric reports, saying, 'Your record and the circumstances of the current crime suggest that you are clearly and fundamentally dishonest to the extent that lying and stealing appear to be deeply embedded in the integral part of your lifestyle.'

How right he was. Released after serving seventeen months, Bints vanished. Scottish cops had warned him that if he returned to his old ways he would be banged up for a considerable period but they knew their warnings would fall on deaf ears. Bints had as much chance of giving up his conning ways as a fish had of crossing the Sahara. There was something in his blood – or his psyche – that compelled him to cheat, lie and steal. Mindful of the damage he had done in earlier years, warnings were issued to hospitals in the Edinburgh area to be on guard against him posing as a doctor. They needn't have worried; Bints had fled south and almost immediately became someone else.

He was now Orlando Pownall, prosecutor in the Barry George case. Using this alias, he managed to talk his way into various hospitals and stole cash and credit cards. He claimed he lived in Hampstead and had crashed his Aston Martin. Hospital authorities believed him and he was admitted for treatment. One consultant even befriended him and took him home. He rewarded her kindness by stealing cash and a credit card. In another hospital he took a credit card from a terminally ill patient in the next bed and used it to pay for a £1,000 weekend with a woman he had met.

It was his Casanova complex that led to his arrest: a female consult-ant he had been trying to win over discussed him with a colleague. The friend was suspicious and reported the matter to the police. When arrested, Bints had papers relating to the case of convicted killer Jeremy Bamber and fake interview tapes labelled 'Maxine Carr' and 'Ian Huntley' (Huntley was convicted of murdering two schoolgirls in Soham, Cambridgeshire and Maxine Carr was his girlfriend).

In October 2003, Bints was jailed for four years and four months for his deceptions and thefts. The court heard that he had a psychopathic disorder that was at the time untreatable. In sending him to jail, the judge said: 'You have caused anguish, embarrassment, loss and difficulty to your victims. You are a serial and practised confidence trickster and you succeeded in fooling people as to your identity and your life. You show a callous lack of concern for the feeling of others. You lack remorse, you have no regrets.'

One Edinburgh police officer summed-up the sheer futility of Bints's criminal career: 'His whole life was a complete lie. I don't think at any time he told the truth. But he makes a pretty hopeless conman because he gets caught all the time and he has gained nothing from his deceptions. He only has the suit he stands up in.'

The bitches from hell
Torture in Greenock

They were known as the Fat Slags, Chucky and Cochise; four young women from Greenock who, over a £40 debt, abducted and held a 21-year-old friend for two days and subjected her to a horrifying series of attacks. Their subsequent convictions earned them another nickname: the 'Bitches from Hell'. Their male accomplice was named as the 'evil puppet master' who had manipulated them into the forty-eight-hour terror orgy. He had a nickname, too. They called him 'The Beast'.

Their tiny victim was Barbara Gillen, who was six weeks pregnant when she was snatched. She had shared a flat for a very brief period with Joanne McCulloch, aged nineteen, who along with pal Marie Davis, also nineteen, were known as the Fat Slags after the characters in the adult comic *Viz*. When Ms Gillen moved out of the flat after only a few days, McCulloch felt aggrieved. She believed she was owed £40 rent and she resolved to have it. Three days before Christmas 1995 they launched their attack. It was supposed to be the season of goodwill but there was precious little of it in evidence when they broke into Ms Gillen's new flat and trashed the place. Barbara Gillen was unlucky enough to show up while they were still there and was immediately grabbed and carted off to another flat where she was given a beating. In addition to blacking her eyes and breaking her nose, they rubbed her face in dog dirt, set fire to her jacket and stole her jewellery.

In a curious move she was then marched around the streets and forced to sing Christmas carols for cash before being bundled into another flat in Banff Road. They were joined there by the rest of the gang: Julie Duffy, Louise Campbell, a 14-year-old girl and Kenneth Woods. High on a cocktail of drink and drugs, the gang of five and their male overseer, a drug dealer, went to work on their terror-stricken victim. They didn't seem to care that she was pregnant. 'They were once my pals,' said their victim, 'but they became monsters. How could they do it?'

During the following two days they locked the five-foot tall woman in a cupboard so small she had to sit doubled up. When they dragged her out it was to assault her, sometimes kicking her in time to the unstoppable beat of rave music. She was stabbed and scalded with boiling water. She was thrown into a cold bath and more boiling water was thrown over her. They stubbed out lit cigarettes on her head and body. She was forced to drink urine, thoughtfully provided by two of the gang. One of the glasses was mixed with grease, turpentine, fish fingers and cigarette ends. Her hair was sprayed with liquid gas and set on fire. And if all that was not enough, they demeaned her even more by forcing her to get down on all fours, bark like a dog and lick their boots. They dehumanised her by calling her 'Beef'.

They fuelled their orgy of violence by cashing their victim's £73 DSS giro and treating themselves to more drink and drugs. And then went back to work again. She was threatened with death. Woods wrapped a wet towel around her neck and choked her. As he did so, he said, 'This is how it will feel when I slit your throat.' He inserted the tip of a long knife into the top button of her shirt and dragged her around the room, threatening to cut her throat. She believed him, for they had spread black bin-liners on the floor to catch the blood. But the expected death blow never came – and she was again thrown back into her cupboard prison to await the next level of hell. And as she hunched up in the darkness, she could hear them outside, taunting her. 'Not long now, Barbara,' they chanted. 'Your throat will be slit, Barbara.'

Believing her life to be in danger, Barbara Gillen tried to escape. She convinced her captors that she needed to go to the toilet and, once locked inside, forced open a small window and slid through. It was snowing outside and she was barefoot but she did not care; she just had to get away from her tormentors. She staggered to a nearby house and battered on the door. The woman who answered was so shocked by the young woman's appearance – her face was swollen and bruised, her skin covered in scald marks, her scalp burned – that she fainted. The terrified and brutalised young woman was ushered into the house and an ambulance and police were called, but still she did not feel safe. As she was being rushed to hospital, she pleaded with the paramedics, 'Don't let them get me.' A doctor who examined her said that she resembled the victim of torture at a Bosnian concentration camp.

Then something even worse happened. Worse even than the torture she had endured for so long. She was told she had lost her baby. 'I told them to stop hitting me but they just laughed,' she said. 'That baby meant everything to me.'

It was a horrifying and senseless crime that shocked experienced police officers. Even tough criminals were appalled by the depravity. Kenneth Wood, who allegedly sold drugs for a well-known local criminal, found himself very much out in the cold as far as his old boss was concerned. The drug baron reportedly offered £5,000 if someone would do Wood over in prison. Someone may have tried to collect the bounty because he was stabbed in the leg while on remand.

Meanwhile, Julie Duffy and Joanne McCulloch were attacked in Cornton Vale prison. Inmates, calling the pair beasts, dragged them to the ground and poured boiling water over them, just as they had done with their victim. Only this time, the water was mixed with sugar to make it cling to the skin.

After a fifteen-day trial in the High Court of Glasgow, the judge called the crimes 'barbarous, disgusting and abhorrent'. His revulsion was reflected in the sentences he handed down to the weeping women before him. Joanne McCulloch was sentenced to twelve years. It was revealed that she and her pal Marie Davis had sent a letter to a prisoner boasting about their crime. Davis pled guilty to abduction and assault and was given two years. Julie Duffy – known as Chucky because she was said to resemble the killer doll in the *Child's Play* movies – was also sentenced to twelve years. Louise Campbell, known as Cochise because of the thick band she wore in her long dark hair, was given eleven years. Her boyfriend, Kenneth Wood, was given sixteen years. He was to be sent to Peterhead prison where, for his own protection, he would be lodged with sex offenders. The other gang member, a 14-year-old girl, was ordered to be detained for five years.

And what of their victim? She stood to gain £100,000 in criminal-injury compensation. In October 1996, against the wishes of her family, she married an older man. Before the end of the year the marriage was over.

Leonard Bowie

The demon barber

The woman trying to board the bus in Aberdeen was obviously injured. The police officer who spotted her later said that 'flaps of skin had been cut on the top of her head, which would have hung loose were it not for the fact that coagulated blood was holding the skin together'. The 51-year-old woman told him she had met a man earlier in the city centre. He had admired her long white hair and said that he was a hairdresser. If she wanted, he proposed, she could come back to his flat where they could have a drink and he would cut her hair for her. The woman agreed.

But once in the tiny bedsit in Devonshire Road, in the city's west end, he attacked her with a razor. And tried to scalp her.

The man was 62-year-old Leonard Bowie, and this was not the first time he had tried to lift a woman's hair. He had been jailed in 1983 for a similar attack on a 40-year-old woman in Bishopbriggs, near Glasgow. The woman had just been released from jail having been convicted of the culpable homicide of her abusive husband. Bowie had promised to put up a curtain rail and had attacked her, then contacted the police himself, confessing to what he had done. Officers found the widow on the floor of her council home. Her hair had been sliced off by a penknife and a pair of hair-clippers. The bloody knife and the scalp itself, ripped from her head, still lay by her side. Bowie told detectives that he enjoyed 'sexual gratification from stroking and cutting women's hair'. However, he had no memory of the vicious act. 'I remember picking up the clippers,' he said, 'but I don't remember using the knife until I saw blood on my shirt and trousers.'

He had once trained as a hairdresser, when he was nineteen. However, he had not continued in the trade, and instead worked for a number of years as a theatre assistant at Aberdeen's Royal Infirmary. After moving to London, he married and fathered two children but the marriage collapsed. He returned to Scotland, taking a job as a barman in Glasgow. It was during his time there that he attacked his first victim. Although sentenced to four years, he appealed against the sentence and it was cut to just one year.

And now, eighteen years later, he was back in Aberdeen and up to his old tricks. His latest victim said that almost as soon as they arrived in his flat, Bowie – almost bald himself – attacked her head with a razor. Ignoring her agonized pleas to stop, Bowie sliced at his victim's scalp, pulling her waist-length hair from her skull, leaving several deep gashes. 'You won't be going out with someone else for a while,' he said as he put her through twenty minutes of agony. Finally, the excruciating pain caused her to pass out and, when she came to, she was on the floor and Bowie was sitting in a chair, calmly watching television. She told him she needed to go the toilet and seized the chance to flee. She wandered the streets in a state of shock until she was spotted by the police officer. In hospital, doctors found an eight-by-seven-centimetre wound on her head. Patches of skin had been scraped to the bone. A skin graft from her leg covered the damage but doctors said there was little likelihood of the hair ever growing back.

The victim was unable clearly to identify her attacker, or even state for certain where his flat was. Nevertheless Bowie's name came up during the investigation, thanks to his previous conviction. When police raided his bedsit they found what was described as a shrine to hairdressing, complete with brushes, scissors and razors, all accumulated over a period of years. One detective observed that it was 'an incredible amount of hairdressing equipment for a man with so little hair'.

They also found a bloodstained carpet, strands of hair and a note about a so-called examination of another victim. It turned out the second victim was a Down Syndrome woman whom he had befriended at the social club where he worked as a doorman. He had invited the 59-year-old to his flat, washed and cut her hair and then sexually assaulted her. This offence was committed on the nineteenth anniversary of his Bishopbriggs crime.

At his trial in the High Court at Perth, Bowie admitted both charges, although his not-guilty plea to a third – that he had scalped a third woman in Aberdeen – was accepted. His defence advocate told the court that he had developed a hair fetish in his teens, leading to his brief sojourn as a hairdresser's apprentice, and that the predilection had continued through his adult life. 'There is no doubt that this is a man with an abnormal interest in hair,' said his QC, Frances McMenamin.

'He has admitted he thought a lot about women's hair and how it featured in his sexual fantasies.'

He was, however, a man with 'an inadequate personality and low self-esteem'. It was stated that depression over his divorce in the 1980s led to excessive drinking. As is often the case, that drinking deepened the depression. This led him into turning his fantasies into reality. His twenty years of heavy drinking had also created another problem – his brain was shrinking. This, though, had not contributed to his offences. He had been examined by psychiatrists and found to be sane and fit to plead. However, doctors could not rule out the possibility that his condition, should it continue to deteriorate, would not make him even more of a threat to women.

Lord Wheatley, in passing sentence, observed that if Bowie got the chance, he would commit further outrages. 'Medical reports indicate this problem is likely to get worse rather than better in the medium term,' he said. 'Your aggression towards women is related to a sexual fetish about hair, which seems impossible to treat.' Given Bowie's background and the horror of the offences, 'which must have caused extreme distress and suffering to the victims', the judge had no option but to pass an exemplary sentence. 'It is clear you remain at present an extremely dangerous threat to vulnerable women in particular, and given the opportunity you are likely to re-offend.' Bowie's defence had even admitted this, saying that he was desperate to get some sort of treatment for his problem to ensure no-one else suffered at his hands in the same way should he be released from prison.

Detectives had already expressed fears that the known victims were only the tip of the iceberg, that there could be other women who Bowie had attacked, physically or sexually, but who had not reported it. In the event, fears that he would reoffend when released proved groundless. Bowie was sentenced to eight years for his crimes but served only eighteen months before his dissolute life caught up with him. He died in Peterhead prison in 2003.

Stewart Boyd

A man called Specky

On Saturday, 28 June 2003 a top-of-the-range Audi TT Coupe crossed the central reservation of a motorway near the Spanish coastal resort of Mijas and slammed into a BMW travelling in the opposite direction. The resultant explosion and fireball killed six people, including a 13-year-old Spanish boy and a 3-year-old Scottish girl. Their deaths, as well as those of the adults who perished in the crash, were tragedies, but that was not why the incident grabbed Scottish headlines. The driver of the Audi was Stewart Boyd, a Scottish criminal known as 'Specky' to the underworld, police and press. And the feeling among some was that the cause of his death was no accident.

Boyd was only forty when he died but in those short years he had carved himself a tasty reputation on the Scottish crime scene. After his death, an unnamed police source was quoted in the *Daily Record* as saying, 'Boyd was known as the enforcer and was a heavyweight player in the crime scene in Glasgow and Spain. He was headhunted by gangsters to carry out hits on rival sites in the security and taxi business. He was a well-known face who has massive street-cred because he got away with so much for so long.'

Like ambitious men in legitimate spheres of business Boyd was keen to make a name for himself in his chosen profession. He had clawed his way up through the often vicious drug world of Barrhead and Paisley. Temazepam was becoming the drug of choice for local addicts and the crooks who furnished their 'highs' were not slow to realise how easily it could be obtained. In the late 1980s and early 1990s there was a dearth of quality heroin around Renfrewshire streets during one of the business's periodic shortages of product, so dealers filled the gap in the market with Temazepam, a prescription drug dished out like sweeties at the time as a sleeping aid. It came in a gel capsule – hence its street name of 'jellies' – and the liquid could be removed, heated and 'jagged' just like the real thing. With smack so rare, jellies were the ideal substitute. However, the criminal world being what it is, there was soon a war raging over control of the market – and Stewart Boyd was in the thick of it. He was working for a Paisley drug baron and he proved himself just the kind of guy you need in a sticky situation.

Come the 1990s and it was time to diversify. If there is one constant in the underworld it is that things change. Bright young gangsters are always on the lookout for new ways to turn a profit and during this period their rapacious eyes fell on the security market. Previously, their main connection with the business was in devising means to put the guards out of commission during robberies. Now they realised that there was a profit to be made; not by beating them but joining them.

In 2004, it was estimated that the security industry in Scotland was worth £180 million a year, and that was too much of the folding stuff for the boys to ignore. Boyd and others were associated with two or three firms over the next few years, allegedly using the companies in a tidy little protection racket that came straight out of mob-world Chicago. The idea was simple: if a company did not utilise their services then their premises were open to vandalism or worse. Ordinary citizens were not immune from the attentions of these rogue companies. Residents of some areas were leafleted by the firms offering to protect them from undesirable elements. By a stroke of coincidence, within weeks, these same areas became the target of vandals and graffiti artists. The security companies themselves were also a neat way of laundering the profits from other illicit endeavours.

Local MP Irene Adams launched a well-publicised campaign against the drug trade and gangsterism in her constituency. She was rewarded with death threats, while the *Paisley Daily Express* was firebombed for its stand against the crooks. Police cracked down on the extortion schemes, the drug dealing and the money laundering but it was not until May 1996 – when Paisley dealer Mark Rennie was gunned down on his doorstep – that the breakthrough came. Boyd was arrested along with his boss in connection with the killing but was cleared. His boss, however, was found guilty. His brush with the courts on a capital crime did little to damage Specky Boyd's reputation; in fact it only served to enhance it. He now looked beyond the confines of Renfrewshire towards the big city and linked up with some well-known underworld faces to expand his empire.

But jail time was just around the corner: in 2001 Boyd was sentenced to eighteen months for intimidating a witness during an extortion trial.

The victim, the boss of a rival – but legitimate – security firm refused to be silenced and spoke out, even though his house was sprayed with bullets. Boyd took to his heels, spending his time between Spain and Scotland, before he was finally caught six months later in Aviemore. Even then, the victim had to be protected round the clock as police learned of death threats against him. Boyd was only banged up for a few weeks, having spent nine months on remand, before he was back out again on the streets. An important player, he was by now the object of keen police attention, particularly by the Scottish Drug Enforcement Agency.

Boyd began to spend more and more time in Spain, on the so-called Costa Del Crime. The area, a playground for the rich and infamous, is a centre for drug smuggling. The cargoes are brought there in small boats and yachts, often from North Africa, transferred at sea or in the Spanish harbours to other vessels and then dispersed throughout Europe. One of his bosses was already hiding out there and for Boyd, not content with the foothold he had already hacked out of the rock-face of Glasgow crime, the sun-kissed coastline was ideal for more than just a tan. There he could make new contacts, and expand his powerbase and his cash reserves. And, if some theories are correct, that was what led to his sudden death on that Spanish road. They say he had forged links with the Russian Mafia but had neglected to cough up for a £2.5 million cocaine shipment that had been routed to Scotland. The 'Cossack Nostra' is not a body of men who accept such unpaid debts philosophically and, the theory goes, a device was fitted to his car.

This theory is supported by one of the first cops on the scene who took one look at the wreckage and concluded that a car bomb had gone off. According to an organised-crime expert quoted in *The Scotsman*, it was not outwith the realms of possibility for Russian gangsters to use such a device. 'They will choose the best time and the best place, where they can be sure of getting away with it, and get someone further down the ladder to do the killing. If innocent people get in the way, that is too bad – it would not stop them. This is business and money we're talking about.'

If it is true then a sudden death was the gamble that someone like Specky Boyd took in following his particular career path. However, innocent people did die in the horror crash: Boyd had just that morning travelled to Malaga airport to meet his daughter, Anna Nicola Gavin, aged twenty-one and her friend, Louise Douglas, also twenty-one, who had flown out from Scotland for a holiday. Also in the car that fateful day was 3-year-old Helen Williams, the daughter of Boyd's girlfriend. Ms Douglas was said to be three months pregnant. They all perished in the crash, along with a Spanish factory manager and his son who were in the other car. Only the Spanish victim's wife miraculously survived.

The feeling was that Boyd was on the verge of something big. Although registered as unemployed back home, he was spending money like it was going out of fashion, while raking it in from his illegal business operations back in Scotland. After his death it was revealed that he was under surveillance by the National Crime Intelligence Service (NCIS) and a spokesman told the press: 'We were well aware of who he was and his involvement in drugs and organised crime. He was the subject of our attention in the days before he died.'

The funeral of Stewart Specky Boyd in Neilston cemetery was a sight to behold as his friends and associates gave him a true gangster send-off. Attended by hundreds of mourners, including many faces from the underworld, it was a ceremony that the Chicago mob in the time of Al Capone would have been proud of. The coffin was adorned with extravagant floral wreaths and, bizarrely, a machete, a magnum of champagne and a gram of cocaine were placed in his coffin. And while the service was being conducted a police helicopter circled overhead watching everything that was going on.

Back home in Scotland, there were fears that a war would erupt in the wake of Boyd's demise, as rival gangsters tried to fill the power vacuum. Within the year, one of his former henchmen had not only had his car torched and been shot at as he drove around the streets but he was also attacked by a three-man hit team as he left the Royal Oak pub, Boyd's former gang headquarters in Nitshill. The man was brutally beaten with a claw hammer and, according to the *News of the World*, would have been knifed if one of the gang had not lost his nerve. Their victim, it was claimed, was engaged in a power struggle with other crooks over control of Boyd's empire.

Then, in February 2004, two men, known associates of Boyd, were shot as they sat in the Royal Oak. It was claimed they were lured there by rivals under the excuse of discussing a drug deal and were blasted by two hired gunmen. Press reports stated that the pub was often at the centre of violent incidents – and in March 2004 the premises were said to have been thoroughly cleaned with industrial-strength ammonia and detergents in a bid to scrub out any trace of deadly dealings.

Meanwhile, even in death, Stewart Boyd was a target. His grave was attacked, the headstone smashed and flowers trampled and destroyed. The two rival drug dealers rumoured to be responsible were warned they were living on borrowed time before Boyd's supporters caught up with them and dished out fierce reprisals.

Time may also be running out for the involvement of known criminals in the lucrative security market. Although it was only a minority of firms that had been infiltrated by the 'faces', it was decided that a crackdown was necessary. England and Wales paved the way early in 2005 with the Private Security Industry Act, which made it compulsory for anyone taking up employment in the industry to have a clean record. The Scottish Executive soon followed suit. In September 2005, plans were announced to regulate the industry by bringing in a licensing scheme for employees. From the end of 2007, it will be necessary for all security guards, bouncers, bodyguards, private investigators, security consultants, closed-circuit television operators and anyone transporting cash or valuables to apply for a licence – and it will only be granted if they have no criminal record and pass other checks.

Elaine Broom

She lived like royalty

It was meant to be a one-off; a quick way to solve a cash crisis. Elaine Broom was desperate for money to pay off crippling debts. So she embezzled funds from her employers. It was so easy that she did it again and again. The ease with which she could take the money, and the joy of spending, became a drug and she was hooked. She seemed unaware, or did not care, that she was on a downward spiral and that sooner or later she would be discovered. The result of her greed would be devastating.

Broom, a senior cashier with an oil company then called Sub-Sea Offshore, was unable to discuss her indebtedness with her second husband, Roger. She hit on the idea of simply writing out a blank cheque on her employer's account and presented it for signature. As she was a trusted employee, it was signed without question. That was the beginning. In a television interview after her conviction, she thought she would have been caught right at the beginning but when she got away with it 'it just mushroomed from there on'.

It mushroomed, in fact, to the tune of almost £1 million. She passed a total of 273 fraudulent cheques in three years.

If the crime was prompted by a dire financial emergency, then it progressed through greed. The Brooms lived in a comfortable lodge on the Queen's Balmoral estate. The family, unwittingly thanks to Elaine Broom's fraud, enjoyed 'a life of luxury well beyond the means of ordinary people,' as the trial judge later said. A yacht was chartered to take the Brooms and their two daughters on a cruise of the Caribbean. The family and three guests flew first class during the summer of 1999 from London to Antigua. When they arrived, the yacht was waiting, complete with a chef specially hired to prepare their meals.

There were shopping trips to London and New York: the Brooms stayed in top hotels and spent small fortunes on luxury goods. Thousands of pounds were splashed out on cars and home improvements; £50,000 alone on building a centrally-heated double garage for the new vehicles. Broom even threw an extravagant party to celebrate the 'opening' of the garage, as one neighbour recalled: 'It was amazing. She had a huge marquee on the lawn with wooden decking. She hired entertainers and had karaoke; she even had portaloos in the garden. The carpets were three inches-thick and they even had perfume for us to use. It was fit for royalty. The Queen herself would have felt quite at home; and all that for a garage.'

To her neighbours the only explanation was that the family had either inherited a fortune or won the lottery. And although the Brooms employed locals to look after their house, and donated a computer to the local primary school, they were unpopular with many of them. As one who knew the family said: 'She was always putting on airs and graces. They had money but no class. It always seemed she was trying to show off.'

But her luck could not last forever. Ironically, it was an argument over cash that resulted in the whole scheme being discovered. It had been decided that the garden at their home, Lochnagar Lodge, needed to be landscaped – including the creation of a footbridge, rockery and even a waterfall – and gardeners, who lived nearby, were brought in to begin the £80,000 project. However, when a cheque drawn on Elaine Broom's employers bounced, the gardeners went to Sub-Sea Offshore to complain. They found out that Broom was not the finance director, as she had claimed, but merely a cashier earning around £13,000 per annum. The firm, now suspicious, launched an internal probe and uncovered 'financial irregularities'. Over £1 million-worth of financial irregularities, they claimed.

In December 1999, three years after she began her life of crime, Elaine Broom was sacked. She later took a job as a £5-an-hour waitress at a Braemar hotel. Naturally, the police had been called and she was charged with embezzlement. At first she claimed that she had been forced to take the cash because she had 'a physical fear of her husband' but that did not work. Her husband denied all knowledge of the crimes and was never charged. He just thought she was doing rather well in her job as a 'financial director', as he later explained: 'I thought my wife was on one hell of a whack. It turns out she was extremely naughty. I trusted her; I guess some people would say I should have guessed something was up.'

Two years later, Elaine Broom appeared in court in Stonehaven.

She admitted stealing £838,709 from her employers. The judge, Lord Marnoch, was stunned that the steady skimming had not been detected for three years. As the accused woman stood in the dock, clutching a teddy bear, the defence pleaded for mercy. The judge, though, was not so inclined. 'I am satisfied that by way of retribution, and to deter others, only a substantial custodial sentence is appropriate.'

He sentenced Elaine Broom to five years in prison for her crimes. Her company, meanwhile, launched a civil action to try and claw back £600,000 but only just over £100,000 was recoverable, it was believed.

In court Elaine Broom had cut something of a pathetic figure. There was little of the confidence that she must have had to pull off her fraud. Nor was there any sign of the high-handed attitude she displayed to those who came in contact with her while she was living the high life, a point made by detective inspector Kenny Lawson: 'It was difficult to believe the extent of her extravagance and everyone who had any involvement with her – witnesses and officers – was gobsmacked by her arrogance and the way she spent the money and lorded it over the mere mortals.'

Broom later spoke of her terror on arrival at Stirling's Cornton Vale, Scotland's only women's prison. However, within a few months her arrogance returned. She had gone from being a neighbour to the Queen to sharing space with common criminals and she bitterly complained about it when interviewed for a BBC documentary on life inside 'the Vale'. Although she was a low-risk, category D prisoner, she resented finding herself talking to 'murderers or drug users or drug traffickers'. She thought prisoners like her should be segregated, perhaps in an open prison.

However, she did have some sympathy for some of her fellow inmates, many of whom were suicidal. 'I don't think the prison staff, albeit they are very good, have the necessary resources to deal with the girls that are trying to commit suicide,' she told the camera. 'These girls are trying to commit suicide because they are totally desperate and they are crying out for help and there isn't the facilities here to help them.'

She was released early in 2004.

Reverend Michael Bunce

The priest who fell from grace

Michael Bunce obviously paid little heed to the Lord's Prayer, for he led himself into temptation and ripped off a charitable organisation, which he had set up, to the tune of £44,000. He carried on with his finger in the till for two years before finally being caught, when there was a further shock waiting for him: his daughter, the apple of his eye, was earning £400 a night as a stripper.

It was in 1989 that this Man of God established a scheme to aid the jobless in Brechin. The St Andrew's Businessman's Association, named after the church which formed the centre of his ministry, was bankrolled by the government-funded Manpower Services Commission to operate training programmes for the jobless. Just a year later, the Association was a roaring success, with several local worthies on its board, fifty trainees on its books, an office staff of ten and an annual turnover of £130,000.

Bunce wanted some of that boodle for himself. He needed the signature of another director to clear cheques and he managed to convince one of them to put her name to them. 'I had some reservations,' said the director at the later trial. 'But if you can't trust the rector of your church, who can you trust?' The crooked cleric would ask his secretary to take the cheques to the director and when she queried the transactions he told her, 'I've done a lot of work. Don't you think I'm entitled to something?'

As it turned out, the 'something' he felt he was entitled to amounted to a decidedly pretty penny. St Paul said the love of money is the root of all evil but the robbing reverend obviously paid very little attention to that part of scripture. When he was arrested he owned a Mercedes, a Daimler and a Porsche. He had bought his daughter a £2,000 pony called Sonny and a Welsh Mountain pony, worth £500, called Mindy. He bought luxuries for himself and his family, he splashed out on paintings, antiques, wine and even flying lessons, he paid his son's school fees.

Bunce's conscience was no doubt troubled by this dishonesty. So he justified it by telling himself that he didn't take a wage. The Bible tells us that the wages of sin is death but for Bunce it wasn't a sticky end that awaited him but a fall from grace. In 1991, suspicions were raised among the other directors and the reverend was offered a salary of £10,000 a year to help pay back the money he had siphoned off. And just to make sure he could not be led down the path of temptation again, his right to sign cheques was withdrawn. The entire matter was discreetly handled. However, it could not be kept a secret for long.

In 1992, Bunce was promoted to the post of provost of Dundee cathedral and after that his sins were brought into the light. Naturally, the police were called in but it took five years before the full extent of his embezzlement was unravelled and he was brought to trial. At first he was quietly confident but as the evidence mounted against him during his five-week trial, he appeared less sure that the Lord was with him. He found his composure at the end for, as he was found guilty, he merely shrugged his shoulders and smiled. But there was a further shock awaiting him.

Reporters, digging into his private life, had found that his stunning 18-year-old daughter Naomi had dropped out of university and was earning £400 a night as a lap dancer in a Midlands nightclub. Bunce refused to believe the reports, saying that his daughter was merely a dancer. Her career burgeoned over the following months and while the newspaper coverage she received would have fuelled her meteoric rise it also resulted in her being pestered by a phone pervert. The gorgeous blonde never seemed to doubt her father's innocence and although she appeared to be still trying to pretend – at least to him – that as a dancer she was more exotic than erotic, she stuck by him.

On bail while awaiting sentence, he was asked about his crimes and he said, 'The whole thing is a mess, a scenario of sadness.' His faith, however, remained unshaken. 'I have my ministry and my faith has always been a total commitment to God. I had a vocation and it's still active.' Having embezzled over £40,000 from a church fund, it would appear he also had something of a commitment to Mammon.

In July 1997, he was ordered to pay a fine of £60,000 or face two years in jail. He was given until the end of October to come up with the cash and it was predicted he would have to sell his £105,000 bungalow. He was also to hand over paintings and antiques he had bought with the embezzled money and pay back £3,800 to a bank to cover the overdraft of the St Andrew's Businessman's Association.

Ronald Bunting

The poison dwarf

Ronald Bunting had a short temper, a propensity for violence and a problem with his height. Put those three ingredients together and you have a recipe for disaster. In Bunting's case, it led to extreme violence, prison and a spell in a mental institution. Ultimately, it led to his tragic death. He was only four feet eight inches tall and it bothered him. As his ex-wife said later, 'He had a short fuse and was totally obsessed about his height.' Herself only five feet and one inch, she said that when they were together he ordered her not to wear high heels.

In 1982, a man made the mistake of taunting him about his height and was almost killed when the little man flew into a rage. Almost ten years later, Bunting was stalked by armed police after he went on a rampage in Airdrie and Coatbridge. The then 31-year-old man had hijacked a taxi and fired at pedestrians with a shotgun before sending customers in a busy pub diving for cover by smashing the windows. He ran riot for five hours before the armed officers arrested him. Sentenced to be detained without limit of time at Carstairs, he was released in 1997 on a conditional discharge, which meant he was to be supervised and could be recalled at any time.

Released into the care of his father in Airdrie, the news came as a shock to his former wife, who claimed that he had 'vowed to kill me and our kids and now I fear for my own safety. This guy is nuts.' They had been together for eight years and when they split she obtained an interim interdict to prevent him from going anywhere near her or her children. However, even though he was denied access by the courts, she said he still found her and made her life hell. She only found out he was free, she told a newspaper, because her mother spotted Bunting in an Airdrie street. At first it was thought that the man had escaped from Carstairs but one phone call to the police revealed that he was officially at liberty.

However, four years later, Bunting was back in custody, having been sentenced to four years for a robbery. In July 2004 his temper brought him to a violent end when, filled with booze and drugs, he got into a fight with 29-year-old John Clark. They had been in Bunting's flat when a violent row developed over possession of three valium tablets. Clark, who had his own previous convictions for violence, admitted to being afraid of the much smaller man. However, when Bunting came at him with a knife, he defended himself with the first thing that came to hand: a tartan golfing umbrella. He jabbed at the man with the pointed end of the brolly and caught him on the face. Bunting fell back, blood streaming from his eye. He later choked to death on his blood as a result of the eye haemorrhage. The post mortem revealed that he had so much alcohol in his system that he would have been a massive three times over the legal driving limit.

Clark was later convicted of culpable homicide when the court accepted he acted in self-defence and was sentenced to seven years in prison.

Robert Cadiz and Paul Macklin
Public-school thrill seekers

There is a belief, often well-founded, that a person's upbringing can lead them into crime. If you are born, they say, into a family of criminals then the chance of you becoming one is greater. If you live in a tough housing estate, surrounded by unemployment and deprivation, then you are likely to become a crook. If you run with a gang, then it is highly possible that as you grow older you will run with even more dangerous comrades. There is a certain amount of truth in this but there are, of course, many exceptions: people who did not join the family business, who worked hard to get out of the schemes, who left their youthful violence behind and became hard-working and honest citizens.

And then there is an even rarer group: those from a privileged background who, despite their good fortune, embrace a life of crime. Robert Cadiz and Paul Macklin are two such individuals.

Cadiz was born in Trinidad, the son of an oil executive and a self-made millionaire, while Macklin's family owned a personnel company and a perfume store. Macklin was a former pupil of top people's school, Gordonstoun, the alma mater of Prince Charles. He was also a thrill-seeker who was an early exponent of skiing-off mountains and para-chuting the rest of the way down. When he met Cadiz at Robert Gordon's College in Aberdeen he found a soulmate. Yet they were bored. They needed something to spice up their lives. Money wasn't enough, fast cars weren't enough, girls were not enough. They wanted more. Much more. And so their minds turned to crime. They would plan and execute daring capers and leave the plodding police in their wake.

In 1994, they planned a wages snatch. A van delivering over £300,000 destined for the pay packets of Aberdeen District Council workers was the target. They had armed themselves with a sawn-off shotgun and a pump-action shotgun for the heist, while their faces were to be covered with SAS-style balaclavas. The pair loitered outside the council's contract-services division in Kittybrewster, where the delivery was to be made.

However, something about the body language of the two young men – Cadiz was then aged twenty-two and Macklin twenty-one – raised the suspicions of a passer-by and the police were alerted. Macklin turned a Russian-made shotgun on the officers who responded – three male and one female – then hijacked a passing car and forced the terrified driver to help him get away. He was apprehended later that night living it up in an Aberdeen nightclub. Cadiz had not been so quick off the mark and was lifted at the scene. Macklin was subsequently jailed for eight years while Cadiz – who was also found guilty of robbing a Clydesdale Bank at gunpoint and making off with £3,000 – was given nine years. Detectives at the time described them as 'adrenalin junkies who glorified violence'.

It was not the end of their criminal career. In September 2000, Cadiz found himself back behind bars after he admitted dealing in cocaine, ecstasy and amphetamines with a street value of £30,000. The court heard that Cadiz had been subject to racial abuse while at school and also bullying because he was dyslexic. This led to depression, which in turn led him into crime. He claimed that, although his wealthy father took care of all his material needs, his emotional life was less than fulfilling. His depression deepened and on one occasion he tried to commit suicide by swallowing an overdose of pills. When convicted of the conspiracy to rob and armed robbery, his parents disowned him. The only member of his family with whom he had any contact was his sister, and it was in her home that police found the drugs. He believed the only friends he had in the world were the men he met in jail and it was on the behalf of one of his new-found chums that Cadiz kept the drugs, it was claimed. When police raided the flat, they found 9,017 ecstasy tablets, 38 amphetamine pills, 13 bags of cocaine and a set of digital scales. They also found over £1,000 in cash under a mattress and in a desk. He was originally sentenced to five years for the drug offence and was recalled to prison to serve the remaining five years of his original sentence. The new stretch was to begin at the end of the old one, although he successfully appealed the drug sentence and had it cut to two years.

Macklin's penchant for threatening police officers was also to land him into further trouble. In May 2003, a gang of masked men forced their way into a flat in Aberdeen's Printfield Terrace and attacked a man with a hockey stick, a baseball bat and a gun. The victim was also punched and kicked. It was claimed that Macklin was one of the attackers and he was also charged with threatening the victim with a hatchet, holding a gun and a knife against his neck and threatening to kill him.

Although he was cleared of attempted murder, with the gun allegation withdrawn by the Crown, Macklin was less fortunate in charges relating to his actions subsequent to the alleged attack. Police officers called to the flat heard someone escaping from an open window and said they saw Macklin running away across the tenement's back green. While two cops chased him through the city streets they said he repeatedly turned round and aimed a silver handgun at them. Eventually, he disappeared down a lane and the officers said they heard the roar of a car engine before they saw the vehicle speed off. The courage of the two officers involved, sergeant Henry Ferguson and constable Simon Reid, later earned them a commendation from the city's chief constable. Sergeant Ferguson told the court about the terror he felt as his quarry turned the gun on him three times. 'It had never happened to me before,' he said. 'It was surreal. I felt sick with dread in my stomach. I felt in immediate danger of my life for the first and only time.'

Macklin was captured and convicted of illegal possession of a firearm and assaulting the two policemen. Despite his claim that he had been in another part of Aberdeen at the time, and denying possession of a weapon and the assault of the two officers, the jury took just over an hour to find him guilty. He was sent down for fifteen years. One of the city's senior police officers said afterwards that, 'Macklin has a violent past and posed a considerable threat to the community and had it not been for the officers' actions, a more serious incident could have developed.'

In 2004, Macklin successfully appealed against his sentence, which was cut to ten years. The Court of Criminal Appeal ruled that a fifteen-year penalty should be imposed only for more serious cases.

James Campbell

'I am an animal'

This 19-year-old was named as Scotland's most evil teenager. His arrest for a sex attack on a 4-year-old girl prompted a storm of outrage when it was revealed that he had been released early from a three-year sentence for assaulting a 91-year-old woman with intent to rape. Campbell himself said to police at the time of the first offence, 'I am an animal. I know I am bad and deserve to be punished.' However, doctors insisted he did not suffer from any mental disorder.

He had been caught assaulting the 91-year-old woman by her daughter-in-law. He was naked and lying on top of the pensioner when the younger woman burst in. He leaped up and attacked the younger woman and struggled with her for several minutes before he finally ran off. In March 2003 he was jailed for three years. Two other charges – one of exposing himself to a young woman and another of trying to abduct a child of ten – were dropped as part of a bargain in return for pleading guilty to the assault on the pensioner. It also meant the young victims would not need to give evidence which, as the **Lee Bell** case shows, can often be as much an ordeal as the original crime.

Campbell was released on parole in May 2004. Two months later he crept into a Coatbridge house and snatched a 4-year-old girl. Minutes later he found himself at the mercy of a howling mob, hungry for his blood – but was saved by the man who had tracked him down.

The child's father had left the back door of their home open for his wife, who was on a night out. Her grandmother raised the alarm when she found the child's bed empty. Family and friends swiftly rallied round and combed the streets for the toddler. Campbell was spotted in a lane with the child. He tried to run off but was chased by local man Ben McGivern, a nightclub bouncer who was more than capable of taking care of himself. By his own admission, he treated Campbell none-too-gently when he caught him. He had caught a glimpse of the child as he ran past and thought she was dead.

'I chased after him,' he told the *Scottish Sun*, 'and pushed him into a fence. Then I cracked him one and punched and kicked him in the face.'

Some youths who had been part of the hunting party arrived and also gave their quarry a few kicks. Mr McGivern took him into his custody, keeping the growing crowd from tearing Campbell apart – and was bitten for his trouble. Campbell sank his teeth into his arm, slicing through the bouncer's coat and into his arm. He hung on like that for almost ten minutes, until police arrived and prised him off.

Later, as word spread through the streets, a mob gathered outside the homeless centre where Campbell had been placed. They wanted the council-run facility closed down.

In September 2004, Campbell admitted abducting the child, detaining her against her will and attempting to rape her. He firmly denied suggestions that he intended to murder her, even though he had stolen a knife from the kitchen. He was, his defence counsel assured the court, 'disgusted at what he has done'. He was sentenced to life, although he would be eligible for parole after ten years. The sentence infuriated the child's family. Life should mean life, they said. Campbell was scum, they said. He should not be allowed to walk the streets, they said. Even television presenter, and Childline-founder Esther Rantzen, commented on the case. 'This man should never have been freed to attack this poor child. It is grossly irresponsible of the psychiatrist who made the decision to release him – somebody should be held to account.'

The decision to release him early became a political football, with opposition politicians using the case to kick at the Scottish Executive. 'Automatic early release is causing needless crime and endless victims,' said one. 'The Scottish Executive refuses to end it. How many more victims have to suffer?' The Executive then announced that the process was to be re-examined by the Scottish Parliament.

William Cordiner

The grandpa rapist

In 1967, William Buchan Cordiner walked free from court when the murder charge he was facing – and had always denied – was withdrawn. In November 1976, by then with twenty previous convictions on his sheet, the Edinburgh man was sentenced to ten years for attempting to murder a garage owner. However, the sentence was quashed on appeal. He successfully argued that one of the charges against him had been committed while he was in jail for another offence. To fight the charge, Cordiner had been forced to tender a special defence of alibi, and in so doing had to reveal his previous convictions to the court, contrary to the Criminal Procedure (Scotland) Act 1975. Three years later, he was jailed for five years in Birmingham for robbery.

Until then, many of the charges against him were related to violence: one of his early convictions was for attempting to extort £1,000 from an Edinburgh man by threatening to torch his nightclub and to 'cut his head from his body'. He was not known for crimes against women. However, that changed in 1983 when he was brought to trial in Jedburgh for raping a 17-year-old girl and assaulting a 16-year-old with intent to rape. Both victims said the offences had been committed in a disused quarry. The courtroom was treated to an incredible outburst from the man nicknamed 'Stein', a contraction of Frankenstein. He claimed police treated him as public-enemy number one. He alleged officers were in the habit of stopping his car and searching it whenever he went out, telling any female with him that she was likely to be raped. He accused the judge, Lord Kincraig, and the prosecutor, Mr Edward Bowen, of knowing the police wanted him put away.

It was not the first time a Scottish court had witnessed an angry outburst from Cordiner. When defending a divorce action on the ground of cruelty in 1972, he stormed out of the court in a rage just as the judge was finding in favour of his wife. When he returned to what he called 'a kangaroo court', he declared: 'All you people will have something to be afraid of. I tell you that you will never sleep in peace.' Unsurprisingly, the judge had him clapped in handcuffs and sentenced him to three years for contempt. He was freed after three months by appeal-court judges who felt he had been sufficiently punished.

Cordiner was sentenced to ten years for the Jedburgh sex assaults but had been at liberty less than six months before he was again arrested for a brutal rape. This time the victim was a 25-year-old mother. Cordiner was accused of attacking her in the stables on the grounds of Old Ancrum House, once used a detention centre for problem boys – including, for a period during the 1950s, William Cordiner himself. The old house had long since been demolished but Cordiner admitted he liked to visit the area to fish and bird watch. The young woman claimed that Cordiner had sold a television set for her and was driving her to his home to collect the cash. He had driven into a country lane, she said, and stopped near the barn. There she was dragged from the car and raped. He also repeatedly stabbed her in the chest, puncturing her lung and narrowly missing her heart. Despite her injuries, the woman managed to run away. Forcing herself to remain conscious, for she knew that if she stopped she would sink into a coma and die, she wandered around, eventually finding help at a lodge.

The prosecution pointed out to the court that the accused had a string of convictions dating back to 1955 and that he had only been released six months before he carried out the attack. Even Cordiner's defence counsel could not deny the extent of his client's previous. He said that the man's record between 1955 and 1985 contained sentences amounting to thirty years, although he had not served the full terms. He recognised that in this case the judge may have been of a mind to impose a sentence of indeterminate duration. However, he pointed out that his client was now fifty-two and asked his lordship to impose a sentence, albeit a substantial one, that would allow him the possibility of release in his later years.

The judge, Lord MacLean, told Cordiner he had a 'lamentable' record. He went on, 'What weighs against my imposing an indeterminate sentence is your age, fifty-two. On the other hand, looking to your record and periods of imprisonment you have served, I feel in all frankness to protect the public that I have no alternative but to impose life imprisonment upon you.'

On New Year's Day 1998, Cordiner of a heart attack in Shotts prison.

John Cronin

'One of Scotland's most dangerous men'

In November 2001, a twenty-stone Scot accused of a bank robbery in the Republic of Ireland asked a judge to order that he be kept in solitary confinement until his trial. His lawyer told the court that 'there are certain things in his past that may leave him open to intimidation. He is worried for his safety in jail.' The man was John Cronin, originally from Tranent in East Lothian, and he was dubbed 'one of Scotland's most dangerous men'.

Cronin first hit the headlines in 1992 when, dressed as a priest, he conned his way into the Edinburgh home of a Conservative Party activist known only as Judy X. He then put the woman through a terrifying and brutal ordeal, battering her with an iron bar and sexually assaulting her. He told psychiatrists that he thought he was attacking his maternal grandfather who, he claimed, had abused him. It was later revealed by psychiatric reports that he had a disturbed childhood, in which he often disrupted classes by urinating and defecating on the floor. These childhood problems led to an untreatable personality disorder. Years later, a police officer told the press that: 'Cronin is set apart by the level of his distorted thinking, and by the attitude towards women he has openly displayed at interview.'

He was sentenced to life in prison for the attack on Judy X but, astonishingly, that sentence was slashed to a mere six years on appeal. The judges' decision quite naturally infuriated his victim and she took the unusual step of speaking publicly at a Tory Party conference condemning the move.

He served only four years and just a day after his release he was picked up in Dublin, again claiming to be a priest. This time he had been stalking female politicians outside the Irish parliament. He was subsequently jailed for a year for stealing £1,180 from the home of a parish priest in County Leitrim.

On his release, he returned to Tranent where he launched a series of threatening phone calls targeted at female members of the Conservative Party. He also posed as a member of a respectable

Edinburgh business family in order to obtain a woman's name and address. Charged with breaches of the peace, he received one year's probation. That same year, 1997, he was back behind bars after being caught posing as a doctor, a businessman and a police officer to obtain personal details of women professionals. Charged with three counts of fraud, he was sentenced to three years but in the end served only twenty months. His lawyer said that he was not motivated in this case by sexual desires but merely to boost his low self-esteem. On his release, he was described as 'a time bomb waiting to explode'.

By 2001, the six-foot-tall, 30-year-old Scot was back in Ireland. Within a month, he was the object of a massive manhunt following a bank robbery in Waterford on the south-east coast. Cronin got away with £2,500 in sterling and Irish currency after thrusting a starter pistol into the face of a shocked teller. The staff knew who he was; he had been in the branch before, claiming to be a businessman inquiring about opening an account. He warned them that he would 'spray them with bullets' if they did not part with the money. He had left a taxi idling in the street and used it to make his getaway. Knowing that the Irish police, the Gardai, were speeding to the locus, he told the driver to take him to Dublin. However, Cronin had not thought his plan through and had no clear getaway arranged. His description was immediately released and roadblocks were set up around Waterford. He was finally caught two hours later by two motorcycle officers thirty miles from Dublin.

Embarrassed police explained that they had known he was in the area and were aware of his past. He had been under observation but somehow had managed to give his watchers the slip in order to carry out the bank raid. It was when Cronin appeared in court that his lawyer made the request that he be kept in isolation; as a known sex offender he would be a target for other inmates, who take a dim view of those who perpetrate sex crimes. Cronin's attack on Judy X, and his photograph, had received widespread coverage and there was the distinct possibility of frontier justice being administered by a fellow con. The judge agreed to the defence's submission.

While he awaited trial, it emerged that Cronin had been travelling round Ireland for some time before he landed in Waterford. Although he had been staying at homeless shelter, he also booked into a guest house claiming to be a successful financial consultant with a wife and two children back in Scotland. While there, he advised regulars at a local pub on financial matters and ran up a £400 phone bill.

In the end, Cronin was sentenced to two years for his bank raid, carried out, it was said, to fund his plan to become a gunrunner, albeit in imitation firearms. It was his intention to ease his straitened finances by buying the guns in Britain and flogging them in Ireland, the land of his father's birth.

On his release in 2003, Cronin flew from Dublin to Manchester and straight into the arms of waiting police officers. They had a warrant for his arrest in connection with a crime in the city two years before: it involved the theft of £75 from an 80-year-old woman who Cronin had befriended through a religious society. He received two weeks for this offence but was back on the streets for only two months before his collar was felt once again, this time for committing no less than fifty-seven frauds since leaving prison. He had told bankers in Oldham that he was establishing a decorating firm, opened an account and promptly set about passing dud cheques to all and sundry. In the almost sixty counts of fraud, he made off with over £13,000-worth of jewellery and other goods. This frenzy of cheque passing netted him a two-and-a-half-year sentence.

In the meantime, questions were asked about why he had been placed in a halfway house for vulnerable people in Oldham without the supervisor being informed of his past. And it was also revealed that he had applied for – and been refused – membership of the local branch of the British National Party, not a body noted for its scruples over membership. Clearly, even they drew the line at the man they called Scotland's most notorious sex beast.

In October 2004, he was a free man again. As his frenzied attack on Judy X had been committed prior to the sex offenders register being introduced, he was able to go anywhere he wished without supervision, once his term of parole had expired. The thoughts of law-enforcement bodies turned to how they could keep track of him. A spokesman for Lothian and Borders Police, which had previously set up a four-man task force to keep tabs on him, said, 'We'll be keeping a close eye on John Cronin following his release.'

Given his obsession in the past with female members of the

Conservative Party, the Scottish chief whip Bill Aitken said, 'Cronin needs to be kept under close supervision. He's fortunate not to be in jail for a long time.'

One method that the authorities considered was satellite tracking, then being tried out in the Manchester area. Around 120 sex offenders and wife beaters were tagged and tracked by a satellite global-positioning-system. Cronin had expressed a desire to stay in the Manchester and West Midlands area, although he said he might visit relatives in Tranent; news that did not please local residents. However, the Scottish Executive said they had no plans to introduce satellite tracking.

In October 2005 he surfaced again, apparently posing as a student at the University of Central England in Birmingham. A Scot studying at the university spotted him on campus, wearing a university jacket and carrying what appeared to be study material. The *Sunday Mail* was alerted to his presence and, although the university stated that student records were confidential, the newspaper discovered that Cronin's name did not appear on the roster of students. However, that did not mean he had not registered under a false name. Also, his previous convictions would not prevent him from studying there, unless he was taking a course that dealt with vulnerable people in society.

James Crosbie

The suburban blagger

On 30 April 1974, two men entered the Glasgow Whiteinch branch of the Clydesdale Bank, armed with a shotgun and a pistol, and fired two shots into the air before telling the staff to lie down on the floor. The shots were designed to let the four workers know they meant business. The men then filled bags with £87,000 in cash and ran out to a waiting car. There was another shot from the car, believed at first to be at a passer-by but later discovered to be accidental, before the car sped off. The haul was, at the time, the biggest-ever from a Scottish bank.

A short time later, a police roadblock waved a cyclist through. The man, James Crosbie, had a rucksack on his back and he smiled at the officers as they let him pass. What the cops didn't know was that Crosbie was one of the raiders and that his rucksack was stuffed with cash. He and his accomplice had driven to high flats at Broomhill – a short distance from the scene of the robbery – where they ditched the car, split up the booty and hopped onto the push bikes they had hidden there. They knew the police would be looking for two men in a car, not two cyclists. Their plan worked and they got clean away, although in Crosbie's case it wasn't for very long.

The 37-year-old Glasgow man had a string of previous convictions for larceny, housebreaking and reset. Now he was married, lived in a nice house in the Glasgow suburb of Bishopbriggs and had a furniture shop in Springburn. But that wasn't enough for James Crosbie. During a separation from his wife, he struck up a friendship with his next-door neighbour, a 40-year-old bank messenger. Soon, talk turned to the inside knowledge the man had about delivery times of cash to various branches of the Clydesdale Bank. Talk eventually turned to action and Crosbie and an accomplice staged their first raid, at the bank's Hillington branch in May 1972. The two armed men walked in brandishing a shotgun and revolver and shouted, 'If everyone behaves, no-one will get hurt.' A holdall was tossed onto the counter and a teller was instructed to fill it with money.

Crosbie and his neighbour then went on a spending spree in America, blowing a lot of the cash on the tables of Las Vegas. Spurred on by the success of the first raid, a second was planned, at Whiteinch in Glasgow. Again, everything went according to plan, no-one was hurt and the weapons were never actually aimed at anyone in the bank. But for Crosbie, things were about to go badly wrong.

He had been having an affair with a 16-year-old girl, the daughter of a couple he and his wife had met at a party. She had become his babysitter and a relationship had developed. He visited her at home almost every day and she played truant from school to see him. Through him she learned how the other half lived. He took her to fancy restaurants and on trips abroad. To her, he meant everything, even though he was more than twice her age. Although she knew nothing at first of his criminal activities, he had asked her to look after a roll of cash and a golf bag which she later discovered contained a gun. Crosbie had also left a locked case in her Possilpark home. Soon, she began to suspect that he was more than just a furniture salesman. He joked about the bank robberies, suggesting that he might be the person the cops were hunting. He seemed to want to talk about his exploits to people, apparently wishing that he could tell everyone how he had outsmarted the police at the roadblock. He also had a habit of flashing his cash, at one point peeling a bill from a thick wad just to pay for a bag of frozen peas. Eventually, he confessed all to his young girlfriend. But she still loved the man she described as 'kind, generous and gentle' and kept his secret. That ended the night she had a party.

Her parents were away and she had some friends round for what the press called 'a teenage pop-record-party'. At some point, a few of the young people found Crosbie's case and managed to open it. To their surprise, they found £40,000 in cash. Some of them dipped into the loot and, over a period of time, took around £13,000. One, though, realised just what the money was and phoned the police. Six weeks after the Whiteinch bank job, cops raided the young girl's house and arrested James Crosbie. Astonishingly, despite facing charges for two armed robberies, which had netted over £150,000, he was released on bail. He then proceeded to execute another robbery, presumably to finance a getaway to foreign climes.

He walked into the Royal Bank of Scotland in Edinburgh's Gorgie

Road, wearing a crash helmet; his face was covered with a visor. He presented a shotgun at a teller, placed a bag on the counter and ordered: 'Fill it up.' At first the bank employee thought this was a joke but when she realised the man was serious she refused to fill up the sack. Thus rebuffed, Crosbie moved to the next position and eventually managed to walk out with over £17,000. He roared off on a motorcycle but was recognised by two eagle-eyed police officers and arrested.

Appearing in court in September 1974, Crosbie had the decency to plead guilty to all the charges and admitted fourteen previous convictions dating back to 1950. The judge, Lord Robertson, said his crimes were of the 'utmost depravity' in which he had used firearms to threaten and subdue citizens going about their lawful business and that he had previous convictions for crimes related to the 'dishonest acquisition of other people's property'. He sentenced Crosbie to twenty years in jail. The neighbour who supplied him with the inside information, but who had not taken part in any of the raids, had earlier been sentenced to nine years. Of the £170,000 taken in the three bank jobs, only £42,000 was ever recovered.

Lorraine Dick

A victim of circumstances?

Lorraine Dick was a victim of a brutal crime in a strange land. To make matters worse it was a crime committed by people she had good reason to trust. Not surprisingly the experience drove her to the very edge of reason and ultimately claimed her life.

She had trained as a nurse but felt she wanted to give something back to the world. She came from a deeply religious family – her father was a minister – and in 1995 she left her home in Kilsyth to volunteer as a surgical staff nurse in a project in Bangladesh organised by the Voluntary Services Overseas. She had been brought up to look for the good in people but in that poverty-stricken country she found that sometimes finding such goodness is not easy. The Scot had only been in Bangladesh for a year when she was attacked by four police officers and systematically raped.

The rape was, needless to say, a traumatic experience for this caring young woman whose only desire was to help others. Her faith in human nature had been ripped apart and, to blot out the memories of the brutal experience, she turned to a substance that is readily available in Bangladesh: heroin. By the time she returned to Scotland she was hooked, an addict who would do anything for the next fix. Like many a drug user before her, she ran up credit-card bills, sold her belongings and ultimately turned to theft to feed her habit. And, coming from the kind of family she did, the shame of her needs and the lies that she told to cover up her addiction made her even more depressed and more in need of heroin than ever. She experienced the duality of feelings that many addicts feel; the need for the drug while at the same time despising it.

Back at home, she blamed her trembling and pale complexion on a stomach bug she had picked up on her travels. In September 2001, she was still struggling with her demons, and the demons were winning. She could no longer hold down a job; in fact, she found herself in trouble in England, where she worked as an agency nurse, after lifting some diazepam. She was, she later said, at an all-time low. She was trying to kick her habit and her needs were gnawing at her nerves and snarling at her resolve. After almost two weeks of cold turkey, her will to live had deserted her. The agony of detox was proving too much and she convinced herself that she would be better off dead. And if heroin was the thing that was ruining her life, then heroin might as well be the thing that claimed it. The problem was she needed money to buy it.

For Pamela Kaur, 20 September 2001 was just like any other day. It could very easily have been her last. Lorraine Dick had selected the Kilsyth off sales in which the 52-year-old woman worked as the source of cash to finance her suicide bid. The desperate nurse entered the shop and began to punch the sales assistant on the head. As Ms Kaur desperately fought back, she was stabbed repeatedly in the chest. Grabbing cash from the till, Dick fled from the shop saying, 'I'm sorry, I'm desperate.'

She bought three £20 bags of heroin from a Glasgow dealer and drove to a car park in the suburb of Bishopbriggs. Once there, she phoned a friend and admitted to robbing the off sales and confessed to what she was about to do. The friend contacted Lorraine's parents and they began a race against time to reach the car park before she spurted the deadly drug into her veins. Her father believed God guided him to his daughter. 'He allowed me to be in the right place at the right time,' he said.

She had, finally, hit rock-bottom. For Lorraine Dick now, the only way was up – but she had assaulted a woman and robbed a store. There was a legal piper who would have to be paid. Luckily for her, her family stuck by her. 'At the end of the day,' her loyal mother said later, 'we love Lorraine and never ever judged her. We just fought with her to fight the addiction.'

In August 2002, she appeared in court where she admitted the robbery and assault. Her defence counsel told the court about her experience in Bangladesh. 'She was raped by four police officers and that had the most awful effect on her,' said lawyer William Thom, showing a flair for understatement, 'particularly being a daughter of the manse and brought up to respect those in authority.'

He spoke of her heroin addiction and went on, 'She is now receiving treatment and has taken on three part-time jobs in an effort to improve her position and become rehabilitated in society.'

Lorraine Dick was lucky. She could easily have been given a custodial sentence, but the court took pity and sentenced her to three years' probation and 300 hours of community service. Relieved to be avoiding jail, Dick pleaded with her victim to forgive her for what she had done. But, at the time, Pamela Kaur said she could not. 'I have to respect the judge's decision but, to me, this is not fair. It makes me angry – I am the victim here.'

In a newspaper interview shortly after her trial, she warned others of the destructive effects of heroin. She told the *Daily Record*, 'what started as a comforter became my hell. Heroin is not a drug you can dabble in or use socially. There's nothing fun, clever or sociable about addiction. It strips you of all the morals, decency and self-respect you had. It is an all-consuming, full-time and greedy companion that soon takes over every bit of your life and will, if allowed, completely destroy anybody close to it.'

In the end, the drug destroyed her. On 22 November 2004 she bought £30-worth of heroin and injected the whole lot into her body. She was found dead in her car outside the flat in Norwich where she had been staying.

Brian Doran

'Half-a-dozen rolls . . . and a snort of coke'

Cocaine was for a long-time the drug of choice for the rich and stupid. Disdaining the lower-class delights of heroin – all that heating and jagging isn't for us, luvvie – they preferred to roll up and snort. Powdering their noses from the inside became a class symbol and people who really should have known better – who were not forced into turning on and tuning out because of unemployment or social disadvantage – worked hand-in-hand with crooks to get their high. All the while, many of them deplored the rising crime rate among the riff-raff.

While Edinburgh drug lord **James Rea** was allegedly leading the way in heroin importation, two otherwise upright Glasgow business-men were doing the same for cocaine. In 1983, one of them faced the courts while the other sunned himself in non-extradition treaty Spain.

Travel-agency boss Brian Doran was already very comfortable when he turned to crime. His company, Blue Sky Holidays, was thriving and he had a loving wife and six children, all living in a luxurious home in the south side of Glasgow. He also had a very close friendship with a gorgeous model. Life for him was very nice, thank you.

But it obviously wasn't enough. He was deeply involved in bringing cocaine into the country from Holland. In Glasgow, he and his asso-ciates arranged for the drug to be cut with lactose to bulk it up. It was then distributed to the city's smart set for as much as £60 per gram. He was unusual in criminal circles in that he was well-educated and his university learning led to him being known as 'the Professor'.

With drugs by now a serious problem in the city, police became aware that, as one put it at the time, 'all of a sudden it was snowing cocaine in Glasgow'. Carefully, they set up a major investigation but it wasn't until 1981 that an anonymous call pointed them to a flat in the city's Highburgh Road, part of the trendy West End. They found two brothers in the process of cutting up an ounce of cocaine with intent to supply. The brothers squealed and named Brian Doran as the West End's 'Mr Big'. They said he had left the drugs with them only hours before.

Other informants also fired in Doran and his friend, a local baker, as the ringleaders. Collectively, the two businessmen and others became known as the Happy Dust Gang. Both men were arrested, but Doran legged it before he was due to appear in the High Court even though, as part of his bail conditions, he had handed over his passport and £5,000. He'd managed to con his passport back but by fleeing he lost the five grand. For most of us, that is not a sum to be sniffed at, but sniffing was Doran's business and he could easily afford to leave it behind. That left the baker alone in the dock.

The court heard that showbiz and sporting figures met with Doran in smart bars and restaurants in the West End and city centre to buy drugs from him. On one occasion, it was later claimed, he used a bag of cocaine to help him and his family get a blessing from the Pope. It was 1982 and Pope John Paul 11 was due to visit the city. The owner of a bar in Glasgow's Byres Road recalled seeing Doran pass a quantity of the drug to a 'sinister middleman' in return for a VIP pass to the scene of the Papal visit. Doran was as proud as punch that he and his family had been blessed by the Pontiff, but it didn't stop him from punting even bigger quantities of drugs.

Drugs, it seems, were also available at a busy bakery in Byres Road. One drug courier told the *Daily Record*, '[the baker] was dishing out coke like Smarties from his bakery. It got to be a joke that you could go in and get half-a-dozen rolls and a snort of coke.' The man quoted and an Amsterdam-based Scot acted as couriers for the Happy Dust Gang but did a deal with the Crown in return for fingering both Doran and his co-accused as the men behind the local trade.

The baker, alone in the dock, was sentenced to four years for his role in importing and selling cocaine. The judge told him, 'I accept that Doran played a major role and yours was subordinate. It must be clearly understood that persons importing drugs and supplying them to others can expect little mercy in these courts.' However, the convicted man was not a dangerous criminal and the effect his conviction would have on his young family was also taken into account. But, said the judge, the part he played in the drug ring 'was an important one'.

His old pal Doran, meanwhile, was secure in his Spanish villa near Marbella, making a living by dealing in property. Known locally as 'El Jock', he told a friend, 'I'm not going back to Scotland, I'd be mad to leave here.' He had little to fear, for at the time Spain had no extradition agreement with the United Kingdom, making it very popular with fugitive gangsters who had turned it into the Costa Del Crime. But Doran did not have everything his own way while abroad. In 1987, his 6-year-old son died in Glasgow and he could not return for the funeral.

But, as Doran found out, the law may not have a long arm but it does have a long memory. However, even when Scots law finally caught up with him, his charmed life would not desert him entirely. In 1987, he was arrested by Spanish police who claimed to have smashed a £50 million hashish-smuggling-ring. 'I'll get off this one and be found not guilty,' he told a friend. 'My days in prison are numbered.' Sure enough, Doran spent six months languishing in a Spanish prison before being bailed pending further inquiries.

Once a free man, he fled the country and took up residence in Holland. That was a mistake. It may have been difficult to have him extradited from Spain, but Holland was a different story. In 1989, at the request of Scottish police, Doran was lifted in Amsterdam and held while proceedings to have him brought back were underway. Naturally, he fought them but was unsuccessful and, in October 1989, he was finally back in a Scottish court facing up to the charges first proffered in 1982. Doran defended himself, treating the jury to a dramatic and near-tearful plea to be acquitted of the charges and be allowed to return to the bosom of his wife and family after seven long years of exile. He had been framed by the police, he insisted, and had never dealt in drugs. His theatrics were partially successful: he was found not guilty of smuggling the cocaine into the country but was sentenced to two years for supplying the drug.

In 1992, he was back in a Scottish court, in Stirling, not for drug-related offences this time but for credit-card fraud. He was fined £100 and ordered to pay £200 to the TSB. His lawyer promised that 'he is resolved not to appear in the courts in the future, both as a matter of honour to himself and to his family'. But almost as soon as the words were out of the lawyer's mouth, his client was formulating other ideas. The credit-card scam was small-time; the next project would be more his style.

Alongside him in the dock of the Sheriff Court in Stirling was

Lanarkshire man Kenneth Togher, later described as a professional fraudster. Together, the two Scots travelled to Colombia, allegedly to form links with the notorious drug cartels. In 1993, Doran and Togher were back in Britain and setting up shop in London. It was there that they sailed into the sights of Customs and Excise, which was targeting some well-known London faces. The probe formed part of Operation Stealer, a three-year investigation that involved dozens of officers and traversed three continents. Doran's name came into the frame in London and soon some of the Customs officers were following both him and Togher. They found that the two men enjoyed a highly luxurious lifestyle, staying at the best hotels, buying expensive cars and even a yacht. Officers said they searched Doran's hotel room and found cash and personal documents relating to bank transfers in false names. They bugged the hotel rooms, a move that would later prove their undoing. Togher's luggage was searched at the airport and £250,000 cash was found lodged inside two suitcases. The man was allowed to go free but was kept under surveillance. There were some minor drug seizures but the main event came in 1995.

The investigators discovered that a huge shipment of cocaine was to be brought into the country on the catamaran *Frugal*. On 10 January 1995, they swooped as the vessel lay at anchor in Pevensey Bay in East Sussex. On board, they found ten plastic-wrapped bales of Colombian sneezing powder, valued at around £34 million. Doran and Togher were lifted the following day. 'You can't arrest me,' said the bespectacled 'professor'. 'I've done nothing wrong.'

A total of forty-four people were taken into custody in Britain, France and Spain in relation to Operation Stealer. Two years later, Doran, Togher and seven other Britons faced a jury in Bristol Crown Court. The former travel boss was dubbed the mastermind and showed no emotion as he and Togher were sentenced to twenty-five years in prison for the *Frugal* shipment. They also received a nine-year concurrent stretch after admitting their part in a £4 million heroin seizure in Madrid in February 1994. Lord Foley told them, 'You are the organisers, although I accept not the only financiers. If this had succeeded you would have made a substantial profit.'

The Crown, naturally, wanted its cut of the profits. Although the men insisted they had no substantial assets, the judge ordered that they must pay £2 million within five years or face an additional ten years in jail.

There was, however, a problem. Three years later, the Court of Criminal Appeal heard that the Customs officers who had bugged Togher's hotel room had broken their own strict rules in that they had neither asked the hotel's permission nor even informed their own superiors. They had compounded their error by lying about it in court. This was enough to have the twenty-five-year sentences quashed, although the nine years for the Madrid charge still stood as the men had already pleaded guilty. The £2 million confiscation order was also deemed excessive and was reduced to £800,000 each or an additional four years. The fallout from the case resulted in a call for a major revamp of Customs investigation techniques.

In August 2005, Doran and Togher were thrown back inside for failing to cough up the cash. They were also informed that, even after they had served the additional prison term, they would still be expected to pay up. Customs officials, who had seen the credibility of their service called into question, were delighted that the pair had been sent back to jail. There was, however, some collective head scratching over why Doran – who it was believed had salted away millions over the years and was ranked by the *Sunday Mail* as one of Scotland's ten richest crooks – had not stumped up what was a relatively small chunk of change.

Perhaps the man they called King Coke was not as a big a drug lord as was thought.

Walter Scott Ellis

'The most inept criminal in Scottish history'

Walter Scott Ellis is not a name that springs readily to the lips of anyone familiar with the history of Glasgow crime, but for a time he was
one of the best-known crooks in the city. Such was his fame following
a sensational acquittal in a murder case that pressmen literally fought
for possession of his slim frame on the steps of the High Court. But
Ellis was soon relegated to the footnotes of criminal history as other
crooks grabbed the headlines.

In July 1961, taxi driver John Walkinshaw was found dead from
gunshot wounds as his cab sat idling in Glasgow's grim Castlemilk
estate. Witnesses said they had seen a man fleeing the scene of the
crime with something that looked like a handkerchief in his right hand.
A second taxi driver identified Walter Scott Ellis as the man he picked
up fifteen minutes later in another part of Castlemilk. At the time, the
suspect was carrying a handkerchief in his right hand. However, no
fingerprints of any evidentiary value were found in the dead man's
vehicle.

When he was interviewed Ellis claimed to have been at his parents'
house in Castlemilk when the taxi driver was killed, although it was
later discovered he had been at a party in Bridgeton on the night of
the murder. He had left the party in a taxi at 1:15 a.m. – half an hour
before John Walkinshaw was killed. Despite strenuous efforts, no cab
driver came forward to confirm that he had picked Ellis up in
Bridgeton. At Ellis's subsequent trial for murder the prosecution used
this to infer that it was, in fact, the murder victim who had picked
him up. A further piece of incriminating evidence was that glass found
in Ellis's shoes could have come from the scene of the crime. In addition, bullets were found in a flat he used. Neighbours of his parents
said they had heard someone coming into the close soon after the
murder but they could not say for certain who it was.

In the days before legal aid, accused persons with no money to
pay for high-priced defence teams relied on the goodwill of lawyers
who were willing to work for free. Surprisingly, given the common

view that lawyers are only in it for the cash, Scottish criminal history is littered with cases where they have elected to conduct a defence *pro bono*, as first the Romans and then the Americans called it. Here Ellis proved fortunate in attracting to his side a defence team that consisted of a young, go-getting solicitor and a gifted advocate who would in years to come forge an almost unstoppable legal force. The name Joseph Beltrami is now legendary in Glasgow legal circles, while Nicholas Fairbairn was first a giant in the courtroom and then in politics. But in 1961 they were hungry young lawyers and the Ellis case would help make their names. Senior counsel for the defence was Ronald Bennet QC.

The prosecution case was totally circumstantial. There was nothing tangible linking the accused either with the murder scene or the victim. The glass found in his shoes was so common it could have come from anywhere. The bullets found in his flat did not match the ones that killed Mr Walkinshaw. The crime appeared motiveless. Witnesses who saw the killer running away failed to identify Ellis. In fact, the defence contended that their client had drunk so much at the party that he was in no condition to walk, let alone run, as the witnesses at the scene insisted. The lawyers could not, however, shake the testimony of the second driver who insisted he had picked Ellis up. Finally, they hammered away at the circumstantial nature of the Crown case. The judge, in his summing up, pointed out that such a case is 'every bit as reliable as other evidence'. However, he warned the jury that, 'In this country suspicion will not do. Proof on a balance of probabilities will not do. The Crown must prove matters beyond all reasonable doubt.'

And a reasonable doubt is just what Ellis's defence raised. After a four-day trial, the jury was out for only half an hour before it returned a verdict of not proven. It was a step below not guilty but it did mean that the Crown had failed to prove its case. Beltrami, Fairbairn and Bennet had done their job and their client was free to go. Outside the High Court, the city's journalists were waiting and when Walter Scott Ellis emerged there was a scramble for the right to buy his story. Nowadays, a deal would in all likelihood have been made prior to the verdict but, in 1961, it was survival of the fittest as reporters and photographers slugged it out to take possession of the hottest story of the day. Eventually, one reporter hauled the man through the crowd and into a waiting car. Unfortunately, it was the wrong car and representatives of a rival newspaper sped off with their prize. Ellis was paid the princely sum of £100 for his story.

It was the highpoint of his career but he soon found that fame is a fickle lover. His name vanished from the papers and the £100 did not go far. In July 1966, he was back in court again, this time for an armed robbery in a Glasgow bank during which a manager was wounded by a shotgun blast. Ellis was caught red-handed with an automatic pistol and sentenced to twenty-one years. Released in October 1980, he was soon back in front of the bench, this time for trying to hold up a licensed grocer in Cumbernauld with a replica firearm. The two plucky shopkeepers were none-too-keen on giving up their profits without a struggle and the drunken Ellis was pursued down the road and swiftly disarmed. The cocky young crook, who had faced the prospect of the gallows in 1961, seemed to have vanished by 1980. He complained that he had been tossed out of prison following his sentence for armed robbery with no training or preparation for the outside world. 'I was besotted by drink and . . . I had every intention of going straight but was tempted by the devil.' He was sent down for three years.

Five years later, the devil lured him off the straight and narrow again. Now aged fifty-three, and having been sentenced to forty-two of those years in jail (although he had not served them all), he was back once again in front of a judge. He and fellow convicted felon William 'Sonny' Leitch admitted attacking two priests in a chapel house in Broxburn, West Lothian. Leitch, then aged fifty, was also something an underworld legend. He became known in 1967 as the 'Saughton Harrier' after he scrambled up two goalposts that had been left leaning against the walls of the Edinburgh jail. Reaching the other side, he stripped down to a vest and shorts and jogged to freedom posing as a cross-country runner. He was at liberty for four months before he was recaptured.

Now he was standing side-by-side with Ellis in court. They had forced their way into the house attached to the church of St Nicholas in Main Street, Broxburn. A 29-year-old priest was knocked to the floor and his wrists and ankles bound. Then a 70-year-old priest was bound and blindfolded before the raiders demanded money. They ransacked the house and threatened one of the priests with a knife if he did not disclose where the money was. They got away with £1,065. After the raiders made their escape, the younger priest freed himself but found the phone lines had been cut so he had to call the police from a nearby old folks home. The thieves had not got far, for police stopped them on the outskirts of the town heading towards Glasgow.

Although Ellis apologised for subjecting the two priests to a terrifying ordeal, he denied he and his co-accused had intended robbery. He said they had gone to Broxburn to 'sort out' a young man named Mooney who had allegedly assaulted one of Leitch's favourite nieces and made her pregnant. Finding themselves in the wrong house, their demand for Mooney was misinterpreted as demands for money! Realising they were in the wrong place, they decided to stage the robbery.

It was a game try but the far-fetched tale failed to impress the court. Lord Mayfield told him, 'You have shown yourself to be a dangerous nuisance and pest over many years. It is my view that the public are entitled to be protected from your dangerous activities.' Ellis was sentenced to ten years and Leitch to eight. On his release five years later, Leitch voluntarily placed himself in what he described as 'the worst jail in Scotland' – Inchkeith Island on the Firth of Forth. He had read that the woman who ran an animal sanctuary on the island for dogs, cats, donkeys, goats and ponies was thinking of giving up because the workload was too great and decided to offer his services. 'The conditions here are worse than Peterhead prison,' he said.

Perhaps in the heady days of 1961, when he had faced the might of Scottish law and beat the gallows, Walter Scott Ellis had imagined a different sort of life for himself. Perhaps he thought he might have become a criminal kingpin, the man they could not hang. In the end, his own harsh words seem to sum him up. 'I am not a dangerous criminal. In fact, I must be the most inept criminal in Scottish history.'

Paul Firth

Scout leader lacked honour

THREE days before this teacher and former scout leader was due to face trial on nineteen counts of child abuse, he sold his house, bought a yacht and fled the country. He was at liberty for three years and was finally caught thanks to British holidaymakers who recognised him when his case was featured on *Crimewatch*.

It was in November 1999 that Firth, then assistant head teacher at St Machar Academy in Aberdeen, was arrested on the child-sex charges. He had been deeply involved in the Boy Scout movement for twenty years, reaching the position of assistant district commissioner, and the majority of the allegations came from former boys who said he had abused them. The offences took place between 1974 and 1996 – although Firth had resigned from the Scouts in 1994 – and by the time charges were proffered some of the victims were in their thirties. The offences were said to have been committed at various locations, including an Oxfordshire vicarage, an Elgin church hall, an Aberdeen flat and campsites up and down the country.

Having been released on bail pending trial, Firth seized his chance to escape. He sold his £80,000 house at Alford, Aberdeenshire, bought the yacht *Romalo* and sailed off into the sunset. He was a seasoned sailor, having previously yachted to Norway and Ireland. His disappearance was not noted until 16 October 2000 when he failed to appear at the High Court in Dundee. The following day, a warrant was issued for his arrest, but he was long gone.

He was spotted soon after at Killala Bay on the west coast of Ireland and then he seemed to vanish. A year later, a Scottish couple on holiday met a Scot who said his name was Doug. 'Doug' was living on a yacht moored at Ceuta, a Spanish-owned port on the Moroccan side of the Straits of Gibraltar. He told them he had previously lived in Spain and Portugal before coming to North Africa. He had with him on board a 10-year-old Arab boy who, the man claimed, was learning English and in return was teaching him Arabic. The couple finally found out the man's real name when they went on an excursion to

Tangier, the historic Moroccan town a few miles to the west of Ceuta. Because they were leaving Spanish territory, the visitors had to hand their passports over to the tour leader. When they were returned, the leader called out the name Paul Firth and 'Doug' stepped up to retrieve the passport.

It was when *Crimewatch* included a report about the fugitive that the couple realised 'Doug' was the man the authorities were hunting. However, by this time Firth had moved on and matters became more complicated. He was now in Moroccan territory and there was no extradition treaty with the United Kingdom. In November 2001, Grampian police announced that they and the Crown Office were working closely with Interpol to recruit the assistance of the Moroccan government in bringing Firth to justice.

Paul Firth then made a serious mistake. Journalists from the *Daily Record* had arrived in North Africa to track him down and discovered that he had secretly sailed back into Spanish jurisdiction to have his boat repaired. The reporters tipped off Spanish police and Firth was finally arrested and packed-off to Scotland to face trail.

However, once again luck was with him; the Spanish authorities would only entertain the extradition request if seventeen of the nineteen charges outstanding were dropped. The offences, they said, were 'too old' and so when Firth finally appeared in a Scottish court he faced only two charges, dating back to 1994 and 1996. The victims, by this time students in their twenties, were sexually assaulted in Firth's home and on camping trips. One said in court that Firth had told him that 'what he was doing wasn't bad – it was just society that made me think it was wrong'.

In October 2003, after a three-day trial, Firth was found guilty at Aberdeen Sheriff Court. He stood in the dock with his head bandaged and his eyes blackened after being beaten up the night before by another prisoner. Later that month he was sentenced to three years in prison, the stiffest penalty the court could impose. He was also to be placed on the Sex Offenders Register indefinitely and supervised for a year following his release. But the sentence came too late for one of his other victims. He killed himself, aged twenty-six, when he was told there was no corroboration to make a charge regarding his case stick. His mother told reporters that, if she had a gun, she would shoot Firth.

But justice prevailed, if somewhat belatedly. In June 2006 Firth was sentenced to eight years for a string of offences that had come to light since his original trial in 2003. At the High Court in Edinburgh, he admitted thirteen charges of indecent assault, and lewd, indecent and libidinous practices on boys aged eight to sixteen between 1974 and 1996.

Hugh Friel and Jason O'Donnell

Like watching a snuff movie

It was a brutal, sickening assault that even horrified one of the culprits when he saw it played back on videotape. Two young men, Hugh Friel and Jason O'Donnell, had been captured by closed-circuit television cameras in a Glasgow street viciously beating another man. The beating was so severe that one police officer was moved to opine that watching the video was like watching a snuff movie. The two men smashed their victim's head against a window before battering him to the ground outside Bennet's nightclub in Glassford Street and kicking and stamping on his head and body. The kicking continued even after the man was unconscious.

They were fortunate that when they were charged, it was only for assault. It could very easily have become a murder case, because when the victim was taken to hospital, doctors said he was lucky to be alive. He almost drowned in his own blood.

The two accused, who both had previous convictions for violence, admitted assaulting the man to the danger of his life and were each sentenced to four years in prison. The prosecuting authorities were appalled at the leniency the two thugs had been afforded and, for the first time, an appeal was lodged against a High Court sentence. In September 1995, the case came before the Court of Criminal Appeal and three judges watched the horrifying tape. This was another first; never before had the prosecution lodged a videotape as evidence in an appeal. Having watched the sickening attack, and listened to the arguments from both sides, the Lord Justice Clerk, Lord Ross, said: 'Having regard to the brutal and merciless nature of this assault, the sentences were quite inappropriate.' The terms of imprisonment for both men were increased to seven years.

Even Hugh Friel was shocked by his own brutality. His lawyer told the court that he was horrified at the thought of seeing the tape again.

There was a further shock ahead for the victim. In January 1996 he was told by the Criminal Injuries Compensation Board that, although he had suffered a prolonged and sustained beating, he had been refused any payment. The board claimed that he had started the violence by throwing the first punch and he also had a number of criminal convictions.

The Grahams

The original family from hell

When 16-year-old James Graham left a 25-year-old woman for dead after ploughing into her in a stolen 2.8 litre Ford Capri, he had no idea the effect it would have on his family. He seemed to care little for his victim, whose leg had been ripped off in the incident, although his mother later said that the sneer he adopted in court hid a more caring heart. 'James has always felt remorse for what happened,' she told reporters. 'James is not what the public make him out to be.' Despite that, her son continued to deny being the man at the wheel.

His victim, though, had identified James Graham as the driver who slammed into her while she cleared snow from her own car. As she lay bleeding and screaming, she saw him speed off, still grinning. A mother's love may have blinded her to her son's failings, but a sheriff had called him 'a very nasty young man' when sentencing him earlier that year to twelve months for slicing a man with a bottle. Now, in September 1994, another sheriff said that Graham's actions merited 'severe punishment'. The maximum penalty he could impose was three years, so the case was referred to the High Court for sentencing. The following month, James Graham went down for five years. Even the boy's own lawyer agreed that a custodial sentence was warranted.

The conviction was the last straw for the residents of the Auchmuchty estate in Glenrothes. They claimed that they had suffered for years at the hands of the Graham clan but had been too frightened to speak up. Now they wanted them out. They alleged that they had been threatened and assaulted by members of the family, that buses had been rerouted because of stone throwing by younger children, that threats of violence had forced Kirkcaldy District Council to suspend collections of rubbish and that drugs had been used and supplied from the house. Neighbours also complained of fires in oil drums and the burning of tyres in the garden. Postmen claimed that they had been bitten by the Grahams' dogs. Things had got so bad, it was said, that the estate had been nicknamed Little Bosnia; and everything seemed to be laid at the door of the Grahams.

Glenrothes Development Agency (GDA), the owner of the Grahams' house, took the claims seriously and began repossession proceedings. Mum Anne Graham – head of the family of five while her husband Gordon was doing time in Saughton prison for a driving offence – said that she and her children did not deserve to be thrown out of their home. 'The neighbours are talking about things that happened years ago,' she said. However, she pledged that they would not go down without a fight. In December 1994, the GDA was successful in winning the right to evict the family. As soon as the verdict was pronounced, neighbours planned a street party.

It was not the first time the family had faced eviction. In 1991, after refusing to pay their rent, sheriff officers arrived at the door to eject them from the property but were faced by an upturned car blocking the door. They were then ambushed with a barrage of missiles and human filth. It was expected that the family would again defend their home to the hilt, especially as Gordon Graham, now released from prison, defiantly vowed, 'We're not moving.'

Meanwhile, there was further public outrage when it was revealed that the legal bill for the eviction could top £29,000 and that it would come from the public purse. Although the sheriff had ordered that the family was responsible for the costs, there was little realistic chance of them coughing up. Had Gordon Graham been working, the GDA could have arrested his wages. Had the family had any assets, they could have been seized. However, Mr Graham was unemployed and the family had nothing of value to impound.

As the family waited for the authorities to make their move, Anne Graham was fined £200 for a dole offence. She had denied obtaining £88 from the Department of Social Security by fraudulent means but admitted to pretending she had not received her giro cheque and obtaining a new one. However, the original cheque had been cashed and her fingerprints were found on it, although this did not prove who cashed it. Her fine was to be paid at £4 per week.

Three months after being given the legal go-ahead, police and sheriff officers moved against the Grahams. The family were unprepared, expecting the authorities to strike the following week. As they were being thrown out, Gordon Graham insisted that his children were no worse then any others, and described the effect the recent events had had on his family. 'My wife is near a nervous breakdown and my daughter is scared to go to school because of the abuse she gets,' he said. One of his daughters, Heather, told reporters that she had been victimised simply because her name was Graham. Speaking after the eviction, the 18-year-old said she had been housed in a hostel with her fiancé and their baby daughter. She claimed it was costing the state £1,000 per week to keep them there and it would be far cheaper to rehouse them.

By May 1991, the family had found a new home, in a seaside cottage. There had been a proposal to create a special commune where the Grahams and other such families could be lumped together, but the plan collapsed. In the meantime, the family had been living with relatives in Aberdeenshire and eventually rented the three-bedroom cottage, giving the landlord a hefty cash deposit and six months rent in advance. The landlord had no idea who his new tenants were and said Mrs Graham had met him very well turned out and driving a new car.

Sandra Gregory

She checked into the 'Bangkok Hilton'

On 3 February 1993, Aberdeen-born Sandra Gregory was caught at Don Muang airport in Bangkok trying to sneak eighty-three grams of heroin out of Thailand in condoms that she had secreted in her body. Obviously, given their location, she knew she had the drugs so had not been duped into carrying them as others have been. She also admitted she had been paid £1,000 to smuggle them to Tokyo. In effect Gregory had become a drug mule; she wanted to raise enough cash to get home. She was not just homesick but physically sick, suffering from dengue fever and amoebic dysentery. She wanted to be home badly and the cash offered by an acquaintance would get her there.

Unfortunately, she had no idea the man she had gone into partnership with was already known to the Thai authorities, who had been tipped off by drug-liaison officers attached to the British embassy in Bangkok. Thai law takes a very dim view of drug smuggling and Gregory was originally sentenced to die. However, because she admitted her involvement in the venture, the 28-year-old Scot had the death sentence commuted to twenty-five years in prison, the shortest penalty available under Thai law. The man who had enticed her was also arrested but, with only her evidence against him, was acquitted, although he was subsequently convicted of another drug offence. He later returned to the United Kingdom where he was arrested again and jailed. As she was sentenced Gregory burst into tears and blurted out: 'He's going home and I'm getting twenty-five.'

Sandra Gregory was an unlikely drug smuggler. She came from a solidly professional background. Her father, Stan, was an oil executive in Aberdeen and she enjoyed all the accoutrements of a middle-class upbringing including ballet lessons and horse-riding. Stan Gregory and his wife Doreen were loving parents who worked hard to provide for their daughter and were no doubt proud when she qualified as a teacher.

Like many young graduates Sandra Gregory wanted to see more of the world before settling down to a career and decided to go backpacking in Asia. She arrived in Thailand at the tail end of 1990 for an eight-week holiday and ended up staying two years. To support herself she taught English to Thai students but did not earn enough to buy a ticket back to Britain. So now she was lodged in the harshest digs she had ever had: Lar Yao jail in Klong Prem – the notorious 'Bangkok Hilton'.

Surrounded by squalor, corruption and almost daily death, Gregory spent four years in Lar Yao. The regime was harsh and, with the prison day starting at 5.30 a.m., sentences somehow seemed even longer. There were up to thirty inmates in each of the tiny cells and sanitary conditions were abominable: an open sewer ran round three edges of the walls and food bowls floated past in bloody, dirty water while women were taking showers. Even the rats in Lar Yao were diseased and without tails. It is hardly surprising that hundreds die every year in the prison from AIDS and tuberculosis.

Corruption in Thai jails is endemic and prisoners have to pay the guards to ensure they are not victimised. Protests by prisoners about their treatment are not recommended, especially from foreigners. When Sandra Gregory lodged a complaint, newspaper cuttings found their way back to the jail and she was victimised by the guards.

All the while, she was supported by her loyal parents, Stan and Doreen, back home. They managed to enlist the help of their MP in a bid to force the hand of the British government who, the Gregory family claimed, did little to help. Finally, she was freed from the Bangkok prison and allowed to come back home. But not to freedom. She was to be incarcerated in British jails for the remainder of her sentence. She had smuggled eighty-nine grams of heroin, with a street value of £9,000, and had already served more time than traffickers guilty of profiting from ten times as much.

Under Thai law, the only appeal is directly to the King and in Gregory's case that took seven years. Had she been Australian, American or Dutch, then things might have been very different, as MP Malcolm Bruce pointed out in Parliament on 17 January 2000. He was questioning the government over its lack of support for this British citizen, the daughter of two of his constituents:

If Sandra Gregory were an Australian, she would receive automatic government support for a clemency appeal. If Sandra were an American, she would have her sentence reduced to take account of time spent in a Thai prison. The Americans multiply Thai prison years by six. Therefore, Sandra's three years spent in a jail in Bangkok would have been regarded as eighteen years in the American system, so that she would have been eligible for parole on her return home and would now have been deemed to have served the entire sentence without remission.

The Dutch, the MP for Gordon pointed out, review the sentence of those transferred from conviction under foreign jurisdiction against the domestic-equivalent sentence. In Sandra Gregory's case, had she been Dutch, her sentence would have been a maximum of four years.

As it was, on her return to British soil, Gregory found herself in some of Britain's toughest jails, albeit they are virtual holiday camps compared to the 'Bangkok Hilton'. She served time in Holloway, Wakefield and Durham maximum-security wing. She was, Mr Bruce pointed out, 'serving the third longest sentence of any woman in a United Kingdom prison'. Amazingly, only multiple murderers Myra Hindley and Rosemary West were serving longer sentences. And all for just eighty-nine grams of heroin accepted when she was in a most vulnerable position, as Malcolm Bruce argued: 'The effect has been that Sandra Gregory – a first-time offender who bitterly regrets her crime and is repentant – has seen professional criminals, with a serious track record of serious crimes, come in and out of prison while she continues to languish.'

It was a ridiculous state of affairs that did the British legal system very little credit. It was thrown even further into disrepute when compared to the case of Patricia Hussain, who was arrested one year after Sandra Gregory trying to smuggle seven kilos of heroin out of Bangkok. She was sentenced to life, but that was reduced on appeal to thirty-five years and then to twenty-five years after a general amnesty was declared. Her appeal to the King of Thailand was heard before Gregory's even though she was arrested after her, and her sentence was reduced to ten years. The appeal was supported by the British Customs and Excise service because Hussain gave evidence leading to the conviction of other traffickers. Patricia Hussain had previous convictions for theft, fraud and prostitution and was carrying seven kilos of drugs – as compared to the much smaller amount Gregory was caught with – yet she found herself eligible for parole while the young Scot was still waiting for her appeal to be heard by the King. The two women met while in prison in Thailand but their subsequent treatment was very different.

Meanwhile Malcolm Bruce was railing against the fact that real drug kingpins in this country were continuing to operate. 'Sandra Gregory is as much a victim of drugs as many others,' said the MP. 'While she faces the prospect of at least another four years in jail before she is even eligible for parole, the serious dealers go free to carry on their trafficking. They have the power to escape while minnows such as Sandra Gregory take the rap.' He concluded, 'Sandra Gregory is paying dearly for her crime. She should not be made a scapegoat for those who are not.'

Finally, on 22 July 2000, six months after Malcolm Bruce made his impassioned plea, the King of Thailand granted a pardon and Sandra Gregory found herself at liberty. 'Coming out was a shock' she said a week later. 'I haven't got a life. Last week I had a life. I was doing things and up to stuff and all of a sudden I'm out and it's like, oh God, I haven't got a life.'

She later disclosed that her Thailand offence was not the first time she had tried to smuggle drugs. She admitted she had not only used narcotics when she was younger but also, aged seventeen, had tried to bring cannabis home from a trip to Amsterdam. However, she said a young American told her she looked too obviously guilty as she approached the customs point and she gave him the contraband. 'I should have known then that I would never make a drug smuggler, but I just couldn't read the signs,' she said.

Once free of the penal system, she revealed that she had also enjoyed a sexual affair with a male member of staff at Durham prison, which she said was the worst prison in which she was held in Britain. She had on more than one occasion contemplated suicide and the intensely physical affair proved to be something of a godsend. 'Durham was such a difficult, horrendous place to be in that I needed something to remind me of the real world,' she is quoted as saying in *Scotland on Sunday*. 'Even now it's hard to believe it happened. But it did and, looking back, I wonder whether perhaps, in some small way, Chris [not his real name] saved my life. Or at least my sanity.'

She said that the sex she enjoyed during the five-month relationship was a means of having something that made her 'feel real again'. However, at one point she was worried that she had fallen pregnant. Obviously, it was a false alarm and the affair began to fizzle out. 'We saw less and less of each other until we stopped seeing each other alone,' she said. For the staff member, such a liaison was extremely dangerous, but apparently such affairs were not unknown in the high-security establishment, although a spokesperson for the prison service dismissed this as 'absurd'.

Though she found Durham to be 'awful', it was, she said, 'the only place where I wasn't pointed out to people as someone who was in a bad way. Every other place the women would say, "things could be worse, you could have twenty-five years hanging over your head like Sandra Gregory".' One of the other prisoners at Durham was serial killer Rosemary West but Gregory believed she was 'not the worst' of her fellow prisoners. 'There were a lot of freaky prisoners in there, let's put it that way,' she said.

Once free, she was determined to make up for her ten lost years. She had messed up, she knew that, and admitted her past was 'embarrassing and shameful'. Within weeks of gaining her freedom, she applied for – and was granted – a place at Oxford, reading geography on a course due to begin in October 2002. She worked with the charity Prisoners Abroad to establish a hospice in the 'Bangkok Hilton' to allow the hundreds of terminally ill patients incarcerated there the chance to die with dignity. She also gave drugs-awareness talks to schools.

George Grey

The monocled major

In Victorian times, a band of crooks known as the Swell Mob would stream out of the thieves kitchens in the slums of London and converge on major events where they knew cash could be made. Mob members were the elite 'buzzers' and 'dippers' of the day, pickpockets and thieves who dressed well enough to mix with the swells who were their marks. Race meetings drew them like ticks to a sheep, for they knew that there was a flock just waiting to be fleeced. Racing, with its links to gambling, has always been linked to the underworld. Of course, not all gamblers are crooks. However, all crooks, by their very nature, are gamblers – risking, if not their money, then at least their liberty. One man who was both gambler and crook, and a spiritual descendant of the Swell Mob, was George Grey. Although not a Scot, it was a daring bank robbery in Glasgow that placed him on the country's most wanted list.

The raid on the British Linen Bank van in the Ibrox area on 19 July 1955 was described in court as 'one of the most audacious crimes of the century'. The story began when a security van pulled up outside the Gower Street bank at about 9.45 a.m. on that Tuesday. Guard Lindsay Currie handed over bags stuffed with cash to driver Gilbert Tait who then carried them into the branch. The two men who emerged from a nearby telephone box must have looked like cowboys in their long, khaki-coloured dustcoats. They climbed into the front of the van just as another similarly-clad pair stepped around the rear of the van. The back doors were lying open and the 56-year-old Mr Currie just barely heard a footfall behind him before he was battered over the head with a cosh. Then the two raiders in the front started up the engine and sped off with the stunned guard on board.

Gilbert Tait came out of the bank only to see his van screeching off at high speed, the rear doors still flapping open. Just as the van lurched round a corner, he caught a glimpse of someone standing at the back, pulling the doors closed, a bank bag tumbling out as he did so. Tait flagged down a lorry and swiftly told the stunned driver what was going on. They took off after the stolen van but lost it very quickly.

The raiders drove the van half-a-mile to a deserted villa on Dumbreck Road where they transferred the loot into two cars and split up. They knew, by that time, that the alarm would have been raised but they also knew the police would be looking for four men travelling together. Later, a warden at the boys home next door heard what he thought were chickens cackling in the garden. He found Mr Currie lying dazed in the rear of the van, his arms and legs bound, tape over his mouth and eyes, blood streaming from his head.

The dust-coated thieves had escaped with over £44,000, making the van raid, for the time, the biggest bank robbery in Scottish history.

Police immediately set up roadblocks on all routes leading south. It was the Glasgow Fair and as witnesses had said they had heard London voices among the gang, detectives believed they might attempt to use the great exodus to England as cover. Vehicles were stopped as far south as Leeds, but there was no sign of the robbers. It seems the raiders had predicted that, too, and had headed north-west of the city; to the Roy Roy roadhouse near Aberfoyle.

When police followed-up a tip that the gang had stayed at the hotel, they found that staff there believed the man they termed the 'Monocled Major' was the ring-leader. Tall, well-spoken with grey hair and a moustache, he was wearing expensive flannels and a blue blazer. On at least one occasion, he wore a monocle. He seemed to be the leader of a group of gamblers who were, ostensibly at least, in Scotland to attend race meetings. The Major was seen at the hotel shortly after the raid with a substantial amount of money. He even paid the bill for all seven of his friends. A hotel employee also saw piles of bank notes in one of their rooms.

The public saw him as a master criminal, a romantic figure from a distinguished military background forced into a life of crime by cruel circumstance. The fact that no-one had been seriously hurt during the robbery helped, as did the suggestion that there were similarities between the Glasgow robbery and a £250,000 bullion raid in London three years before. The reality, though, was somewhat different.

Meanwhile, the police dragnet spread over most of the country. One of the cars used in the eventual getaway was found abandoned in a Perth car park. Inside, were two of the dustcoats, keys to rooms at the roadhouse and fingerprints. The coats featured prominently in a

He was poison! Dr Paul Agutter is led away from the
High Court to start a twelve-year stretch for the
attempted murder of his wife.

(courtesy Mirrorpix)

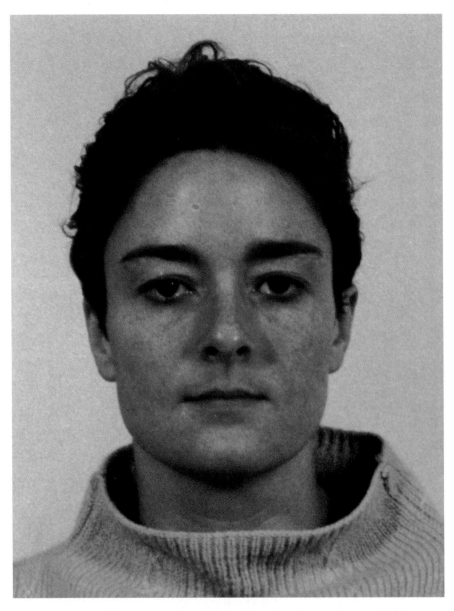

Alison Anders. In 1988 the girl from a top public school
planned Scotland's biggest-ever fraud with her married lover.
She came within a whisker of getting away with it.

(courtesy Mirrorpix)

Walter Scott Ellis (*centre, facing camera*). He sensationally walked free from a murder rap in 1961 following a not-proven verdict. But he was later convicted of a number of serious offences.

(courtesy Mirrorpix)

Not a care in the world! But Sandra Gregory was
distinctly unhappy in 1993 when she was sentenced to
twenty-five years in a Thai jail for drug smuggling.

(courtesy Mirrorpix)

Power to the people! Matthew Lygate looks completely
harmless as he feeds the birds in Glasgow's George Square.
But the 'Tartan Trot' was the mastermind behind a
series of bank robberies in the early 1970s.

(courtesy Mirrorpix)

Terrorist or freedom fighter? Andrew McIntosh
wanted to free Scotland from the
'yoke of English oppression'.

(courtesy Mirrorpix)

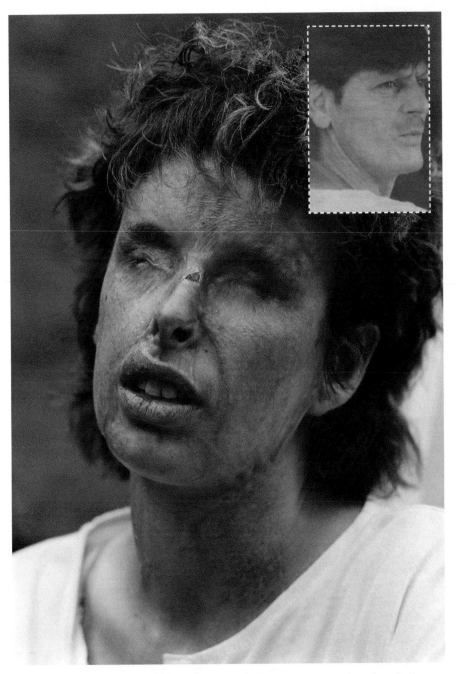

Jealousy led Gordon Modiak (*inset*) to instigate a plot that led to sulphuric acid being thrown in the face of his wife, Louise Duddy. Her injuries were horrific (*main picture*).

(*courtesy Mirrorpix*)

Lee Bell. A brutal assault led to his teenage victim committing suicide.

Lucille McLauchlan (*left*). The Scottish nurse was convicted of murder in Saudi Arabia and of dishonesty at home. She is pictured here with her former husband.

John Cronin. 'One of Scotland's most dangerous men.'

Roddy 'Popeye' McLean. Adventurer, soldier of fortune, drug smuggler and supergrass.

special broadcast on national television on Monday, 25 July, an unusual step in those pre-*Crimewatch* days. The appeal for information brought immediate results when an AA patrolman recognised a coat as one that had been lifted from his car in Fulham. The abandoned car had also been stolen in London and so members of Scotland Yard's famed Flying Squad were drafted into the investigation to noise-up city villains in their own inimitable fashion in an attempt to scare-up some information.

Meanwhile, hotel staff were taken to Govan police office where they were shown books of photographs. They picked out six men as having been at the Rob Roy during the period in question.

In September, the normally quiet roads around Dunblane were the scene of a high-speed chase as police pursued what they believed was the second vehicle seen leaving the Dumbreck Road villa. Five police officers were injured when their vehicle collided with an armoured lorry. The police driver was detained in hospital with chest and facial injuries, while his four colleagues suffered cuts from flying glass. Their quarry escaped.

Finally, police officers began to swoop on the men they believed to be responsible. Two men were arrested in Dublin, one during his honeymoon. A third was picked up in London. Three more were caught in other parts of the country, including Glasgow. Some of the money was recovered.

But of the Major there was no sign although it emerged that he had already slipped through their fingers. In August, a policeman had questioned the owner of a black Rover parked outside a Killin hotel. The man gave his name as Ian Stewart of Bath and while the officer went to check his details by phone the man slipped out of a rear entrance. A search of his room turned up £240 in ten-shilling notes, various items of clothing . . . and a monocle.

He was finally caught in Yorkshire in October. But the Major was nothing of the sort. George Grey, an Australian aged fifty-six, was simply a petty thief, arrested after a series of housebreakings. Police spoke to him in Wandsworth prison and he told them where to recover twelve bank bags, which had been hidden beside a road near Callander. They found the bags, but the loot inside amounted to a threepenny bit and a penny.

The trial for the Scottish 'crime of the century' began in January 1956. But 'Major' Grey was not among the accused. He had already been sentenced to seven years in England and under the laws of the time he did not need not to appear in a Scottish court unless he volunteered to do so. Naturally, George Grey was not about to volunteer. Ultimately, only three of the six accused were sentenced, one to eight years the other two to six each. The charges against the rest were found not proven.

The man seen as the ringleader, though, would not escape Scottish justice. Although he had not stood trial, a Scottish Office official hinted darkly that things might change. And change they did. In November 1957, Grey was brought to the High Court of Glasgow where he received six years for assault and robbery, but only as an accessory after the fact. There was no evidence that he took an active part in the raid while police were now satisfied that he was not the leader of the gang.

Fifty years after the robbery, two mysteries remain. Grey was a petty crook who was unlikely to have planned and executed such a daring caper. So who was the real mastermind? And what happened to the loot? Of the £44,000 taken, only £6,000 was ever recovered.

Martin Hamilton

A penchant for cruelty

For many crooks, crime is a business. Sometimes that business calls on them to be tough, perhaps even ruthless. But violence, while often part and parcel of their chosen profession, is used only when necessary. It is not something to be savoured; it is simply a means to an end. But for Martin Hamilton – the so-called 'Blackhill Butcher' and, it is said, a one-time ally of Glasgow 'Godfather', Arthur Thompson – it was reportedly a source of pleasure. He was described as 'a major player in the Glasgow crime scene' and his past was peppered with allegations of attempted murder, armed robbery and illegal money-lending, allegations that brought him to trial twelve times in seventeen years. In ten of the cases he avoided conviction, making him 'the man they couldn't nail'. Witnesses, it was said, were too afraid to speak out, fearful of the backlash if they did.

One Glasgow police officer was quoted as saying that Hamilton thought nothing of inflicting terrible injuries on those who crossed him. 'He's almost psychopathic,' the cop said 'and never shows any sympathy for the truly evil things he's done.' The underworld also feared, and hated, him, prompting four attempts on his life by fellow criminals.

By the year 2000 Martin Hamilton was based in the Broomhouse area of Edinburgh, where he was attempting to carve out a niche in the city's drug market, allegedly on behalf of a well-known Glasgow crook. He had a firm foothold in both Broomhouse and Sighthill and was looking to step into the lucrative Drylaw and Granton areas. It would, however, be the year that the law finally caught up with him for what one appeal judge called 'crimes of the utmost depravity'.

According to official court papers, the 39-year-old gangster had 'developed some kind of sexual obsession' with a 19-year-old man. The young man, though, did not reciprocate the feelings and grew so scared of Hamilton's continual overtures that he worked out a murder plan with a friend. He even went to the length of getting his hands on a gun. Hamilton, though, pre-empted the murder plot. One evening in March 2000, he turned up with a man called 'Hendy', later said to be David Henderson, at a flat in Edinburgh's Glenalmond Road where a small-time drug-dealing pal of the young man lived. The 19-year-old was in the flat with his friend and others when Hamilton and his two sidekicks arrived. Everyone but the object of Hamilton's affections and his friend was ordered to leave and Hamilton said to them, 'Do you think you're smart not to answer the phone to me? We'll see how smart you are now.'

Hamilton ordered Henderson to give the young man a beating. The victim was punched and kicked on the head and body while Hamilton watched, chuckling. 'Don't mark his face,' he said, 'he's got a pretty face.' But the hiding was not enough, for he told Henderson to slash the teenager, again warning him not to damage his face. Henderson gave the boy a few more punches and kicks then sat him down at the table, placed his hands on the surface and tried to slice-off his pinkie. The removal of a finger is commonplace among the Japanese Yakuza crime mobs but not so popular in Edinburgh housing schemes. As it was, the threat was not carried out, although the youth's finger was cut in the process. The victim ended up with bruised ribs, several bumps and contusions and, despite Hamilton's orders not to damage his face, a broken nose. He was convinced that he would not get out of the flat alive that night.

Then Hamilton turned his attention to the other young man. He, too, was punched about the head before Hamilton decided that the youth's eye offended him – so it was to be plucked out. Henderson took a teaspoon and attempted to force it into the victim's eye socket. As the young man was subjected to this terrifying and agonising ordeal, it was claimed Hamilton sat watching, clearly enjoying what was going on. Henderson stopped his digging at the flesh around the young man's eye and, again on Hamilton's instructions, took a lighter to his hair. This victim later said that he had never felt pain like it in his life. Still Hamilton was not satisfied. The youth was then beaten with a carpet sweeper on his head, arms and body so severely that the long handle snapped.

The two young men were told that they were then to pay Henderson's wages and around £70 was handed over. This, however, did not satisfy Hamilton who said that more should be obtained from the second victim's mother, so another of their friends – who lived in the same flats – was sent to collect it. When he arrived back with a further £20, he, too, found himself at the mercy of Hamilton's fury. 'Here's the other one,' he said. 'You're the cheeky one who gives us cheek on the phone.' This third victim was then attacked with a piece of wood, poked in the head, struck on the ribs, punched and kicked. He was also forced to kneel on the floor and lick the men's shoes. He later said that Hamilton was 'having a good laugh' at it all. The men threatened to cut this young man's legs to the ankles but left the three of them, badly injured, with the warning that if they contacted the police, Hamilton would be back to kill them. They had no doubt that the gangster meant what he said. Even so, two days after the assaults, the first victim spoke to a policeman, although he refused to make a formal statement.

Horrific though that night was the entire ordeal lasted only thirty minutes, although it probably felt longer to the victims. Hamilton and another of his cronies later took a teenage couple hostage and subjected them to fourteen hours of terror. At one point during the attack, police turned up at the door, having been alerted to the screaming. Hamilton and his bully boy, Martin Byrne, hid the couple in a cupboard and convinced the police that there was nothing amiss. When the police left, the men went back to work.

During the fourteen hours they repeatedly punched and kicked the 18-year-old boy about the head and body, forced him into a bathroom and then into a bath. He was told to take off his top and a knife was plunged through his cheek. As if that wasn't enough, he had boiling water poured over his head and body and was racially abused. At the same time, his 18-year-old girlfriend was grabbed by the hair and dragged to the floor, punched, kicked and stabbed on the face. She was also told to take off her clothes, and had boiling water poured over her head and body. Her attackers then threatened to bury her alive.

When Hamilton was brought to court, he and his two co-accused faced a total of twenty-one charges, although by the end of the six-week trial the Crown had withdrawn a number of them. Still, the list of charges for which Hamilton was found guilty was impressive. They included the assaults on the three young men in the Edinburgh flat; the abduction and assault of the teenage couple; assaults on three other men; and being involved in the supply of diazepam. Byrne pled guilty to two charges of assaulting the couple; Henderson was found guilty of the charges relating to the three young men.

Due to fears that witnesses would be intimidated, the trial was held virtually in secret and amid high security in Inverness between 29 September and 3 November 2000. Police wearing body armour and brandishing assault rifles and side arms surrounded the court. There was also a number of police dogs in evidence. The judge ordered a ban on media reporting of the proceedings. In the end, Hamilton was jailed for life with a recommendation that he serve a minimum of nine years. The trial judge, Lord Kingarth, said: 'You showed yourself capable of taking sadistic pleasure in the infliction of pain, and the inspiration of real terror over long periods. . . . It is clear to me that you pose a substantial danger to the public while at liberty.'

As for his partners in crime, David Henderson was given six years while Martin Byrne – who gave evidence against his former boss and was described as a 'slave' to Hamilton by Lord Kingarth – received three years. Before he jailed Byrne the judge sought reassurances from the Crown that special arrangements would be put in place to protect him in prison. These precautions were undoubtedly necessary: defence counsel Ian Hamilton told the court that Byrne had been told in an anonymous phone call that, 'No matter what jail you go to, you will be found and killed.'

In 2004, it was Hamilton's turn to be injured, when a younger prisoner fought back and stabbed him repeatedly. According to press reports, Hamilton had been pestering the younger man for sex and, according to an unnamed inmate quoted in the *News of the World*, 'when he got a response, it wasn't the one he wanted'. Hamilton survived the attack and was brought to Falkirk Sheriff Court for the young man's trial. Surrounded by six police officers, he denied the accused was the knifeman.

Torturer he may have been, grass he wasn't.

The Haney clan
'Get it up you!'

Big Mags Haney was a journalist's dream. The sixteen-stone, 60-year-old bleached-blonde matriarch of a notorious Stirling clan – dubbed 'the family from hell' by a sheriff – had a string of offences to her name, including breach of the peace, fraud and contempt of court. But that was not what made her good copy. She turned 'family values' spokesperson when she campaigned to have a convicted child molester removed from the Raploch housing estate, which at the time was her family's home. Alan Christie had been found guilty of lewd and libidinous behaviour towards a four-year-old girl and Big Mags was none-too-pleased at him being housed in the estate. She led a group of around seventy demonstrators who massed outside the hostel where Christie had been placed by social services. They battered the doors and windows of the building and chanted 'Beast out'. Eventually, police officers smuggled Christie out a back door and away from the estate.

Mags, then fifty-four, said she was proud of her neighbours for standing up for their rights. 'They have rid the community of a convicted child molester by the strength of their actions,' she said. 'This is a deprived community but we love each other and every one of our bairns and we want them to live in peace.'

But as later events proved, the community did not love Mags and her family quite as much as she thought. Neighbours grew tired of the family's thieving and dealing and banded together to hound them out of the estate. Neither did her concern for the wellbeing of local youngsters prevent Haney and members of her family from supplying them with drugs.

Big Mags and her crime dynasty were outed by the *Daily Record* during the tabloid newspaper's often controversial 'Shop a Dealer' campaign in December 2000. Joseph Haney, her 25-year-old son, was jailed for twenty-one months and daughter Valerie for thirty months after being found guilty of dealing in heroin near the family home in Stirling's Lower Bridge Street. Then her daughter Stella, aged twenty-seven, was jailed in March 2001 for possession of fourteen grams of heroin, stashed in a condom inside her body.

Police had being watching the Haney home for seven weeks

before they pounced on Stella and she admitted she had the drugs hidden inside her. The condom of heroin was worth £1,500. Stella, herself an addict, wept as she was sentenced to three-and-a-half years after pleading guilty to being concerned in the supply of the drug, possession with intent to supply and supply. She told the court she had intended smoking half of the stash herself and selling the rest. As she was led from the court she pleaded 'take care of my wean'. She had already had one of her two children adopted while the other was in care.

Mags herself was hoovered up in June of 2001. Drug Squad detectives rammed their way into what had become known as 'Hotel Haney' – the council-owned homeless unit in Lower Bridge Street, which had been the family's headquarters for two years – as well as seven other flats in Stirling and Alloa. The operation involved over sixty officers and netted them, in addition to Big Mags, other members of the family, including her estranged 71-year-old husband John, who lived nearby. As Mags and others were led out in handcuffs, a crowd of locals – some of whom may well have informed on them in the first place having grown disgusted by the drug dealing – cheered. Haney, still in carpet slippers and holding a packet of cigarettes in her hand-cuffed fist, yelled, 'Get it up you!'

For the next three hours, a succession of rubber-gloved cops and handlers with sniffer dogs moved in and out of the tenement block, removing a vast amount of evidence.

It took almost two years for the case to reach court. Mags, her address by then given as Mill Street, Alloa, stood accused along with her daughter Diane, 35, son Hugh, 31, and niece Roseann, 40, of dealing in heroin. Ex-husband John had his plea of not guilty accepted and he was freed. Mags Haney, it was claimed, 'sat like a queen at the centre of a huge drugs empire'. The court was told that the accused had traded in the drug between 2000 and 2001 from their cluster of flats in Lower Bridge Street, which they had all but taken over after other tenants moved out. The tenement was so well known that local addicts called it 'The Shop' and often phoned Diane Haney's mobile asking if it was open.

Big Mags, it was revealed, received state benefits of £1,200 a month, but she supplemented it by earning £1,000 per day from selling drugs. Mags was 'the controller' of the organisation, overseeing the cutting of the drugs every morning into bags, which were then distributed through a series of runners. The loud-mouthed matriarch went down for twelve years, Diane for nine, Hugh for five and Roseann for seven. A grand-daughter, Kim, was sentenced to twenty-four months for contempt of court after she refused to give evidence. A total of £10,740 cash found in their possession was seized by the Crown. The Crown also planned to probe the family finances under the Proceeds of Crime Act to claw back more of their ill-gotten gains.

While in jail, the 60-year-old grannie suffered another blow. She was diagnosed with cervical cancer. One friend told the *News of the World* that she was 'a changed woman. She's really scared of what the future holds.' Another unnamed source said that she was 'terrified of dying behind bars'. However, her attempt to have her sentence reduced failed.

But even with Big Mags behind bars, the Haney family was seldom out of the public eye – or the tabloid press. In April 2004, 17-year-old grandson Thomas Haney was pictured giving a defiant two-fingered salute after appearing at Alloa Sheriff Court. He pled guilty to stealing a handbag from a woman in a cemetery. The victim was placing flowers at her mother's grave while Haney pretended to tend a nearby plot. He lifted her bag and a shopping carrier as she knelt to place a bouquet of red roses at the headstone, then sold the handbag and its contents, including jewellery and a mobile phone, to buy drugs, 'Cannabis, ecstasy, valium, heroin – whatever I could get my hands on,' he said.

Sentence was deferred until May for social enquiry and community-service reports but when Haney failed to turn up a warrant was issued for his arrest. He was found and in June 2004 sentenced to fifteen months.

With Mags experiencing the delights of Her Majesty's penal establishments, leadership of the depleted clan passed to her daughter, Catherine, who had already served time for robbery. In September 2004, tenants in Alloa's Hawkhill estate paraded the streets to register their protest at the suggestion that Catherine, known as 'Crackers', was to be rehoused there. Banners declaring 'Haneys R Scum' and 'No Haneys Here' were raised, while graffiti displayed similar sentiments. In the end, Clackmannanshire Council changed its mind and announced that the Haneys would not be gracing the estate.

Joseph Howard

From a 'frightening' family

Edinburgh pensioners Harold and Elizabeth Snook had already fallen victim to callous crooks once before. It was in early 2001, when bogus workmen stole £3,000 from their Newington home. That should have been enough for the old couple who, as one police officer put it, 'should have been able to live out their final years in peace and quiet'. But fate had something much worse in store for them.

Later that year, in October, 83-year-old Mr Snook answered his door to two men. Without so much as a by your leave they burst through the security lock and threw him against a wall, banging his head. They took him and his wife into a room and tied them up. One of the raiders told them to keep quiet and they would not get hurt. The raiders then ransacked the house but managed to find only a paltry £128 before fleeing the scene, leaving their elderly victims still locked in the room. The pair did not spare a thought for the old man and woman as they went on their way. All it would have taken was an anonymous phone call to the police, tipping them off. But they remained silent.

The Snooks lay in their prison for three days, with no food, water or heating, until a neighbour heard their weak moans. When police forced their way in, they found the old couple lying on the floor. They were starved, severely dehydrated and had suffered kidney damage. Mr Snook was unable to move his arms and his hands were badly swollen after being tied up. His wife was 'gravely unwell, confused and bedridden'. Naturally, both were badly affected by their nightmarish ordeal. They were taken to hospital, where Mrs Snook died in February the following year, although a pathologist stated that her death was not due to her treatment at the hands of the raiders.

By that time, police had swooped on 20-year-old Joseph Nelson Howard and his 25-year-old brother, Joseph Downie Howard. The Dundee-born brothers were snared when DNA found on a mask at the scene matched the younger Howard. The duo were said to be 'of the travelling community' and from a 'frightening' family. The younger brother had links with gangs of bogus workmen who specialised in targeting pensioners. He was locked up at the age of fifteen for robbing a Carlisle bowling alley at knifepoint. At seventeen he was ordered to get counselling after assaulting a man.

In this new Edinburgh case the two brothers had originally been charged with attempted murder but, by the time the case opened, a bargain had been struck in the name of legal expediency. The younger brother admitted a reduced charge of assault to severe injury, while the older brother had his not-guilty plea accepted and was released. In so doing, the Crown spared the still weakened Mr Snook the stress of appearing in court to give evidence. In court, his lawyer said that Howard 'accepts his behaviour was appalling and he regrets what happened'.

However, the plea bargain enraged many, including police officers. 'We are stunned that the Crown has chosen not to proceed with the attempted murder charge,' one detective lashed out. 'We can't understand their logic. If tying up an elderly couple, leaving them without food or water for days and making no attempt to alert others to their plight is not attempted murder, then I don't know what is.'

John Snook, Mr Snook's son from a previous marriage, said: 'My father has been informed and I speak for him when I say he is completely devastated. I am angry with the entire judicial system for allowing this to happen.' He added, 'How can this be called justice?'

In April 2002, Joseph Nelson Howard was caged for ten years. The judge declared he had committed 'a monstrous crime'. He went on, 'It is one of the most cruel and cowardly crimes it has been my misfortune to deal with.'

'He deserves every hour of that ten years – and more,' said John Snook. 'He is a danger to society – especially innocent old people – and always will be.' He also launched another attack on the plea-bargaining system. 'Plea bargaining should never be allowed in crimes of this magnitude. My parents were not given any chance to bargain when they were tied up in that locked room.'

Meanwhile, Harold Snook, still in hospital six months after the crime, said he wanted his house burned down.

Some memories are too hard to live with.

The Inverness prison riots
The gang of four

They called them 'The Cages'. They were actually specially constructed rooms in the segregation block at Porterfield prison. There were five cells, and in each was a tiny cage with a bed that was little more than a board nailed to the floor with a mattress on top. There were no chairs, no tables, nowhere for inmates to store any personal possessions, no toilet facilities except a pot in which to urinate. A sixth cell was the so-called 'silent cell', for use when an inmate grew too unruly. This was the same as the other five but was soundproofed. Food was pushed to the prisoners like feeding time at the zoo – for to the prison authorities, the inmates in the unit, hard men with a history of rioting, assaults and 'dirty' protests, were little more than animals and were to be treated as such. In December 1972, the four who were quietly raging behind these bars were described as the 'most violent men' in Scotland. And that rage was about to boil over.

Jimmy Boyle is perhaps the best known. The 29-year-old Glasgow man had been sentenced to life for murder in 1967 and was a troublesome prisoner from the off. He had refused to fall in line with the system and had been accused of attacking a prison governor and a variety of guards in Barlinnie, Peterhead and also Inverness.

Larry Winters was also doing life for murder and had proved a violent handful for prison guards.

William McPherson had been convicted of bank robberies to raise funds for the Workers Revolutionary Party (see **Matthew Lygate**) but had been involved in a riot in Peterhead prison.

Howard Wilson was a bank robber who turned cop killer, gunning down two officers in Glasgow, and had also been involved in the riot at Peterhead in August 1972.

These four men were now penned together, albeit separated in their iron cages. They socialised for only two hours a week, in the unit's recreation room, and it was here that their hostility, their bitterness and their outrage at the brutality they claimed to have experienced at the hands of the prison system over the years erupted into violence.

The only people who knew what really went on inside that tiny little room were the prisoners themselves and the prison officers involved. For there are two different stories told about the 'Inverness cages riot'. The guards claimed that the men had launched an escape attempt; that their plan was to take one of them hostage and use his keys to help them get out. When that seemed to fail, they had decided to kill as many officers as they could. For their part, the prisoners insisted that they had started a peaceful demonstration; a protest over the brutalities of the prison regime. No violence had been planned but when the warders came at them with batons they had fought back, using home-made weapons.

Boyle, it was said, was the ringleader. In his book, *A Sense of Freedom*, he writes that he had in fact advocated violence, supported by Winters, but neither Wilson nor McPherson had gone along with them. Reluctantly, he agreed to the peaceful protest, linking arms with the other three in the middle of the floor. He claimed the fight broke out when an officer cracked him over the head with a baton and he smashed a radio into the man's face. After that, by his own admission, he used his sharpened piece of metal to stick as many prison guards as possible.

The prison officers said that Boyle came at them with a knife in his hand screaming, 'kill, kill, kill!' He stabbed one officer fifteen times before he was overpowered. Another officer tried to reach the alarm bell but was stabbed and battered as he pushed his way across the room. He managed to get to the bell, then turned, he said, and came face to face with Larry Winters. The prisoner had a knife in his hand and was coming at him as if in slow motion, 'with a smile on his face'. Luckily, reinforcements arrived and Winters was also overpowered. During the fight, a third officer lost an eye. Both McPherson and Wilson were also restrained, the former later admitting he was not a very good fighter and claiming he had been 'tossed all over the place' during the so-called riot. Once subdued, the prisoners claimed, they were treated to the attention of a prison batter squad, Boyle being severely injured.

Later, the authorities claimed that they found a rope made of sheets in McPherson's cell. After the riot, a document was discovered on the prison grounds which, it was alleged, had been written by the men.

This note seemed, in part at least, to back up their claim that they were protesting over conditions and treatment. It stated that society throws men like them into 'concrete boxes' and 'steel-barred cages' and they call it 'mollycoddling'. It went on, 'you set your black-clad thugs on us and you call it restraining. You brutalise, dehumanise and degrade us. Worst of all, you give us no vestige of hope.'

The note went on to say that if their demands were not met within sixteen hours, they would murder their prison-officer hostage. It also warned that they were not to be approached or accosted by prison officers or police or their escape publicised in the media. A transistor radio, alleged to have been found in a cell after a previous search by three officers, was to alert them to any publicity. The men themselves dismissed the allegation that they had written the note as 'sheer fantasy'.

Amid high security, with police helicopters buzzing the skies above Inverness, the four men appeared in the High Court charged with attempting to murder six prison officers. The men denied the charge, again stating that they had embarked on a peaceful protest that had turned violent only when the prison guards attacked them. The Crown insisted it was an escape attempt and that the men would not have hesitated to kill; and had indeed tried to do so. Both Boyle and Winters had gone to the recreation room with weapons and showed themselves ready and willing to use them. Both sides believed they were fighting for their lives in that tiny room.

In the end, after two hours and ten minutes of deliberation, the jury returned to find the men not guilty of attempted murder of the six officers but guilty of assault on five guards and of attempting to escape. Lord Wheatley sentenced each of them to six years, to be served consecutively to their current term.

Following the cages riot, Boyle became one of the first prisoners at a new experimental 'special unit' in Barlinnie prison. The approach here was not the dehumanising policy of other prisons, but a more humane regime where the prisoner was treated with respect. It was as if the prison service had learned that brutality only causes more brutality and the controversial unit was an attempt to find a new way to deal with troublesome inmates like Jimmy Boyle. Housed in the former women's wing at the Glasgow jail, the unit was never popular with certain elements of the press and right-wing politicians. The idea worked, though, and Boyle is perhaps its greatest success. It was here that he learned there was a new way to deal with the world other than hacking and slashing. He found he could write and sculpt and when he finally completed his term he was accepted by the artistic world, even if some elements of his old world could not believe he had changed his ways.

Larry Winters was also sent to the special unit but his ending was more downbeat. He, too, discovered he had some talent as a writer but died of a drug overdose before he could fully explore it. His death led to an inevitable tightening up of the liberal regime but the unit went on to prove that it was a sound notion for the rehabilitation of violent offenders, with many successful 'graduates', until its critics finally managed to have it closed down in the late 1990s.

Howard Wilson and William McPherson were both sent back to Peterhead. Wilson is still in prison but McPherson died in 2005 of a heart attack while serving another term for a drug offence.

As for the notorious Inverness cages, they were closed down for three years following the escape attempt. They have now been completely dismantled.

Eamonn Kelly
'A serial killer in the making'

Eamonn Kelly might have got away with his crimes if he had not had an argument with an uncle. As it was, the assault and subsequent police investigation led to him being convicted of viciously assaulting two prostitutes.

On 19 July 2000, working girl Alison Wallace was found lying at the side of Drumpellier loch, Coatbridge with serious head injuries that led to her being treated in hospital for over three months. Even after treatment, the 27-year-old woman would never make a full recovery from the brain injury she sustained during the attack and years later still suffered from flashbacks to that terrifying night.

She had been selected by her attacker in Glasgow's red-light district, the grid of streets between the former Anderston bus station and Sauchiehall Street. The soft-spoken young man who picked her up in the white car seemed safe enough. After that her mind was a blank until she woke up in the city's Southern General hospital. Almost three years after the attack, she still suffered memory lapses. 'My memory is so bad that that I've often got to ask for a question to be repeated,' she said in court. She also said she heard 'banging noises' when she was awake or asleep. 'The banging is what he was banging my head with,' she said.

She told the court the left side of her body had been permanently affected by the attack. She suffered a permanent limp and could not bend her knees. The mother-of-two said she had twice tried to take her own life.

Strathclyde Police, with a string of unsolved slayings of vice girls on their books, launched a major operation to catch Alison Wallace's attacker. The subsequent publicity revealed that another prostitute had been attacked a month earlier by a man answering the same description. Amanda Ryan had also been picked up in Glasgow city centre and driven out of town. She, however, was not attacked right away. She had sex with the man and received her fee. But then he drove his car up a quiet country road that came to a dead end, where he hauled her out.

Wearing surgical gloves, he attacked her with a silver knife and beat her over the head with what may have been a baseball bat. She ended up in some water and, as he reached for his knife again, she made a bid to escape the man she was certain meant to kill her. 'I don't know how I got the energy but I got out of the water and ran to the car to press the horn,' she said. 'Dogs started barking and he panicked and drove away.'

But despite the descriptions provided by both victims, police were unable to track down the brutal attacker. It was not until May 2003 that the break came.

The man responsible for the attacks was 24-year-old Uddingston man Eamonn Kelly, known as the 'Ratcatcher' because he used hawks to hunt vermin on rubbish dumps. After the attack on Alison Wallace, he asked a friend to set fire to his white Ford Orion to destroy any possibility of forensic evidence linking him to the crime. However, he had forgotten one very important piece of evidence that would ultimately connect him to the brutal attacks. In the meantime, he moved to Brighton where he found work under an assumed name and lived for the next two-and-a-half years.

Finally, believing the investigation had wound down and that police had other, more important, matters to deal with, he moved back to Scotland. But, in May 2003, he had an argument with an uncle that degenerated into a fight. Police were called and the uncle revealed that Kelly had previously confessed to battering a prostitute. He had made the admission on his twenty-first birthday, the same day that Alison Wallace had been left for dead on the banks of Drumpellier loch.

Police took DNA from Kelly, which matched a sample found on a condom left at the scene of the brutal assault.

Tried in November 2003, sentence was deferred while risk assessments were made over whether he posed a significant danger to women. In December, Lord Menzies said that he represented 'a menace to young women and a real risk to their safety if you were to be at large'. He sentenced the Ratcatcher to nine years in prison.

Gerald Lafferty

On the run for thirteen years

A gang of masked and armed men ambush a security vehicle as it makes a delivery to a bank, abduct the guards and during the getaway engage in a shootout with officers who are in hot pursuit. It is the kind of robbery that is common in police dramas on television. But it still has the power to shock the public when it happens in real life.

It was on Wednesday, 20 November 1991 that two men wearing masks bearing the likeness of former Soviet leader Mikhail Gorbachev, and a third with a balaclava pulled over his head, ambushed a Securicor vehicle as it delivered cash to the Clydesdale Bank in Stewart Street, East Kilbride. A gun was placed to the head of one of the van's three guards while a second guard was dragged back into the cabin and forced to lie on the floor. One of the raiders tried to start the van but a coded ignition key prevented the engine from kicking into life. An alarm was finally switched off and the van was started but then a second alarm sounded due to a door still being open.

Throughout all this, the third guard was sitting in the back of the locked van. The gunmen drove the armoured truck to Greenhill Park in High Blantyre, just a few miles away, where another vehicle was waiting with a fourth man, the getaway driver. The two guards who had been taken hostage were dragged round to the rear of the Securicor van and a warning shot was fired at the door, it was later claimed in court. Eventually, the van was opened and the men unloaded £2.5 million into the getaway vehicle.

It had been far from plain sailing for the gang so far and it was about to get worse, for armed police arrived and chased them as they tried to drive off. More shots were fired before they abandoned their own vehicle and tried to escape on foot. Police followed them and, it was alleged, dodged bullets. Finally, three men were arrested but a fourth man escaped and has never been identified.

In April 1992, three men appeared in the High Court at Airdrie charged with assaulting and attempting to murder the three security guards, detaining them against their will, discharging a firearm and robbing them of the £2.5 million. They were also accused of attempting to murder three police officers. But still the drama was not over. No sooner had the trial of Gerald Lafferty, William Barbour and the third man started than it was interrupted: the court had to be cleared because of a bomb alert, the second in two weeks. Nothing was found and the trial resumed – only to be halted again when the case had to be deserted *pro loco et tempore* because defence advocate Tom Dawson QC was tapped on the shoulder by prime minister John Major to become solicitor-general for Scotland. The three accused would have to wait for a retrial.

That was when Gerald Lafferty took his chance to go on the run. Incredibly, he remained at liberty for thirteen years. Fife-born Barbour denied he had anything to do with the crime but was eventually found guilty and sentenced to life with a recommendation that he serve a minimum of fifteen years while the third man was found not guilty.

Police launched a search for Lafferty but found little trace of him. In 1997 they were told he was living in Donegal using the name Hugh Docherty but the lead took them nowhere. They heard he was in Kent lodging with relatives but again they drew a blank. Then they were told he had been seen drinking in Glasgow and raided twenty places in an attempt to snare him but again came up empty-handed.

For thirteen years Gerald Lafferty managed to evade the long arm of the law, but he was certainly not living the life of Reilly. The fugitive moved from place to place, mostly in England, never staying in one location too long, finding work as a labourer. Occasionally he returned to Scotland but only for very short visits. His years on the run had a disastrous effect on his marriage and it ended in divorce. He lost touch with his three children and he found that life on the lam can be very, very lonely.

Finally, in May 2005, he decided he'd had enough and, accompanied by a lawyer, turned himself into the police. In court later, defence counsel Tony Graham said, 'Lafferty had lived a solitary existence as a non-person without the ability to get medical or other benefits. He gave himself up because if he was to have any meaningful quality of life, he could no longer run. He wants to serve his sentence and try to contact his children.'

He continued strenuously to deny any involvement in the 1991 robbery but that really did not matter anymore: the Crown had announced that the passage of time meant he would not be prosecuted for it. There were 164 witnesses and scores of documents to find and the Crown took the view that it would be impossible to track them all down. He was, however, brought to court for attempting to pervert the course of justice by failing to appear for the 1992 trial. His plea of not guilty to the part of the indictment that stated he was conscious of his guilt when he escaped was accepted by the Crown, further underlining the fact that he would never be tried for the raid.

In October 2005, by now sixty-one years of age, Lafferty was sentenced to eighteen months for jumping bail.

Matthew Lygate
Power to the people

Glasgow has long had a reputation for left-wing sympathies. The struggle between the workers and the bosses has often turned bitter in the city, and just as often turned violent. It was, after all, the Second City of the Empire and its industrial and commercial growth had been meteoric. This, naturally, caused the already disparate classes to move even further apart as the factory owners and employers seemed to line their pockets thanks to the sweat and blood of the workers. In many cases it was true and that, in turn, helped breed a strong streak of radicalism among the people on the factory floor. In the eighteenth century it was the Radicals and the Chartists who carried the flag, although it was not yet red.

Markets must both boom and bust and life was fine in the good times but, when the lean years came, so did the bitterness. Meanwhile, the French Revolution had given the British government the jitters with its motto of Liberty, Equality and Fraternity. In 1820, there was a weak attempt at rebellion by weavers, led by John Baird and Andrew Hardie, a forebear of Labour Party co-founder James Keir Hardie. That ended with a skirmish to the north of the city and the execution of the ringleaders. Later the Chartists took up the cause by pressing for political reform. Again there was violence, but still there was no revolution.

The ousting of the Russian royal family by the communists gave the government of the day as much to worry about as the French Revolution. In 1919, concerned that a strikers' rally in Glasgow's George Square was the beginning of a Bolshevik revolt, they sent in the troops to put it down. Batons were drawn, the Riot Act was read and, when the crowd of thousands refused to disperse, skulls were cracked. In the days that followed, tanks and armed troops patrolled the city streets. Among the ringleaders arrested were socialists Emanuel Shinwell and William Gallacher. Three years later, the city stunned the country when it returned no less than ten socialist MPs to Westminster. Two thirds of the city's constituencies had gone over to the Labour Party and the term Red Clydeside was born.

In years to come, they would discover just how many reds were indeed under the Glasgow bed – in particular John MacLean who was, in the 1920s, made the first Soviet consul of Britain by Lenin. MacLean was, and still is, an influential and charismatic leader. Although his dream of a Workers Republic of Scotland never came to pass, his beliefs helped to inspire a young man decades later. And that young man, if the case against him was correct, also had a dream of liberating the working class. But, to do that, he needed money. And to raise that money, he turned to crime.

Matthew Lygate was thirty-four when he became a household name in Scotland. Until then he had just been one of a number of young radicals who wanted to change the world. Born in Glasgow's south side, he first became passionate about politics after leaving school at the age of fifteen. Training as a tailor's cutter, he joined the Young Communist League and realised that he wished to dedicate his life to bettering the lot of his fellow working man. He spent six years in New Zealand, not a country known for spawning revolutionaries, but while there he developed a deeper interest in what he called 'the struggle of the oppressed worker against capitalist doctrines'.

By the mid-1960s he was back home in Scotland where he became part of the brand new Workers Party of Scotland. It did not have many members – perhaps around seventy nationwide – but it did demand a very high membership fee: one day's pay every month. Lygate soon became party chairman and in return for those duties, as well as running the party headquarters in the Vanguard Bookshop on the city's Paisley Road West and editing the party magazine, he received a wage of £8 per week.

In 1969, like his great hero John MacLean, he stood as the party's candidate for the Gorbals in a by-election. However, red though the Clyde may have been, the masses were not prepared to send a man with his extreme left-wing views to represent them in Parliament for Lygate finished bottom of the poll. Only seventy people put their cross beside his name, less even than the official Communist Party candidate received. This failure did not deter him, however, for he travelled the country rallying support for his cause and his party and, as time passed, he became something of a fanatic in his passion for workers rights.

And there were many people willing to listen. The country may never have had it so good in the 1950s and 1960s but there were still plenty of disaffected men and women who would find something to agree with in his arguments. The boom time of engineering and ship-building was in rapid decline. The lines at the unemployment office were lengthening. Radicalism was again on the rise, whether it be for workers rights or the independence of the country from London rule. Naturally, his activities brought him to the attention of the authorities and, by extension, Special Branch, who kept him under surveillance.

Back in his bookshop headquarters, he produced propaganda material espousing his party's views and, according to evidence, plotting direct action against the Establishment. He held certain Stalinist views and the notorious Soviet leader had, in the early days of his party, robbed banks to finance the cause. Lygate, it would appear, was about to follow in old Joe's footsteps in targeting what he called 'bloated banks' and 'capitalist parasitic vermin'.

In 1972, Glasgow was hit by a series of four bank robberies in which hooded men wielded sawn-off shotguns and clubs and made off with more than £13,000. In one of the raids, a twelve-bore shotgun was fired through a wooden door that a young bank teller had locked behind her in a bid to get away. In court, it was pointed out that this could easily have been a case of murder because whoever fired the weapon had no way of knowing if the woman had moved out of the way. In another, a young employee had his head cracked open by a wooden club. There were more raids, on a haulage firm and on a British Rail wages office, during which around £9,000 was taken. According to the authorities, the man behind three of these robberies was none other than Matthew Lygate. He had, they claimed, decided that the best way to get political power was through the sawn-off double-barrels of a shotgun.

Police said they received information suggesting that Lygate was behind the crime wave and when they raided the Paisley Road West bookshop they found – in the basement – guns, ammunition, hoods and bank notes, many of which were new and bearing consecutive serial numbers. They also searched Lygate's flat in Albert Road and found further weapons and cash, as well as a radio tuned into police broadcasts.

The would-be revolutionary was arrested, along with fellow party members William McPherson, aged thirty-one, and Colin Lawson, who was thirty-five. Another man, 23-year-old Ian Doran, was also arrested. He was not a member of the Workers Party of Scotland because, one newspaper stated, being English he was not allowed to join. It seems the party that wished to fight for the rights of the working man was not yet ready to accept Sassenachs! All four were faced with a twenty-five-charge indictment that included armed robbery, assault and forming a criminal conspiracy.

Both McPherson and Doran were identified as being the men who had raided the haulage firm because they had, somewhat surprisingly, not worn masks during the robbery. Witnesses had said that one of the men carried 'a Luger-type' pistol and such a gun was found in Doran's flat. However, when it was shown to the witnesses they said it looked different somehow and it was presumed that during the raid a silencer had been fitted. However, much of the remainder of the evidence was highly circumstantial, particularly against Lygate. There was the material found in the shop and flat and it was also pointed out that two of the banks robbed were fairly close to both. He admitted that he had agreed to store the weapons and money in his shop – the material in his flat was planted by police, he claimed – but insisted that he took no part in any of the robberies.

Although Lygate supported the concept of robbery to further political aims, he had declined to participate because he felt that it would negate his political struggle. He admitted he had 'associates in many parts of the world involved in guerrilla tactics on behalf of the working classes'. He went on, 'Last year, I was approached by some of these people and asked if I was prepared to participate in bank robberies. I refused as I felt this would jeopardise my position as a political organiser and chairman of the Workers Party of Scotland.' His reasoning makes a lot of sense. Lygate must have known his views and speeches would have made him a target of Special Branch attention, so to keep the material in the shop and his flat was bordering on lunacy. However, it also has to be said that stranger things have happened.

The trial lasted eleven days and shortly before its conclusion Lygate sensationally sacked his defence lawyers. Given that it was the Glasgow dream team of Nicholas Fairbairn and Joseph Beltrami (see

Walter Scott Ellis) along with Edgar Prais QC, the move was puzzling. However, he dismissed his counsel on the understanding that he would be able to give his own closing speech to the jury and also a plea in mitigation. Perhaps by then Lygate had sensed the way the winds of justice were blowing and knew he had little hope of leaving the courtroom as a free man. He was right. In March 1972 he and his three co-accused were found guilty. The judge, Lord Dunpark, was as good as his word and allowed Lygate the opportunity to tender a plea of mitigation prior to sentence. But his patience soon died for what was supposed to be a plea for the judge to be merciful only succeeded in making things worse.

It was acts of violence against the working classes that had brought him to court, Lygate asserted, although he did not seem to refer to physical violence but something more metaphysical. It was such violence that had left 150,000 in Scotland out of work, he claimed. It was such violence that had caused the withdrawal of free milk to schoolchildren, he insisted, leading to the return of rickets among the nation's young.

Lord Dunpark interrupted here, pointing out that these matters were irrelevant in regard to the sentence he was about to hand down. However, he allowed Lygate to continue in similar vein before he broke in again, this time with irritation in his voice: 'I have given you a good deal of licence. You must not make a political speech.' Lygate, whatever else he was, was a political animal and was not about to yield the floor. People could not get work, he went on, and their only alternative was to join the army and then be sent to Ulster to fight 'and murder Irishmen and women'. Lord Dunpark was having one of that: like unemployment, free school milk and rickets, violence in Northern Ireland was nothing to do with the matter in hand. Lygate went on talking about the oppression of the working class and ended his peroration with a slightly sinister prophecy: the day would come when those who judged him and the other men in the dock would themselves be judged.

As pleas in mitigation go, it at least had the benefit of being impassioned. But as pleas in mitigation go, it went unheeded, which was no surprise to any of the accused. Lord Dunpark slapped Lygate, who had no previous convictions, with a hefty twenty-four years in jail.

It was, at the time, one of the longest prison sentences handed down in a Scottish court for robbery. However, the judge believed Lygate was a highly dangerous insurrectionist and that he and the others had executed a lawless and ruthless campaign. 'The raids were serious enough in themselves,' he went on, 'but together they formed a frightening pattern of criminal conduct which might have continued to this day had someone not have given information to the police.' He had no doubt that had anyone got in their way, the shotguns would have been used while Lygate, viewed as the leader, supported such robberies 'presumably because they were aimed at capitalist institutions'.

McPherson – the former soldier who was credited with the military precision with which some of the crimes were carried out – admitted five previous convictions and received twenty-six years. Doran, the cockney car salesman who had fled to Scotland originally to escape the law in London, put his hands up to eleven previous convictions and was given twenty-five years. Lawson, a former monk and Lygate's assistant in the bookshop, was found guilty of being involved in one bank raid and was given only six years. As they were being led down to begin their new lives behind bars, Lygate – defiant to the last – joined McPherson in raising clenched fists in a salute and cried out 'Long live the workers of Scotland.'

The authorities were happy that four dangerous revolutionaries were safe in the arms of the prison service. The members of the Workers Party of Scotland were not so pleased and began to distance themselves from the men's actions. Although Lygate had resigned as chairman, the party's 71-year-old secretary, Thomas Murray, told a press conference that there may yet be a time when his party would stage such robberies in order to raise cash to finance the overthrowing of the capitalist system. That time, though, had not come. The working classes had the right to fight capitalism, he argued, and suggestions that bank robberies could be carried out had been raised at party meetings but no agreement had ever been reached to act on them. Those who carried out such raids were wrong. The speech condemned their former members without actually condemning what they had been found guilty of. The Workers Party of Scotland itself did not survive very long after the convictions.

The following year, a fifth man was sentenced to three years for taking part in one of the robberies. Workers Party member, Alexander Watt, aged twenty-three, had fled soon after Lygate and the others were arrested. The Edinburgh native escaped to Holland where he joined a religious group known as the Children of God. In November 1972, his conscience moved him to give himself up to the British consulate in Amsterdam, saying he wanted to get 'a heavy burden off his shoulders'. In January 1973, he admitted to his part in a bank raid in which thirteen people were menaced with shotguns.

After the convictions, further details were revealed about Lygate. Press reports revealed he had been meeting with Chinese officials in Paris and London, had actually appeared on the platform of a meeting of Maoist sympathisers in Britain and pointed out that on one occasion he had flown to Algiers to meet with other guerrillas and revolutionaries such as Yasser Arafat. He also had links, it was claimed, with an Irish organisation known as Saor Eire (Free Ireland) – a group said to make the IRA look like cub scouts – which carried out bank raids to finance terrorism. All of this assured the reading public that a dangerous fanatic was safely off the streets.

However, not everyone agreed with the portrait. Lygate's father in particular and unsurprisingly defended him. He was first quoted in one newspaper just after the trial as saying 'There is no doubt that Matt robbed banks to finance a workers revolution. I am certain he would have used the money to buy arms and create a big propaganda machine.' His son went to prison happily, he claimed, because he was convinced that a revolution would take place in Scotland within five years and he would be freed. But within a year, John Lygate wrote to the *Glasgow Herald* declaring that he believed his son had been wrongfully convicted and that the severe sentences were 'a reflection of the security service's reaction to a crumbling system that values profit and property above people and social welfare'.

There may be something in what he said, for Lygate's sentence was particularly heavy, especially when you consider that murderers had been sentenced to similar periods in jail and sometimes less. Until his death – which was caused, it has been suggested, by the strain and heartache of his son's conviction and the subsequent fight for justice – Mr Lygate continued to believe in his son's innocence, even hiring a private eye to find new evidence.

But Matthew Lygate remained in prison, a martyr or dangerous reactionary, depending on your political viewpoint. He continued to express his left-wing views but replaced championing workers rights with those of his fellow prisoners and organised a food strike in Peterhead prison. Having been turned down twice for parole, he said after almost ten years inside, 'I suppose I could have made out that I had seen the light and become religious or something but even if it means I must stay here and serve my full sentence I still could not compromise my integrity, honesty and principles.'

Lygate was finally freed in 1983, after his third application for parole. He was later nominated for the rectorship of Glasgow University but was knocked out in the first round of voting. Other nominees included Yasser Arafat, Jeffrey Archer, comedian and actor Rikki Fulton and Menzies Campbell QC, now leader of the Liberal Democrats. Former Glasgow Lord Provost Michael Kelly (who was also a director of Celtic Football Club) was the eventual winner.

In 1973, McPherson's name was back in the headlines, this time alongside notorious, but now reformed, Glasgow crook Jimmy Boyle, convicted cop killer Howard Wilson and murderer Larry Winters for their involvement in the **Inverness prison riot**. The prisoners claimed they had been making a peaceful protest in the recreation room of Inverness's Porterfield jail when trouble erupted. The prisoners said they and others were regularly subjected to regular beatings by prison staff and were merely displaying their objections to the regime when officers lunged at them with batons. The warders countered by claiming that the inmates started the violence when they came at them with knives. Whatever actually happened in that room, one officer was stabbed repeatedly and another lost an eye. The four accused were found not guilty of attempted murder but did receive an additional six years each for assault.

By 2003, McPherson was free but once again in trouble. In October that year, he was arrested in Glasgow's Firhill area with two kilos of heroin worth £200,000 in his possession. The 63-year-old former soldier was at the time living in Ayr and he claimed that he had been offered £100 to collect 100,000 cigarettes. In December 2004, he was jailed for five years but died of a heart attack after a year inside.

Ian McDonald

A blagger with ambition

At first glance, the couple were just like any other in the Chinese restaurant, simply out to enjoy a good meal and each other's company. However, a close observer would note that the man seemed unusually edgy and was regarding some of the other diners with suspicion. The woman appeared to be attempting to reassure him that everything was all right. But the man had good reason to be nervous for everything was far from all right, at least for him. He had spent some months on the run from the law after a botched bank job in England and he was sitting in the Glasgow eating house with a loaded gun lodged in his waistband. What he didn't know, although he suspected something as he wolfed down his chicken curry, was that just about everyone else in the restaurant that night was an undercover cop – and they were just waiting for the nod to take this notorious Glasgow crook down.

The man was Ian McDonald, known as 'Blink', it was said, because he would kill someone without blinking (even though he has never been convicted of murder). He was brought up, in the early 1960s, a gunshot's distance away from Glasgow's feared Barlinnie prison, the son of a strict railway engineer who made tracks when the boy was just fifteen. By that time, the young McDonald had already been knocking around the streets with a wild bunch of lads but his father's desertion sent him off the deep end. A punch thrown in physical-education class, at the teacher no less, saw him sent to an approved school. On a weekend break, he stole a car, assaulted a pursuing policeman and ended up in Longriggend remand centre. A spell at a young offenders institution really set him on the road to becoming one of Glasgow's most feared hard men. He turned to thieving and fell in with a young man named Paul Ferris. Together they made a criminal living out of jewel raids and unwound at night getting into fights, their weapon of choice being ultra-sharp carpet knives. 'I probably assaulted a dozen people and cut people's faces,' said McDonald years later to a newspaper. 'It wasn't for money – it was just the way things were, I'm afraid. I didn't feel nothing – some of these people were trying to hurt me and I was trying to get in there first.'

Although they remained friends, the young desperadoes went their separate ways. Ferris went on to become one of the most notorious – and feared – gangsters in the city's history, famously beating a murder rap after being accused of gunning down former pal Arthur Thompson Jr. McDonald went back to lifting jewels but, by 1983, when he hit a police officer with his car in a bid to escape arrest, he realised that life was getting a bit too hot for him. He took off to Benidorm, where the heat was more climatic. Even there, he risked falling foul of the very tough Spanish police by shoplifting leather jackets and perfume to sell on to gullible and bargain-hunting tourists. It was his first experience of a foreign land and he would return to Spain many years later.

However, he decided to come home after six weeks and was promptly arrested. Doing time for a jewel robbery and running down the police officer, he widened his circle of criminal contacts. On his release, he wasn't at liberty for long before he was banged-up again, once more for police assault. Enjoying the dubious hospitality of Barlinnie, he learned the hard way not to cross the prison staff. After assaulting a prison officer and an assistant governor, he claimed he was treated to the attentions of a batter squad. 'Officers lined up and passed me along them,' he later said. 'Everyone got a punch and kick and they were smashing my testicles.' When the doctor was called, McDonald said the incident was transformed into a serious fall down some stairs.

It was on one of his infrequent spells of freedom that he fell for attractive blonde Sheila McGourlay and began a long-term, if spasmodic, love affair. By this time, McDonald had graduated from shoplifting and beating up policemen to post office and bank blags. He and Sheila lived the high-life filled with good food, good clothes and good times and, with his ill-gotten gains, he bought a pub in Springburn. He continued to rip-off security vans and in 1990 was accused of gunning down a Glasgow gangster. However, the weekend the man had been shot in Glasgow's Merchant City, McDonald and Sheila were on the Isle of Bute with their one-year-old son. Actor and film director Sir Richard Attenborough owned a holiday home on the island and McDonald had managed to meet him. When police arrested him for the shooting, Blink trotted out his famous alibi.

Doing banks, post offices and security vans was bringing in steady cash but not enough for the ambitious McDonald, so when an old friend approached him in 1991 with a scheme to lift as much as £6 million from a Torquay bank he jumped at it with both feet. However, the job was to go seriously wrong and land him the longest jail stretch of his career. His motivation at the time was to make this, his biggest haul, his last. With his cut of the £6 million he could retire and live a life of luxury with Sheila and his son. There would be six men in the gang and McDonald, like television's 'Del Boy' Trotter, looked forward to being a millionaire this time next year.

However, despite meticulous planning and careful surveillance, the plan went badly pear-shaped. The one person the gang needed to come into the bank that morning – the person entrusted with the key to the final gate that led to the millions held in the vault – was late. The men had turned up armed and one of the shotguns went off, tearing a clump of hair out of a female teller's head. Their scheme in tatters, the gang ran out of the bank, leaving their weapons and empty loot bags behind. They had been staying at a local caravan park while preparing for the job and that was where McDonald was grabbed by an armed police officer. But as he was led back to a police caravan, he realised his handcuffs were insecure. He climbed through an unlatched window, managed to evade recapture and made his way back to Glasgow.

Disappointed that his big score had failed to materialise – and knowing that his telltale fingerprints were all over items left in Torquay – he picked himself up a gun and set out to wreak revenge on the two brothers who claimed that he had pulled the trigger in the earlier shooting in the Merchant City. Speaking at length to the *Daily Record* years later, McDonald said that by that time his life 'was nuts'. 'I was on the run for five weeks running about Glasgow looking for these people with a gun and I was just going to shoot him in the street. I thought I was going to get twenty years anyway, so why not sort a few grievances out?'

He never did sate his desire for vengeance and it was while he was out for dinner with girlfriend Sheila McGourlay that armed officers finally tracked him down. They had kept her under surveillance and even tapped her phone in a bid to trace the runaway robber. The couple were out for their meal in the Poa San Chinese restaurant in Glasgow's East End when the law swooped. Almost every other customer in the place that night was a cop and it was when they saw McDonald's hand nervously wander towards his gun that they leapt up with their own weapons in their fists. Luckily, there was no gunplay and McDonald was huckled roughly out of the restaurant.

He received two-and-a-half years for possession of the loaded gun and later, at the Old Bailey in London, a further sixteen years for his part in the bungled bank job. It was his longest stretch yet and as he did his stir, he must have wondered if he would ever achieve his ambition of becoming a millionaire. He was now in his thirties and time was running out. Sheila stuck by him at first but eventually their relationship faltered. He said he was 'gutted' by the break-up but understood the pressures of conducting a love affair where one side of it was being shuttled from jail to jail on a long prison term.

In 2001, he was freed and back in Glasgow. He said he'd learned his lesson but there were disturbing tales that he and old pal Paul Ferris, also recently at liberty after serving time on a gun-running beef, were back in action together again. A feud with another gangland figure led to Ferris having his licence revoked and being whisked back inside. Blink, meanwhile, was told that there was a contract out on his life – and that two Serbian hitmen were out to get him. Eventually, the pipe of peace was smoked between the warring parties and an agreement reached. McDonald was also said to have become involved with Ferris in a security firm. Reports that he had become inveigled in other illegal activities prompted Scottish police to ask for his licence to be revoked and he be put back behind bars to serve the remainder of his sixteen-year sentence.

One of the alleged crimes was the extorting of a hefty sum of money from businessman Pat Sweeney, who had been dating Sheila McGourlay while McDonald was inside. There were reports that he had put a contract on the millionaire's head from behind bars because he was livid that Sweeney could give his former girlfriend and his son the things he never could. But McGourlay later said she had grown tired of Sweeney's growing drug habit and had finished things. Sweeney, meanwhile, had gone on the run to escape the price on his head. Allegedly, that contract was lifted when he agreed to part with £400,000.

However, McDonald was apparently extremely irritated over the claims that he had placed a bounty on Sweeney's head, pointing out that it would have ruined his parole. 'Blink wouldn't pay that kind of money for a hit,' Sheila McGourlay was quoted as saying. 'If he wanted to kill someone he would just do it himself.' A gangland source said that the real reason McDonald, a lifelong non-user, was furious with Sweeney was that the businessman had taken drugs in front of his son. Whatever the truth, Sweeney did have to part with £1.9 million in a divorce settlement to his wife. 'I went off the rails at one time and mixed with the wrong people,' he confessed. 'I have now learned my lesson and now work very hard and live very clean.'

Linking up again with ex-flame Sheila in Spain – although both said they had found new loves – McDonald was also renouncing his past life. He told the *Daily Record*, 'I want to put the violence behind me and spend time with my family but I'm not a hypocrite. Who knows what will happen? Never say never.'

He also did not scotch the rumours of his latest activities. 'People think I'm into extortion now and that I'm a millionaire. I can't say if that's true because I'm out on licence but I'm not denying it.'

Early in 2003, police got their wish when McDonald was hauled off back to the clink thanks to a bust-up in a nightclub. Armed police officers descended en masse on the home of his mother in Glasgow, as well as his brother's house near Stirling and his new girlfriend's gaff in Kirkintilloch. But McDonald was not found at any of the locations. He was, at the time, on the Costa Del Sol with McGourlay, where she was helping him look for a villa to buy. Although furious when he heard of the heavily armed cops bursting into his mother's home, McDonald handed himself in and was returned to prison.

A bid for parole in September of that year was rejected after police informed the authorities that he was planning payback on a man who had stabbed his younger brother. However, the man who McDonald was supposed to have asked to carry out the revenge attack was in jail on the day they were reported to have met, according to his family. Police, however, insisted their information was concrete.

By April 2004 he was out again. A new appeal was granted and he learned he was to be freed while serving at Castle Huntly prison in Dundee. He was doing day-release work with the Salvation Army at an OAP lunch when he was told he was a free man. According to the *Daily Record*, fast becoming the Bible where McDonald was concerned, he enjoyed his first meal as a free man in a converted bank in Glasgow. He joked, 'It's nice to be back in familiar surroundings. But this time all I want is a good breakfast.'

Margaret MacDonald

From convent girl to madame

In the 1960s, Fernande Grudet – a famous French procurer who used the name Madame Claude – once observed, 'There are two things that people will always pay for, food and sex. I wasn't any good at cooking.'

It is unknown whether Margaret MacDonald was a dab hand with a skillet but she certainly made a bundle out of sex. At the height of her business, she employed 453 girls and 30 gigolos in a worldwide sex-for-sale empire that reputedly earned her £100,000 each and every day. When her story broke in 2003, it made headlines across the globe. For as Margaret MacDonald proved, sex sells.

Her mother and father were Scots. Dad John McDonald was a sergeant in the RAF and in 1957 he married shorthand typist Tilly in Thornliebank, near Glasgow. Mr McDonald left the air force and went into the private sector as a quality controller for technology companies, then graduated to company chief executive. Originally stationed in Buckinghamshire, the family moved into a stylish Georgian style house in Windsor.

Margaret was born in 1959, followed by a sister in 1961 and a brother five years later. The young Margaret was sent to a convent school in Windsor and then to another in Slough, where great stock was placed on old-fashioned teaching and good manners. From there she attended Windsor High, then she took evening classes in maths. She was a bright student, teaching herself to speak German, French, Italian and Spanish – all to come in very handy in her later chosen profession – and she won a place at one of France's top business schools, Reims Management School. She also took a course at the country's famed Sorbonne University. She added Greek, Arabic and Japanese to her roster of foreign tongues. It was in France that she subtly changed her name, adding an 'a' to her patronymic to make it MacDonald.

When she graduated, she told her family she had become a market researcher – and in fact, she had. But the cash she made in that modern-day profession was not enough for her and she had found her way into a somewhat older one. It is a risky step for anyone to take, for no girl can be certain if their next client might prove to be their last, but Margaret seemed to do well enough. But as time passed, she must have realised that her career as a high-priced call girl would have a limited shelf life. So she went into business for herself, recruiting a stable of beautiful girls by poaching them from other 'escort agencies' and finding her clients through discreet advertisements, the internet and word of mouth. Eventually, she had business outlets across Europe, Asia and the United States.

Often, she dealt with clients herself, finding out what sort of girl they wanted as an 'escort' and then arranging an assignation. Her girls were exquisitely turned out – they had to be, for they had to blend in with the fragrant customers at five-star hotels – and although it was claimed that sex was never mentioned, the girls were clear about what was expected of them. It was later noted in court that every girl on her books signed a contract saying they would not have sex with clients.

However, the girls knew that these men were not paying up to £800 an hour simply for the pleasure of their company. There was other pleasure on the menu here. In a cash-on-the-nail business, 40 per cent of what the girls made from clients went directly to the boss lady. Operating out of France as a headquarters meant she was running all the risks: prostitution itself is, rightly, not illegal although open solicitation on the streets was banned in 2003 after pressure from the moralising far right. But pimping, or managing prostitutes, is illegal and carries with it the threat of jail time and a hefty fine. If everything went bottom up, it was Margaret MacDonald who was exposed.

That end came after one of her girls broke away from her iron fist. Laura Schleich set up her own agency and made little secret of what it offered its clients. It was a bitter break-up, each side claiming the other became a phone pest, with threats being relayed. MacDonald likened Schleich to Glenn Close's character in the hit movie *Fatal Attraction*, saying the German girl bombarded her with phone calls day and night. Schleich later claimed that MacDonald threatened to have acid thrown in her face. Finally, someone tipped off the gendarmes about Schleich's business and when they swooped, the 24-year-old rolled over on her former boss.

Vice cops tracked MacDonald across Europe with difficulty. The 43-year-old woman moved constantly, travelled under a variety of aliases and had no permanent home. Her lawyer later characterised this as something of a sad life, with his client spending her time drinking alone and taking Prozac. She saw her family at home in England seldom, the last time they got together being the funeral of her father in 2001. The highly moral, strait-laced man was spared the shame of the publicity following his daughter's arrest the following year. When undercover officers pounced on MacDonald in Paris's Hotel Tivoli, she was found with fourteen mobile phones and a lap-top containing a list of her employees and their clients.

Margaret's defence was simple. 'I was running a legitimate escort business offering solace to lonely businessmen,' she said. It was her contention that if the girls offered the men anything extra, then that was their business. 'When a man and a woman have an intimate dinner, then things can happen afterwards . . . I used to tell the girls, "if one thing leads to another, do what you like but I don't want to know about it".'

In court she admitted that she practised what she preached. On occasion when she could not find a girl for an escort job in time, she would take the contract herself. 'I have fallen into bed with a client, but only if I liked the look of him,' she said.

Even the police could barely conceal their admiration for her. 'She is an exceptional suspect,' said the head of the vice squad in Paris, 'brilliant, distinguished, truly a class operator'.

As she sat on remand in the Fleury-Merogis prison outside Paris, charged with 'aggravated procuring of women for the purpose of prostitution', Margaret MacDonald, or prisoner 32686-S as she was now known, filled her time adding further languages to her already impressive linguistic skills. She was, however, attacked by another inmate and slashed on the face with a broken plate. For some time she was incarcerated not far from her former partner, Laura Schleich. However, when the younger woman was released on bail she promptly vanished from France.

MacDonald's arrest and subsequent trial had reopened the controversy over prostitution. At the lower end of the profession there is, without a doubt, a great deal of abuse and exploitation. But at the upper end of the scale, where Margaret MacDonald and her girls worked, it was wondered exactly who is exploiting whom? Her books were filled with young women who were, by day, teachers, housewives, would-be models or actresses and air hostesses.

As far as is known, there were few, if any, complaints of mistreatment, although the madame could be somewhat testy when the girls did not meet her exacting specifications. She insisted that they did not smoke or give out their personal phone numbers. They had to dress smartly and always brush their teeth before meeting a client. They had to wear only black or white underwear. And for those who were unused to such intricacies, she taught them how to operate a condom using a courgette as a model. Many said that she cared for them and protected them. Through her they had managed to make more money than they would have done in their day jobs. However, one former employee who had supported her throughout her trial later turned on her saying that 'We escorts are not like sisters. And Margaret is a hard woman who treated us very badly.'

The Establishment in France seemed intent on making an example out of this well-groomed British woman with no prior offences. 'Lesser sentences have been demanded in these courts for gang members who have kept their women locked in cellars,' said her defence lawyer. 'There was no wickedness in this woman. She does not deserve to be in jail.'

But jail time is what she got. Margaret MacDonald was sentenced to four years, including time already served on remand. She was also fined £100,000, which would have been pocket change had she been making the millions the authorities and the press claimed. But when police seized her bank accounts they found them empty. It was believed that she had spirited the money she had earned over the years into untraceable accounts but she could not explain where the cash went. She knew how to make it and she knew how to spend it. Keeping it was beyond her.

In February 2005, Channel 4 broadcast a documentary on the British 'Madame Sin' – and a darker side began to show itself. One of her former girls revealed that from prison MacDonald had plotted to wreak revenge on Laura Schleich, the former employee who had ratted her out. One plan was to have her brought back from Germany to face the French legal music. Another, more sinister, allegation is that MacDonald wanted the woman kneecapped. At one time MacDonald and the former escort girl who made these claims had been friends but after the vice boss's conviction the woman began to distance herself. It has been suggested that this may have been more to do with the fact that MacDonald could no longer help keep her in the style to which she had grown accustomed. Meanwhile, the furious vengeance plots could merely be the wishful thinking of a once-powerful woman who had lost almost everything.

If it was true that Macdonald had banked a personal fortune of £40 million, then there was little evidence of it when she was released from prison. It was reported that she lived in a cramped council flat in Paris, and had taken two jobs as a clerk and in an old people's home. The terms of her parole meant she was under strict supervision and could not leave France without permission for two years. A trip to try and build bridges with her shocked and disappointed mother had to be cleared in advance. She seemed to have little to show for her high life. Even the promised film of her life has yet to materialise. Perhaps, some time, an enterprising television producer will recognise the story as an ideal subject for a mini-series.

Andrew McIntosh

Terrorist or freedom fighter?

In 1707, the parliaments of Scotland and England were united. The two nations had been ruled by a single monarch since 1603, when Scotland's James the Sixth assumed the throne of England on the death of Queen Elizabeth. But the two nations had remained politically separate, with Scotland retaining its own parliament, the Three Estates. In 1707 that was disbanded and the northern country became a part of the United Kingdom. Opponents proclaimed that the Scots had been sold out by a parcel of rogues for a handful of gold. They've been saying it ever since, although the country was once more granted its own form of Parliament – the Scottish Executive.

There have been armed rebellions. First there was the Covenanters, who were not fighting for an end to so-called English rule but rather for religious freedom. Then came the Jacobites, who were also not interested in splitting the northern kingdom from the south but merely returning the throne of the united nation to the Stuarts. Their hopes came to a bloody end in 1746 on Drummossie Moor near to Inverness, better known to history as Culloden. In the two hundred years since, the cry for freedom, although not stilled, was muted. The first Scottish Office, complete with a secretary of state, was founded in 1885, round about the same time as the first Scottish Home Rule Association, the forerunner of the Scottish National Party, which itself was created in 1928. They wanted complete secession from the Union and for Scotland to rule its own affairs.

Despite the growing political swell towards some form of independence, political violence was not endemic, unlike with our Celtic cousins across the Irish Sea. That does not mean it was unknown. In 1982–3, members of the Tory party, including Margaret Thatcher, Michael Heseltine and Malcolm Rifkind were the targets for letter bombs. In November 1982, there was a small explosion in Downing Street and the following year a larger device went off at Woolwich Arsenal. Glasgow's Lord Provost Michael Kelly received a bomb through the post on the day of a visit to the city by Princess Diana.

All were the work of the Scottish National Liberation Army (SNLA). In 1984, two men fled Scotland amid claims that they were at the heart of the bombing campaign. One was Adam Busby, who continued to act as a spokesman for the SNLA from exile in Ireland.

In 1993, the organisation was back in the news after another letter-bomb campaign and a series of hoax calls in Aberdeen, Dundee and Glasgow. The man at the heart of the campaign was a 38-year-old Aberdonian courier with a passion for weapons.

On 17 March 1993 the Samaritans in Aberdeen received a phone call from an anonymous male, using a code word that proved the caller was genuine. He said that there were bombs hidden in or near the headquarters of four major oil companies in Aberdeen. Police evacuated the offices of Shell, BP, Elf and Conoco, sealed off the immediate area and diverted traffic while they launched a search for the devices. They found four suspect packages at the first three sites and all were made safe by bomb-squad officers. However, they found nothing at the Conoco building – until the caller phoned a newspaper office and warned them that the search parties had missed one of the bombs. A further hunt was launched and another package was discovered and dealt with. All five packages were hoaxes.

Five days later, a genuine letter bomb was delivered to the offices of the water-registration division of the Scottish Office in Edinburgh, although it did not go off. A similar device was received by the atomic-energy plant at Dounreay in Caithness and another at the headquarters of Anglian Water in Huntingdon. The latter bomb went off and slightly injured an 18-year-old office worker. The power plant was chosen because of fury over the siting of a controversial nuclear facility in Scotland, while the government office and the English company were both closely linked with the unpopular privatisation plans for Scotland's water. Police, though, were still very much in the dark over who was sending the devices and causing the havoc – until an alert 11-year-old boy brought them their big break.

Apart from the nuclear controversy and the selling-off of Scotland's resources, one of the other great bugbears of nationalists is the buying up of their country's rural properties by 'incomers', either for use as full-time homes or as holiday cottages. An extreme group called Settler Watch took it upon themselves to agitate against the so-called white settlers. In May, two female members of the group were arrested as they put up anti-English posters in Royal Deeside. The young boy had spotted them pinning up the offensive material, and his mother had phoned the police. When taken into custody, the two women were found to be driving a red Vauxhall Nova registered to an Andrew McIntosh. The name of the car's owner was duly noted for further investigation.

Eight days later, 10 May, the campaign took another turn. Yet another coded message was issued to the Samaritans, this time warning that, to coincide with a visit by Scottish Secretary of State Ian Lang, a number of explosive devices had been secreted in Glasgow's city centre. Traffic was brought to a standstill as police and bomb-squad officers searched the city centre. They found three suspect packages in post boxes but each proved to be a dummy. Further calls to the Samaritan telephone helpline claimed that more bombs had been planted in both Edinburgh and Dundee. Again searches were mounted and a total of seven suspicious packages were found, each one a hoax. One final fake bomb was discovered in a sorting office in Portsmouth.

Someone was playing with them, showing exactly what could be done if they had a notion to really commit mayhem. By this time, Andrew McIntosh's background had been fully probed and his nationalist leanings uncovered. He had been a member of the SNP but had left the political party because it was not radical enough for him. He had then allied himself with the splinter group *Siol nan Gaidtheal* (Seed of the Gael), young radicals who had veered away from the party in the late 1970s to pursue their own aims.

However, although their views were not as moderate as those espoused by the SNP, they still were not extreme enough for McIntosh. He believed in taking direct action, and the SNLA beckoned. At the time of the bomb campaign, he was the organisation's area commander for the north-east of Scotland. According to spokesperson Adam Busby, he commanded a cell of freedom fighters ready to strike. McIntosh himself believed he was one of the last Scottish warriors prepared to help free his country from the yoke of English oppression. At work, for an oil company ironically enough, he often called colleagues 'English bastards', although he tempered his views when it was pointed out that one of those English bastards paid his wages.

Police found out that on the days of the hoax bomb threats, McIntosh was not at work. That, his background and his connection to Settler Watch was enough for them to close in. They raided his second-floor Aberdeen flat and found a cache of weapons, including pistols, rifles and a Kalashnikov automatic. They also found a number of dud mortar bombs that could easily have been made operational, it was later alleged. Not all the arms found in his flat were illegal. He enjoyed target shooting as a hobby and was a member of the Peterhead Gun Club as well as a founder member of an Aberdeen club. He loved firearms and spent many weekends dressing up in military-style uniforms and playing war games. In addition, it was revealed that he was a former Territorial Army paratrooper and during his two years with them had been given specialised weapons training.

The raid also uncovered a number of Settler Watch posters and SNLA literature as well as a book, *The Urban Terrorist's Cookbook*, which gave advice on how to make bombs. When he appeared in court he faced a total of eighteen charges, including conspiring to further the aims of the SNLA by active means with the intention of coercing the government to set up a separate government in Scotland, sending letter bombs and planting hoax bombs. As he stood in the dock he did not look much like a freedom fighter or a rebel warlord. He had been dismissed as an 'inconsequential loner' by acquaintances and in court he looked like a sad little man in glasses with ideas above and beyond his abilities. But Adam Busby saw him differently. McIntosh was, in the words of the SNLA spokesman, 'A soldier patriot' who was ready to 'face the judgement of the British state and of the 'Scottish legal system' and with 'courage and determination' was prepared to 'defy and defeat them'.

Advocate-depute Michael O'Grady dismissed McIntosh's aims as 'a dangerous fantasy'. He continued, 'A fantasy that he and his companions were the last great hope of the nation, a group of warriors and the only ones who would liberate us from the English yoke. And if that took illegal arms, if that took CS gas, if that took letter bombs, if that took causing chaos to city centres, and if that took frightening a young girl opening a letter half to death so be it – the end justifies the means.'

The jury agreed that McIntosh was a danger and found him guilty of a variety of charges at the end of the eight-day trial. Lord Morison said his actions had 'caused severe disruption in Scotland and very serious alarm. The crimes of which you have been convicted are extremely grave.' McIntosh showed no emotion as he was sentenced to twelve years for the conspiracy charge and further sentences ranging in length from two to seven years for the remaining charges against him. The sentences were to run concurrently.

Although tartan-terrorism experts dismissed the SNLA as 'a one man and his dog operation', Adam Busby, speaking from the safety of Ireland, assured the British government that the organisation was very much a force to be reckoned with. Busby said the campaign to free Scotland would continue. He also warned that the deaths of members of the public would have to be accepted as part of that struggle. The campaign that McIntosh waged was carefully planned and involved a number of the SNLA's cell in the north-east. The arms uncovered in his flat were only a very small part of the arsenal available to them. The message was that there were other soldiers out there and they were ready to take up arms where McIntosh had left off. Years later, another expert said that McIntosh was 'a fanatic who believed heavily in his cause'.

Eleven years after his conviction, McIntosh once again grabbed the headlines. By then forty-nine, he was arrested with two other men in South Queensferry. He had been freed in 1999 and had told a friend that he never wanted to return to prison. He said that going back inside would kill him and he would do anything to avoid it. He also claimed that he had put his terrorist leanings behind him. But he found himself back behind bars when armed cops picked him up on firearm charges just hours before the Queen opened the new Scottish Parliament.

Ten days later, on 18 October 2004, he was found dead in his cell at Aberdeen's Craiginches prison. He had hung himself shortly before he was due to appear in court by tying a ligature to a tap. A fatal accident inquiry in April 2005 heard that no-one had suspected he was a suicide risk and therefore he had not been placed on any special supervision. It would seem that the man who was willing to kill to free his country was willing to kill himself in order to be free from prison.

Lucille McLauchlan

Death in the Kingdom

Had Lucille McLauchlan stayed at home to face a Scottish court instead of fleeing abroad, she would have been spared a murder charge and the hell of life in a Saudi Arabian jail with the prospect of being flogged, or worse, when found guilty. But flee she did and when a South African nurse was found battered and stabbed to death, McLauchlan and a fellow nurse were arrested. The case, with the threat of beheading hanging over the accused women, made headlines across the globe.

At the age of thirty-one, in August 1996, McLauchlan left her native Dundee to take up employment in the King Fahd military hospital in Dharan. There she met Deborah Parry, 41, from the Midlands, and Yvonne Gilford, a 55-year-old South African whose brutal murder was to place both women in fear of their lives. Her body – stabbed, beaten and smothered – was found in her flat on 11 December 1996. Ms Gilford's murder was the fourth killing that year to rock the expatriate community in Saudi. A Filipino laboratory assistant with the hospital had been stabbed and then an American couple were murdered. Two years before, the hospital was at the centre of another murder mystery when a nurse, again a Filipino, was knifed.

Within days McLauchlan and Parry were arrested and undergoing gruelling interrogation by Saudi police. According to the investigating officers, both women confessed to killing Yvonne Gilford by stabbing her with a kitchen knife and beating her with a teapot before robbing her, although initial reports stated the weapon used was a hammer. The two accused later gave a very different version of events: they insisted the confessions were coerced, that they were completely innocent of the crime and that one of the Saudi guards in the compound where they lived had carried out the murder. It would be the responsibility of a Saudi court to decide who was telling the truth, and human-rights groups in the West were far from convinced that the women would receive a fair trial.

These misgivings were dismissed by the Saudi authorities, who were adamant that their legal system was above reproach and that the women would have an impartial hearing. Although they would be tried in accordance with *Sharia*, or strict Islamic, law there was still a presumption of innocence and guilt had to be established beyond reasonable doubt. The women's pre-trial confessions would not necessarily be admissible, as the court had to be convinced they were given voluntarily and not under duress. Critics, though, were unimpressed by the assertions. They pointed out that as both accused were women they would be seen as second-class citizens. They would also not be allowed direct access to defence attorneys in the court and there would be few, if any, facilities for translation.

At home, Lucille McLauchlan's family were convinced of her innocence. They were proud of their daughter, who had left school at seventeen to take up nursing and had proved herself to be a top student. However, neither her mother nor her father knew she had been dismissed earlier that year for gross misconduct from her nursing post at King's Cross hospital in Dundee and that she was facing a charge of bank-card fraud. When reporters asked them about the allegations, they refused to believe them, pointing out that if it was true, how was she able to obtain references from her previous employer to get the post in Saudi Arabia? The answer to that question would take a number of years to surface.

The criminal charge in Scotland was small beer compared to what McLauchlan was facing in the Middle East. There were fears that, if convicted, she would be beheaded, for the kingdom of Saudi Arabia was, and is, very fond of capital punishment. In 1996, the year of her arrest, seventy people were beheaded, mainly for drug offences. None, though, were European and although the threat was real, experts deemed it highly unlikely that the women would be put to death if convicted. But experts can be wrong.

There was a ray of hope. Saudi law holds that a victim's family has the right to demand the death penalty but it could be waived on payment of a *Diah*, or blood money. However, the ray dimmed when Ms Gilford's brother Frank in Australia took the view that the two women should be beheaded. The hope almost died when Saudi police announced that not only did they have the confessions, but also that the women had repeated them in front of three judges and had recreated the crime for them. They stated that the women had argued over 'personal relationships' – the accusation was that there was a lesbian love affair in the mix – and that Parry had stabbed Ms Gilford and then McLauchlan had smothered her. In addition to the confessions, they claimed to have found the women's fingerprints in the flat and photographic evidence of Lucille McLauchlan using the dead woman's bank card.

The accused denied everything. They were not lesbians. They did not kill Yvonne Gilford. They did not steal her bank card. Yes, they had confessed, but they had been told they would be deported without being prosecuted if they admitted the killing. The re-enactment of the murder was carried out after police told them what to do.

Back home in Scotland, Lucille McLauchlan's family consulted a lawyer to help them make sense of what was going on thousands of miles away – and for the first time ever, the internet was to play a part in a defence case. Peter Watson, of Glasgow firm Levy and McRae, requested that witnesses in Saudi who had relevant information should contact him via the web.

The trial began in May 1997. Aware of the intense international interest, the Saudi authorities bent their rules and allowed the accused to have defence counsel present during the hearing. However, even before it began, Ms Gilford's family had asked the three judges to impose the death sentence. It soon became clear that all the prosecution had against the women were their confessions. The fingerprint evidence was never produced, neither was the photographic evidence of Lucille using the dead woman's bank card. Despite that, the court still found them guilty of murder, although the length and nature of their sentences were not made clear. Finally, it emerged that Lucille McLauchlan, viewed as an accessory to the murder, had been sentenced to eight years in jail plus 500 lashes. Deborah Parry's sentence was unknown, although unconfirmed reports suggested that because she was deemed the prime mover in the murder, she had been sentenced to death.

McLauchlan was never flogged and she and Parry spent seventeen months in a Saudi prison before being released. Conditions were primitive. They were locked up twenty-four hours a day in a crowded cell with twelve other prisoners. The heat was intense. And the only toilet facility was a hole in the ground. McLauchlan later said that the stress of imprisonment under these conditions made her hair fall out. Her only consolation was that men were forbidden from entering the women's quarters.

While the two nurses were inside, intense diplomatic efforts were underway. They eventually succeeded in convincing Saudi Arabia's King Fahd to pardon them both. Prime Minister Tony Blair had even raised the case during an official visit to the country. The way was eased considerably by the payment of £700,000 to Yvonne Gilford's family. Over half of the sum, said to have been put up by British businesses, was to go towards the establishment of a ward in an Adelaide hospital dedicated to the dead woman's memory.

Not everyone was overjoyed about the pardon. Owen Joyce – who had a passionate six-year relationship with Yvonne Gilford in South Africa – was enraged. He believed that McLauchlan and Parry were guilty and should have been executed. He firmly rejected insinuations that his lover was either a lesbian or a dodgy moneylender. 'She was the most gentle, loving, caring human being. She was the love of my life,' he said. And he bitterly criticised the prime minister for his part in the release of the two nurses who had, he believed, killed the woman he hoped to marry. 'Tony Blair has been gutless, heartless and uncaring. He has shown no feelings towards Yvonne's feelings. And I think he has blood on his hands. I think he should be ashamed.'

Nevertheless the two nurses were free and once they were back on British soil, newspapers went to war over the rights to the their sensational story, with six-figure deals allegedly being proffered. The *Daily Record* won the bidding war for Lucille McLauchlan's exclusive story, prompting much moral indignation from other papers, some of which had also bid for the rights. Such was the frenzy, that one Sunday tabloid allegedly offered to double the highest offer she received from rival editors. The news was greeted with disgust by maverick MP George Galloway, always quick to defend the Middle Eastern powers from criticism. He said that 'criminals are not supposed to profit from their crimes'. The women disputed they were criminals. They may have been convicted but they were far from guilty; they were the victims of a miscarriage of justice. McLauchlan also argued that she had enormous legal bills to pay and that her family had spent considerable sums on flights from Dundee to Saudi Arabia to visit her.

Lucille McLauchlan gave her version of events in a series of interviews with the *Record*. She said that when she was arrested she was tortured and threatened unless she confessed to the murder (claims that were vehemently denied by the Saudi police). She was beaten, denied food and water and continually menaced. Worst of all, McLauchlan later said, was the sexual abuse. She claimed her male interrogators told her: 'We are going to fuck you. We are all going to fuck you unless you sign.'

Then, she said, her ordeal took an even darker turn. Desperate to go to the toilet after hours of being interrogated, but refused permission to leave the room, she said that she wet herself. 'I couldn't hold on, I was ashamed that I should do such a thing in front of these men but I couldn't help it.' Her trousers and knickers were then taken away from her, leaving her with nothing apart from a T-shirt. It was then, as she told the *Record*, that the sexual touching really began. Finally, she said, she would have confessed to anything, even assassinating the Queen, just to get them to stop. The officers also played the two women against each other, promising that they would not be prosecuted, merely deported, if they admitted the crime.

After the interviews, McLauchlan planned to go on a delayed honeymoon with her husband Grant Ferrie. She had met him five years before she left for Saudi and they had intended to wed on her return. The murder charge, naturally, got in the way of those plans but they were married – in a Saudi court house with court officials, police and lawyers as witnesses. Now it was their intention to fly off to the Caribbean for a much-needed holiday.

Soon after their release, BBC Television's *Panorama* screened a documentary on the case in which a forensic psychologist studied their alleged confessions and decided that they had, in fact, been dictated. Another expert witness asked to examine the evidence believed that the descriptions the women provided of the crime did not tally with the actual wounds on Ms Gilford's body. The programme used personal accounts of both McLauchlan and Parry, smuggled out of Saudi Arabia while they were in prison, to recreate certain scenes. The families of the two women had asked the BBC to delay the screening until after they were released, for fear that the Saudi authorities might take umbrage and change their minds. Memories of the controversy over the ITV drama-documentary *Death of a Princess*, which caused a complete diplomatic breakdown between Britain and the Gulf state, were still fresh in the mind.

It was not the end of Lucille McLauchlan's legal troubles for she still had the theft charge to face in Dundee. There had been some doubt whether the authorities would press charges, given her ordeal in the Middle East but, in December 1998, after a number of delays, she was finally brought before Dundee Sheriff Court.

It was alleged that while working as a nurse she had stolen the bank card of a vulnerable 77-year-old patient and, while acting with others, taken almost £2,000 from the woman's account. In addition, it was also claimed that she had forged the references she provided for her Saudi job to hide the fact that she had been sacked for dishonesty. In Saudi, it was claimed that she had been caught on camera siphoning cash out of the Yvonne Gilford's account. That evidence was never produced but in Scotland similar evidence was ranged against her, and on this occasion it was produced. Video from a bank cash machine showed her using the patient's card to withdraw £300. The prosecution claimed that the woman's PIN number had been written in a diary, which was also stolen while she was in hospital.

McLauchlan denied the charges, saying she was somewhere else when other cash withdrawals were made. However, she was found guilty of what the sheriff called 'a gross breach of trust' although her Saudi punishment helped her avoid a jail sentence. For this despicable crime she was sentenced to 240 hours community service and was ordered to pay £300 compensation to the family of the by-then deceased victim.

In Australia, Frank Gilford was asked his reaction to the news of her Scottish conviction. 'What has happened is in the past and what's happened to her now is her problem,' he told reporters. 'I reckon she deserved it. How can you go out and steal from somebody in your care? That's one of the worst types of crimes you can get.'

With her legal troubles now behind her Lucille McLauchlan settled down to what she must have hoped was a happy life. She had two children with husband Grant and wrote a book about her experiences. However, in January 2005 she was back in the news, when it was revealed that her marriage had broken down. The union was forged in a time of great stress and it was suggested that what she had suffered in Saudi Arabia had taken its toll on their married life.

Roddy McLean

Adventurer, soldier of fortune, drug smuggler and supergrass

The owners of the Streatham bed and breakfast had no idea the man they knew as John Nicholson was so notorious. They had hired him for a few days only, as a stand-in caretaker, while their regular man was on holiday. The job carried with it a room and it was there that 'John' died in bed, apparently of natural causes. Obviously, police were called, as they are to any sudden death, but it seems even they did not appreciate exactly who they had lying on their mortuary slab. It took a few weeks for the results of a fingerprint test to reveal that 'John' was actually Scotsman Roddy McLean, a convicted drug smuggler who had legged-it from an open prison months before.

Ordinarily, the man's death would have closed the file. But Roddy McLean was no ordinary villain. Questions had already been asked as to why he had been placed in a low-risk prison facility only six years into a twenty-one-year sentence for a smuggling operation that resulted in the death of a Customs officer. Suspicions were raised when it took prison chiefs two months to announce that he had absconded. Now eyebrows were heading skyward over the length of time it took to cross-match his fingerprints. And then there was the alleged involvement of Britain's security services . . . .

If ever there was a Scottish crime story crying out to be filmed, the story of adventurer, soldier of fortune, drug smuggler and supergrass Roddy McLean is it.

Roderick McLean was born in Fife in 1944 but brought up in Edinburgh. At the age of twelve he was expelled from school following an assault – an early example of showing he was well able to take care of himself in a violent situation – and five years later he took that ability with him into the Scots Guards. By 1964 he had bought himself out and was earning a crust as a gun-for-hire in war-torn Congo. It was claimed that during this period he attracted the attention of the spooks in MI6, always on the lookout for a good man to use in a bad situation. And Africa in the 1960s and 1970s presented one bad situation after another, with colonial rule breaking down and

148

various political factions limbering up for bloody power struggles.

But a year later McLean was back in dear old Blighty and getting married. Civilian life, however, proved hard on a man who needed thrills to feel alive and soon he had drifted into crime, taking part in an armed robbery in Newcastle in 1966. Unbelievably, he then became a prison officer but that, also, was not for him and so in 1971 he opened Boston's – a shop selling second-hand goods – in Edinburgh. However, the store was also a front for a massive fencing operation that had McLean raking in the readies. His business saw him rubbing shoulders, shaking hands and exchanging coin of the realm with crooks from all over the country. A keen sailor, earning him the nick-name Popeye, McLean took to sailing to Norway to smuggle stolen jewellery into that country. With a brothel operating in Edinburgh's Albert Place also swelling his coffers, McLean bought the city's Royal Yacht Club for £200,000 in 1984.

But still this was not enough for his restless spirit. He seemed to crave excitement and danger. Being one of Britain's biggest fences didn't push his buttons, neither did his gem smuggling nor prostitution operations. He wanted more and, in 1986, he went back to Africa. There was a rebel uprising in Mozambique and he ran guns in his ships, the *Boston Belle* and the *Boston Trader*. He was not, though, operating totally outside the law. His new business was, according to rumour, being operated with the full knowledge and co-operation of both the British and South African security services.

He returned to Africa in the early nineties, with a new vessel – ironically given later events – bought from Her Majesty's Customs and Excise. He continued to smuggle arms and, in a new wrinkle, drugs. He was still trading under the auspices of the spooks in Whitehall, for part of their remit is to gather intelligence on international organised crime, while the political instability of many African countries is also of interest. Mozambique was a training ground for terrorists as well as a centre for diamond and drug smugglers and slave traders. Popeye played both sides of the field. He was making a fortune from smuggling drugs into Britain while ensuring his protection from the law by steering intelligence to the security services and grassing on rivals at home to police and the Customs.

It was not all plain sailing for the swashbuckling, but utterly ruthless, former soldier. In 1996, he lost £10 million-worth of cannabis destined for Britain when his boat, *The Dansk*, caught fire in a Spanish port and sank. He was now deeply in debt and needed a quick hit to bail out of trouble. A mystery man threw him a financial lifeline by proposing a single transaction with Dutch crooks to bring three tons of hash into Britain. The man said he would buy the boat, which McLean could keep or sell after the job was completed. The initial cost of the vessel would be deducted from his cut. McLean agreed, although he had some reservations.

The deal was transacted in the icy waters of the North Sea and McLean, his son and their crew steamed back to Scotland with the cannabis. What they did not know was that the entire transaction was being monitored by Customs officers. On 29 July 1996, they intercepted the consignment just off the coast of Caithness. In a bid to destroy the evidence, McLean set fire to the boat and, in the ensuing bedlam, Customs officer Alistair Soutar died after being crushed between the drug boat and his own.

McLean, his son and the crew were arrested and brought to trial. The death of the Customs officer had inflamed the passions of the authorities and McLean was sentenced to twenty-eight years in jail, although this was later reduced to twenty-one on appeal.

The operation, codenamed Balvenie, had netted one of the country's biggest drug dealers. It had, though, gone tragically wrong with the death of Mr Soutar. Questions were asked, not the least by McLean himself. For it was his contention that he had been set up by Customs and Excise, that they had been running a sting operation, that they had financed the whole deal, through the mystery man he met in Spain, in order to set him up. He insisted the death of the Customs officer could have been avoided but the service wanted a high-profile and dramatic raid for their own purposes. Mr Soutar's death was a tragic accident that would not have happened if the team shadowing them had simply allowed them to dock before boarding.

The senior management of Customs and Excise denied the accusations of entrapment, of course, but all attempts by Mr Soutar's family to discover exactly what happened in the cold waters off Caithness have been blocked.

There was another version put forward: that McLean was part of the operation from the beginning and that the whole thing was contrived to bring the Dutch crooks to justice. The accidental death of Mr Soutar scuppered the plan and McLean, instead of receiving the expected slap on the wrist, went down for the full term. In February 2002, *Scotland on Sunday* obtained documents that confirmed McLean was asked by police in Thurso on his arrest whether he was a registered Customs informant. Although McLean had refused to answer, a former associate was quoted in the newspaper saying that Popeye had told him that they were all working for the government.

The plot thickened with an amazing series of bungles by the authorities. McLean was, at first, deemed a category A prisoner and penned-up in various tough Scottish jails. That should have been the end of it. If he kept his nose clean inside, he would have become eligible for parole about two-thirds of the way into his stretch. According to the rules, at some point, his security category would probably have been reduced and he could have found himself in a more liberal regime. In McLean's case, this happened a mere five years after he was sentenced, when he was plucked from the Scottish prison system and placed in the care of Leyhill open prison in Gloucestershire. Peopled by low-risk prisoners, the jail was notorious for inmates simply walking out; in the year up to McLean's own escape, eighty-two men had made the big bid for early freedom. And on 14 November 2003, Roddy 'Popeye' McLean became one of them.

It took the prison service six weeks officially to confirm that he had failed to return from his twenty-first day release. Meantime, officers from the Avon and Somerset force, investigating his disappearance, were unaware that the man they were hunting was a drug kingpin. They believed he was a category D prisoner who was in the open prison completing a sentence for tax evasion and did not step up their hunt until reporters gave them the facts. On 29 December, Interpol was alerted and an all-ports-warning was broadcast to keep an eye out for the fugitive. However, after fifty-one days this seemed like a pointless exercise.

Politicians demanded answers as to why the prisoner had been downgraded in the first place while journalists, scenting something sinister, had a field day. McLean's story was dusted off and revisited. Police and underworld contacts were questioned and soon there were stories appearing about the missing man's career as a supergrass.

At first, it was suggested that police helped him escape in return for his naming more names in the drug trade. Then it was whispered that McLean – who was thought still to be a wealthy man – had paid off prison officials to smooth his way to freedom. Then came the bombshell. The *Daily Record* floated the idea that he had also been working for the security services – and that they, and only they, had the muscle to set the escape plan in motion and to keep it secret for as long.

This particular revelation was made on 10 January 2004. Four days later, the man hotel staff knew as John Nicholson was found dead in bed, apparently of a heart attack. It was a further month before the Metropolitan Police formally identified the body through fingerprints as that of Roddy McLean. Although a post mortem was carried out as a matter of course, no toxicology tests were made to determine whether the heart failure was natural or otherwise. It was left to Avon and Somerset, still nominally in charge of the inquiry, to order the tests the day before the body was due to be cremated. They came back negative.

So what happened to Roddy McLean after he walked out of the open prison? According to press reports, the dead man's diaries and *Cut-throat* – a book written by McLean's nephew based on conversations he'd had with his uncle – McLean was met by secret-service contacts who wanted him to infiltrate a dangerous Turkish crime syndicate operating in London. McLean had other ideas, however. He planned to double-cross his old handlers and use his contact with the Turks to flee the country and start a new life in Cyprus, which does not have an extradition treaty with the United Kingdom. Before he could be smuggled out of the country, he died in the bed and breakfast in Streatham. He was sixty years of age.

Conspiracy theorists suggested he had been silenced by the security forces. Others claimed that the Turkish gang, having read the press reports, decided he was too hot a property – and far from trustworthy – and so had him killed. But perhaps the truth is more mundane. The 60-year-old man drank and smoked heavily. He had been under considerable stress for some time – drug smuggling, coupled with being an active informant, is not the most relaxing lifestyle – while he had been on the run for two months. Perhaps Roddy McLean simply fell victim to that Scottish serial killer: heart disease.

Dean Martin

Some might call it murder

A trip home from a disco-dance class ended in tragedy for three families. Two of the families had loved ones die when a young man, high on drugs and drink, slammed into them with his speeding car. The third had to come to terms with what their 23-year-old scion had done.

Eight-year-old Ashley Martin was a keen disco dancer and it was while she, her mum Anne, friend Michelle Sneddon with her children Ross, aged five, and a two-year-old daughter, were walking to their Glenrothes homes one Sunday afternoon after a class that the horror struck. Dean Martin – no relation to Anne – had been drinking all Saturday night and that morning he had decided to supplement his intoxication with an Ecstasy tablet. His sister tried to stop him but he told her, 'it's cool'. But what he was about to do was far from cool. Some might call it murder. He took the keys to the family Vauxhall Vectra and, with two pals in the back, went on a joyride around the housing estate in which he lived.

The two women and their children had originally intended to go to the shops after the class but changed their minds. Ross was keen to show his dad what he had learned at the dance class. As they crossed the road, Mrs Sneddon pushing her daughter's pram, they heard a screech of tyres and turned round in time to see Martin bearing down on them at high speed. Instinctively, Michelle Sneddon pushed the pram out of harm's way and reached back for the other children.

But by then it was too late. Careering ahead at seventy-five miles an hour, the drunken driver bulldozed into the four people, catapulting Mrs Sneddon into the air. She later said all she felt was 'a thud and then silence'. Anne Martin had bounced off the bonnet of the vehicle and smashed into the windscreen before her body was tossed aside. Ashley was flung to the side while Ross was thrown fifteen feet, his neck broken.

When Michelle regained consciousness, she heard people milling around and lots of crying and shouting. She opened her eyes and found little Ashley Martin lying dead on top of her – and beyond her she could see her son Ross lying in the road. Anne Martin also lay dead. Mrs Sneddon dragged herself over to her boy, who was still alive. 'Someone was standing next to me saying "don't move" but I had to get up and find Ross,' she said later.

Meanwhile, Martin kept driving, weaving around the road. His friends in the back were pleading with him to stop even before the accident but he had ignored them then and he ignored them now. Finally, though, he completely lost control and slammed the car into a wall. But still he kept going, finally screeching to a halt outside a house. There he climbed out and staggered off in search of more drink. His two friends jumped out of the back seat and ran back to the scene of the accident to see if they could help. A man watched Martin weave away, saw the car's front bumper and grille were missing and grew suspicious. He phoned the police and then went out to see if he could find out what had happened. That man was Andrew Sneddon – and he had no idea then that the young man he saw running away had just killed three people, one of whom was his 5-year-old son.

Little Ross was still alive when his severely injured mum reached his side. He was lying on the road, she said, 'with his usual cheeky grin on his face'. He often had that grin, which prompted his grand-mother to observe that he would break a thousand hearts. And he had it in those last few moments of his life as his mother held his hand. Andrew Sneddon then arrived. He saw the bodies of Anne and Ashley Martin already covered in blankets and, as he knelt by his wife's side, he knew in his heart that there was no hope for their son. But he spoke to the boy, telling him that he had bought him a 'Ghostbusters' pack he had wanted. They would go home and play with it when he got better.

'I gave him a wee kiss and told him not worry,' said the distraught father to the *Scottish Sun*. 'I was saying "hang in there, you'll make it". He was a magic wee man.'

But as the traumatised parents watched, they saw the 5-year-old's grin simply fade away and the magic wee man was gone. Mrs Sneddon started to scream hysterically, holding her son, begging him to wake up. Andrew Sneddon saw the missing parts from the damaged car out-side his house lying next to the scene and he realised then he'd seen the man who had done this. 'If I'd known at the time I would have done more to stop Martin. I don't know what I'd've done if I'd caught him.'

Meanwhile, the idiotic driver who, like all drunk drivers, thought he was stronger than the substances he had taken, had run off. Later, his horrified sister took him to the police station where he was breath-tested. He had an alcohol reading of ninety-one, almost three times the legal limit.

Michelle Sneddon was permanently injured in the incident. The force of the collision knocked out all her teeth and surgeons had to restructure her face with metal plates. She will now always walk with the aid of a stick. For Joe Martin, Anne's husband and Ashley's father, life would also never be the same. He told the *Daily Record* that even five months after their cruel death, he thought he could still hear their voices echoing around the house they had once shared. 'I keep hoping I will wake up from this terrible nightmare and I will have my wife and wee girl back with me,' he said. 'I see their faces every day and I can hear them speak to me but I know it is just grief playing tricks on my mind.'

He said that in his mind he hears his wife shouting and waits for his daughter to rush into the room and give him her usual cuddle. 'I just sit in the silence for hours with tears rolling down my face just praying for a miracle – but there is only ever silence.'

The only consolation, he told the newspaper, is that his wife and daughter had died instantly – and together. 'Anne lived for her wee girl,' he went on. 'If Anne had survived and Ashley had died, I know that Anne wouldn't have been able to go on.'

In June 2004, Dean Martin pled guilty to culpable homicide, fleeing the scene of the accident and attempting to defeat the ends of justice. His defence counsel said that his client had asked him to 'take this opportunity in the presence of the bereaved and wounded to express his profound sense of shame and deep sense of remorse. He knows know no words will heal – let alone resurrect. And he knows that no punishment, that no price, will ever repay the price of this tragedy.'

As Martin was led away, the packed courtroom seethed with shouts of 'scum' and 'rot in hell'. Outside, the families of the victims were in no doubt as to what price they would like to him to pay. 'He should be locked in a room with a group of mothers – including me,' said Michelle Sneddon. 'He would come out in a million pieces. He would get ripped apart.' She went on, 'Hopefully he'll commit suicide. I'd love to dance on his grave.'

Her husband believed that Dean Martin was guilty of premeditated murder. 'He willingly and knowingly got into that car with God knows how much alcohol and other drugs in his system. It was totally avoidable.'

Joe Martin later said that he thought about getting himself arrested in a bid to get close the 'scum' who had killed his family. 'If I could, I would kill him with my bare hands,' he said, 'or at the very least, I would cut off his hands and legs to make sure he never drives again.'

Dean Martin was sentenced to eleven years for the killing of the woman and the two children and the injuring of Michelle Sneddon. He was also banned from driving for life. The sentence angered the bereaved families. 'Eleven years for three lives?' said a furious Andrew Sneddon. 'I think it should have been that for each life he took.' The judge had explained that Martin, amazingly, was entitled to a two-year discount for pleading guilty. The bargain-basement style of justice only infuriated the families even more, although they were aware that it was not the judge's fault. 'He works for the justice system and it is the justice system which has let me down and let the victims down,' blasted Andrew Sneddon. 'But you don't get a discount for taking someone's life. It's incomprehensible and it just doesn't seem fair.

Joe Martin said 'Scum like Dean Martin should rot in hell for what he did to my family. He has taken everything from me and destroyed my whole life. All he got for murdering three people was eleven years.' He continued, 'Martin should have been given three life sentences but the judge could only give him a maximum jail term of thirteen years [less the two-year discount]. The law must be changed to stop scum destroying other people's lives.' He and his brother-in-law joined forces with the Sneddons to campaign for judges to be given powers to slap killers like Martin with heftier sentences.

Gordon Modiak

'There are no eyes there'

Gordon Modiak put his attractive wife Louise through years of hell. Insanely jealous, he subjected the former model turned hairdresser to incessant beatings. It was claimed during the subsequent divorce proceedings that he once stabbed her in the leg and refused to allow her to seek medical treatment until it was about to turn gangrenous.

'If I went to a disco and I looked the wrong way, he would wait until we got home and then he would beat me up,' she would later tell the High Court. But when she finally decided enough was enough and plucked up the courage to tell him the marriage was over, the then 26-year-old woman found just how vicious this man she had once loved could be. She obtained a divorce in November 1990 and was granted custody of their two sons.

The 38-year-old Edinburgh man chose St Valentine's Day 1991 to show just how twisted his love had turned. Louise had returned from an interview for a job as a hairdresser/beautician and was feeling optimistic. She picked up her two sons from her parents' house and stopped at a corner shop to buy some cigarettes. It was as she returned to the car that her husband's hired help struck. She didn't see him coming; she only felt the agony as the pint of sulphuric acid hit her face.

In court the following July, she took off her dark glasses and the plastic facemask she had been wearing ever since she left hospital to reveal to the jury the extent of her injuries. 'The acid that was thrown burned my eyes out.' she said. 'There are no eyes there.'

Her 8-year-old son said he felt something splash onto his face and there was 'a sort of burning' sensation. The court was cleared to hear his testimony and the judge and the lawyers present all removed their wigs to appear less intimidating to the young boy. He had seen a man he knew as Kelvin lurking near a bush as his mum went into the shop. He recognised him as his aunt's boyfriend. The man started to walk along the pavement as Louise returned to the car and the boy could see he had a glass jar in his hand. The man threw the contents

157

of the jar at his mother and some splashed onto his face, leaving a four-inch burn mark. His mum, meanwhile, was 'screaming and kept falling'. The boy ran into the shop and help was called. Louise was taken to a nearby house and submerged in a bath of cold water before being rushed to hospital where she would spend the next three months.

Modiak pleaded guilty to plotting to throw the acid on his wife but claimed the attack was not meant to scar her for life. He had been jailed for three weeks and thought his wife was responsible, so had planned the attack as payback. He said he offered martial arts expert Kelvin Greenhalghse, his sister's boyfriend, an interest-free loan of £3,000 to do the deed as he could not bring himself to do it personally. He claimed the original idea was to squirt ammonia in her face but there was a danger that Louise would swallow some and might die. 'I refused to have anything to do with that,' said Modiak, 'so he got acid.'

He said he drove Greenhalghse around the streets that day looking for Louise. When she was spotted, Greenhalghse got out and Modiak drove to another street to wait for him. A short time later, Greenhalghse came back and said simply, 'That's it done.' Later, when he found out the extent of his ex-wife's injuries, Modiak was so guilt-stricken that he fled the city and wound up in Derby where he tried to take his own life by swallowing two grams of heroin.

The alleged assailant, however, had a different tale to tell. He told arresting officers that if he hadn't done it, he would have been shot. When he threw the liquid in the woman's face, he thought it was battery acid and that it would only give her 'a wee burn'. Modiak had provided the jar and the contents. Greenhalghse said on his arrest, 'I did it but I didn't know how severe it was going to be.' He also said that he didn't want to do it but he'd been given a choice: do it and get three grand or don't do it and get a bullet.

In court, however, Greenhalghse, who denied the charges, told yet another story. He said that it was Modiak who had actually thrown the acid and he was told that if he didn't take the blame he would be shot.

The jury, though, did not believe either tale. The fifteen men and women took two hours to find Greenhalghse guilty. Modiak, of course, had already admitted his part in the plot. Both men were jailed for twenty years. The judge, Lord Maclean, told them, 'In the long catalogue of crimes with which this court has to deal, it is hard to find one that is more cowardly, more wicked, more premeditated and more devastating.'

It was predicted the two men would find life in prison hard. The shocking crime had turned the stomachs of many a hardened criminal and the prison authorities had already foiled one plan to dish out some rough justice. On the eve of their sentencing, it was learned that prisoners were planning to stage a riot as a diversion to allow a group of men to isolate the two accused and give them a severe beating. Prison officers were tipped off and security was tightened around the two men.

Modiak had known life was going to be tough from the beginning. The *Daily Record* reported that he had been overheard offering £10,000 to anyone who would help spring him from Saughton prison. There were no takers. 'No-one on the outside wants to know Modiak after what he did,' an unnamed criminal source was quoted. 'He's yesterday's man as far as his old mates are concerned. He'll have to spend every day in prison looking over his shoulder.'

Meanwhile, Louise reverted to her maiden name of Duddy and tried to get on with her life. She moved to Paignton in Devon but returned in 2000 after she broke up with her new boyfriend, who had revealed himself to be a love cheat. She had two children and she moved into a house near her parents in Edinburgh. It was while she was living there that she met the new man in her life, through her local church. According to a report in the *Sunday Mail*, her youngest son got the man to propose to Louise, saying he wanted him to be his dad. The man had lived in America for a time and so did not know what had happened to his new love. He believed she had been injured in an accident.

But even behind bars, Modiak fixated on his young wife. He placed her again in fear for her life when he hired an ex-con to take pictures of her, which he then sent to her. She dreaded the day he would be set free.

That day came in November 2004 when Modiak, by then fifty-two, was released having served only thirteen years. By law, he had served two-thirds of his sentence and had to be freed. The news terrified Louise Duddy, who was living the life of a shut-in. Neighbours said that they hardly ever saw her and her curtains were always drawn. The terrified woman, now forty, did not open her door to anyone but close family.

Modiak, meanwhile, was said to have fled Scotland out of fears he would be a target for vigilante attacks. According to a report in the *Edinburgh Evening News*, city criminals had warned him that if he showed his face on their streets he would be killed. A policeman was reported as saying that Modiak was 'offered the chance to be rehoused in Edinburgh but he refused because he was scared of what would happen if he went back'. The source continued: 'He said he was frightened people would target him for what he did to Louise and said he was scared for his life. There have been rumours about contracts out for Modiak and people looking for revenge and it looks as though that has got to him.'

But Louise Duddy, speaking from the home that had become a prison, was not so certain her former husband would not come back to haunt her, as she told reporters:

> I know Modiak jumped on a train and headed for England the moment he got out of jail. He's probably practising his driving skills for a wee trip back up here. I've got to be careful for my safety. I've got two kids to protect. I've got no eyes; I've got to have people around to help me all the time. I've been through hell the past fourteen years and I don't want anything to start again. I just want to put it all behind me and move on – try and live a normal life.

A neighbour said that although Louise had a guide dog, 'She is out so infrequently he acts more like a sentry for people knocking on her door she doesn't know. Now Modiak is out the nightmare has started again for her.'

It was true that the newly-released Modiak had left Scotland, but only for a few months. He relocated to Liverpool for a while but eventually returned to his native Edinburgh. Mindful of the strong feelings against him – not to mention the threats – he adopted the alias Wood and stayed first with his brother, then with his mother. In September 2005, he was reported by the *News of the World* as saying that Louise had brought the attack on herself by driving him wild with jealousy. He had even convinced himself that she still had some sight in one eye. 'It's a shame how it's all turned out because I've been made to look like a nasty bastard and that's not the case,' he allegedly told an undercover reporter. 'I'm called the acid monster but in my heart I know I'm not that person.'

He also said, 'I'm not a bad person. I've just been made to look bad because of what I've done.'

Frank Murray

Trouble in Thailand

In October 2001, Dundee-born Frank Murray was found beaten unconscious in his new-found home in Thailand. He had second-degree burns covering 40 per cent of his body – and had been so badly mutilated that the tattoos on his lower arms had been completely burned off. Thai police searching the blood-soaked bungalow found a household iron with scorched flesh still clinging to its base. The wounds were severe but the fact that the victim was doped to the eyeballs with Valium may have meant he had felt little pain.

The house was in a British enclave in the resort of Pattaya known as the Railway Village. The Saturday before, a neighbour had been called in to help dress some cuts and bruises Murray had received. Murray's estranged wife Margaret was there at the time. 'She told me she was his wife and that I should not bother helping him,' the neighbour is quoted as saying. 'She said she had wasted thirty-seven years on him. She said he was a worthless man.'

The following morning, the neighbour looked in and saw blood everywhere – but his wife was nowhere to be seen.

The man she dismissed as 'worthless' had allegedly left Dundee following a fall-out with crooks over a bootleg-booze scheme. He had been living with Margaret for fourteen years before they married in 1985. But in 2001, friends of his wife told reporters that he was an abusive man who cheated on her many times. They claimed that at one time he was a taxi driver and used the job to meet women for a series of one-night stands. They also claimed that he was a bit too fond of the drink he smuggled and often beat his wife while drunk. 'He breaks hearts like he breaks open his next bottle,' one was quoted as saying.

On fleeing Scotland, Frank Murray ended up in Saudi Arabia where he found a job as a transport manager for a local company but seemingly lost little time in setting up an operation supplying illegal booze to European ex-pats. Islamic law forbids the consumption of alcohol but, to an extent, a blind eye is turned to foreigners enjoying a drink or two, as long as it is kept clandestine. However, anyone caught smuggling the stuff into the country or selling it is dealt with very severely. Murray apparently started off making home-brewed beer and a local mixture called *siddiqui*. From that small beginning he allegedly graduated to full-blown smuggling.

Murray seemed to lead a charmed life in Riyadh, leading some to believe that certain officials were not averse to a pay-off or two. Whether that is true only he and the officials themselves can say, but he lived in the city for twenty-three years and, according to reports, set up a multi-million-pound business bringing whisky, vodka, brandy and champagne into the country in oil tankers and then passing it onto illegal drinking dens. He was so successful he was able to give up his job and concentrate on his business.

But then something went seriously wrong. He told friends that he was going to have to disappear because he knew 'something big was going down'. Whether that 'something big' was a tip-off that the authorities were going to crack down on his operation, or that rivals were going to get heavy, is unclear. Whatever the truth, a few weeks later, a British engineer was killed when a car bomb exploded in his four-wheel drive. His wife was injured in the blast. Shortly thereafter, another man was blinded when a bomb hidden in a juice carton placed on his windscreen exploded. Saudi police, announcing the terrorism was the result of a turf war between rival bootleggers, made a show of cracking down on the trade.

Among the innocent Europeans hoovered up to face the ire of Saudi law were Glaswegian Alexander Mitchell and Glasgow-born Canadian William Sampson. They appeared on local television apparently confessing their part in bomb attacks and acting as spies for the British government. Their families said at the time the two men looked as if they had been drugged and they later retracted their confessions. Their lawyers insisted that there was no direct evidence linking them to the crimes and that their confessions (like that of **Lucille McLauchlan**) were the result of torture comprised of sleep deprivation, long-term solitary confinement and beatings. The men were found guilty and sentenced to death by beheading, although in August 2003 they and others being held were granted clemency and allowed to leave the country. They all denied being involved in the bombings which, it was claimed, were more likely to have been the work of local insurgents with links to Al-Qaeda. A Greenock fireman was also arrested following the Saudi purge and sentenced to 300 lashes and a year in jail.

Speaking from the safety of Thailand, where *Daily Record* reporters had tracked him down, Frank Murray firmly denied any involvement in the bombings and said he did not believe they were anything to do with the illegal drink business. 'I don't believe those television confessions,' he said. 'A much more logical answer is that the bombings were an Islamic fundamentalist reaction to the behaviour of expatriates.'

He went on to claim that the Saudis knew all about the smuggling business and the drinking dens but 'as they were in foreign compounds they left them alone. We could not possibly get booze into the country without the help of Saudis in positions of power,' he alleged.

As soon as his whereabouts were revealed, the Saudi authorities began extradition proceedings to have him brought to back to face their courts. However, before that could happen, fate somewhat brutally stepped in.

Once in Pattaya, 100 miles east of Bangkok, Murray bought a bar for £10,000 and spent a similar amount fixing it up. Calling it Papa Frank's, he said it brought him a comfortable income but not enough to retire. Later, following the publicity, he renamed it The Highlander. He had left everything in Saudi, he said. But now he had a new home, a new business and a new 'wife' in 22-year-old local girl, Orn, although that liaison apparently did not last. Back home in Scotland, his wife read the report and decided to pay her wandering husband a visit. The 57-year-old woman arrived on the day before her husband was attacked in his new home. Reports stated she had a copy of the *Daily Record* interview in her hand.

While the alleged booze king of Saudi Arabia lay critically injured in hospital, a search of his bungalow revealed that a large amount of cash he kept stashed had vanished, as had any credit cards. A note was found, however, pledging financial support in perpetuity for his wife. The note read, 'I, Frank Murray, upon request of my wife, Mrs Margaret Murray, hereby declare that I will support and provide for her during the rest of her natural life.' Mrs Murray, aged fifty-seven, had been seen last leaving the house with a suitcase. It was believed she had flown home. Although local police had at first wanted to interview her regarding the assault on her husband, they eventually decided to treat the incident as a domestic squabble between foreigners and that unless a formal complaint was made, there would no prosecution.

Whoever was responsible for the attack, Murray survived – and spoke to the *Scottish Sun* about the incident, claiming that he had burned himself while ironing a shirt. 'It was down to my own stupidity,' he was quoted as saying. He was depressed, drank a bottle of vodka and took an overdose of Valium. He had done it all himself, he said, and his wife had nothing to do with it. 'Margaret wouldn't have the bottle to do something like this,' he said, although he did admit she was furious over reports that he had married the Thai girl.

In November 2001, he returned to Britain for skin grafts on his face, chest, arms and groin. Despite his colourful lifestyle, Frank Murray appears never to have been convicted of any crime in Scotland, Saudi Arabia or Thailand.

Paul Murray

'An utterly callous act'

There seemed to be no reason for the murderous shotgun attack, apart from a dislike of the police. The victim, a police officer, was chosen at random. Even the accused's defence attorney called it 'a strange and bizarre' case.

On 20 July 2003, 19-year-old Paul Murray was seen hanging around outside Shettleston police station in the East End of Glasgow dressed in camouflage clothing. He walked into the front office and was asked by PC John Cunningham, manning the front desk, if he could help him. Murray left without saying anything. When he returned a short time later, he carried with him a sawn-off double-barrelled shotgun. He loaded the weapon and fired at the shocked police officer at point-blank range as he rose from his chair. The 53-year-old veteran was hit in the chest and stomach. Although he was not killed by the shotgun blast, he was severely injured.

In the resulting furore, Murray got away, leaving the weapon behind him, but was spotted three days later and armed police arrested him at his home in Barlanark, part of the jigsaw of housing schemes that sprawl across the far east of Glasgow.

While awaiting trial, Murray was examined by psychiatrists but none could explain exactly why he had calmly blasted the officer. Murray himself could not even say why he felt the need to try to kill a policeman. The shotgun and ammo, he had said, was found abandoned in a rucksack in an old railway yard near Parkhead used by him and others as a drinking den. At the time of the incident he was drunk, depressed and felt that life was not worth living. But instead of using the weapon on himself he walked into Shettleston police office and started blasting. Had the crime taken place in the United States, or even in parts of Europe where officers are routinely armed, he may have been gunned down and his death would have been what is termed 'suicide by cop'. But not in Britain, where uniformed officers are invariably unarmed.

In December 2003, Murray admitted attempting to murder the

police officer. Sentencing him, Colin MacAulay QC called the crime 'callous and cold-blooded'. He continued, 'Your victim was chosen at random and he is a man who had dedicated over thirty years of his life to loyal service as a police officer. By your actions you have deprived him of continuing in his chosen career.'

The judge believed that a clear message had to be sent: anyone who deliberately attempted to murder police officers would be dealt with severely by the Scottish courts. However, when passing sentence he took into account the accused's drink and drug problems, his age, his lack of any serious previous criminal convictions and his remorse. He also factored in the young man's 'extremely sad and deprived' background, which left him with little or no family support. His father, it was heard, had committed suicide when he was eleven years of age.

Murray was sentenced to ten years and the injured officer's wife and family immediately condemned the jail term. He would be free in five years, they said, and still be a young man while they would have to live with the results of his actions for the rest of their lives. John Cunningham still had 200 pellets in his body, one behind his heart and others lodged in his spine. He had difficulty walking due to permanent numbness in his right leg. During the operation to save his life after the attack, doctors had to remove the right side of his colon and dead tissue from his back. In addition, he suffered from post-traumatic stress. The veteran police officer was unlikely ever to return to work.

Police officers also did not feel that the sentence sent as clear a message to would-be cop killers as it could have. The judge could have sentenced Murray to life, it was pointed out. 'We fully expected this person to be put away for at least ten years,' said Norrie Flowers, chairman of the Scottish Police Federation, 'but this sentence is effectively five years behind bars and that wouldn't be appropriate. The prospect of Murray only being off the streets for five years is quite worrying.'

Lord Advocate Colin Boyd QC agreed and took the case to the Court of Criminal Appeal to argue that the sentence was far too lenient. The judges took into account that Murray had experienced a normal childhood until he was aged eleven, when his father took his own life. Following the trauma, his mother turned to drink and within two years Murray himself was drinking and taking drugs. By the time he tried to murder PC Cunningham, he had come to think his life was not worth living. However, although the intended victim was chosen more or less at random, the shooting was, in fact, premeditated.

In conclusion, Lord Osbourne, one of the three appeal court judges, said, 'The crime of attempted murder can only be seen as a very serious one. The various aggravating features in this case render the crime one of the utmost gravity.' He said that they considered it the duty of any court dealing with offences of this character to keep 'prominently in mind the need to deter others from such quite appalling behaviour'.

A further cause for concern was Murray's lack of explanation for exactly why he did what he did. 'It appears he may have had some general animus against the police at Shettleston police office, but there is nothing to suggest that he had any reason to mount an attack on [PC Cunningham]. His assault upon him must therefore be seen as an utterly callous act.'

At the end of the review, in August 2004, the three judges saw it the Crown's way and increased Murray's sentence to life, with a minimum of ten years inside. In December 2004, it was announced that the stricken police officer John Cunningham had left the force due to his injuries.

David Neill

'Captain Bird's Eye' got his comeuppance

It was a love of the sea that drew David Neill's young victims to him. The pleasure cruiser *Waverley* had been saved from the scrapyard in 1974 by enthusiasts from the Steamship Preservation Society who paid the princely sum of £1 for it. They then set about restoring it in order to turn it into a popular and well-known attraction on the west coast of Scotland and beyond. As its skipper from the very beginning, Neill would have cut a very attractive figure to young boys who, even today, dream of a life on the ocean wave.

The ship's chaplain – Reverend **Clem Robb**, who was convicted of abusing young boys in 1994 – introduced some of the potential victims. With the ship being described as 'a mecca for young boys' there were fears that the two men used its attractions to lure victims to a paedophile ring. However, apart from the reverend and the captain, no other convictions have followed. It was in 1995 that Robb called police to see him in jail and he put his old friend in the frame for crimes against innocence. Detectives investigated the claims and found young men who were willing to stand up and say that David Neill had violated them on board the ship.

The pattern was very simple. The young boys were drawn to the ship by their love of the sea, sometimes introduced by Clem Robb. The smartly uniformed captain would invite them up to the bridge. Some were invited to work on the vessel. They would then be sounded out. Questions were asked about their sex lives and, finally, they might be invited to the captain's cabin where he would sexually assault them. One victim awoke to find Neill interfering with him in his bunk. Another was invited to the captain's home in Darvel, Ayrshire, ostensibly to see films on paddle steamers. He stayed the night and, while Neill's daughter slept in a bottom bunk, he was molested. A third was assaulted after he inquired about a summer job aboard ship and was told that workers had to be sexually mature. Another was targeted as he stood on the pier at Rothesay, one of the ship's regular stopping points. He was invited aboard, his father's unwitting permission was obtained – and so began three years of sexual abuse.

A total of five young men told police of their experiences at his hands. One outlined a life of broken marriage, career problems and depression caused by the sex abuse. The boys and workers on board ship called Neill 'Captain Bird's Eye' or 'Old Fishfingers'. His depredations only came to an end when Robb, who had introduced boys to the boat, turned him in. At least two young victims had suffered abuses by both Robb and Neill. Later, one observed, 'Looking back on it, there is a distinct possibility he [Robb] took me to Captain Neill for one reason and one reason only and that was so he could use me as a sexual plaything.'

In 1998, Neill was finally brought to court for abusing the five teenage boys in his cabin. The sheriff who heard the case had some strong words for him. Sheriff Daniel Convery told him, 'With some of the boys you exploited your considerable authority by sexually interfering with them and you did so in a manner and on a scale which was systematic and cynical.'

Neill's defence counsel told the court that his client had a terror of being sent to jail. 'His psychological health is not robust, given his feelings of anxiety about the prospect of a jail sentence.'

But the court had little regard for his psychological health. The 53-year-old disgraced master of the *Waverley* was sentenced to three years.

Dora Noyce

The blue Danube

Edinburgh is not only Scotland's capital, but also its tourism centre. The world-famous castle, Holyrood Palace, Arthur's Seat and the city's place in the country's turbulent history have made it for centuries the place to visit in Scotland. But there is a dark side behind the tartan-and-shortbread image it presents. Edinburgh has its own place in the annals of bloody crime. So-called bodysnatchers Burke and Hare are synonymous with Auld Reekie, as is the seemingly upright, but downright crooked, Deacon Brodie.

Prostitution has been a booming industry since time immemorial but whereas Glasgow seemed to concentrate its sin industry on the working girls in the streets, the more genteel city to the east tended to hide its sexual commerce behind closed doors. That's not to say that Edinburgh did not and does not have prostitutes touting their wares on street corners – traditionally around the port of Leith – but in general it has specialised in houses of ill repute. These days, it is mostly seedy saunas and dodgy massage parlours that provide the girls with the premises in which to ply their trade.

However, it was not always thus. Starting in the latter part of the eighteenth century, brothel-keeping was one of the city's major growth industries. In 1775, the city's dandies compiled a sort of *Which* guide to the best whores the city could offer entitled *Ranger's Impartial List of the Ladies of Pleasure in Edinburgh*. The guide listed the various women's best attributes and just how skilful they were in their profession. What is also clear from the list is that most of the brothel keepers were women.

From the end of the second world war until the late 1970s, one of the most celebrated brothels in Edinburgh could be found in a respectable street in the city's New Town. The house at 17 Danube Street was known the world over, thanks to its steady clientele of sailors and businessmen. Its owner, the outwardly prim and ever so proper Dora Noyce, became the best known madam in Scotland, thanks to her many court appearances and her willingness to talk to the press.

171

Dora Noyce was born in 1900, the daughter of a knife maker, in Rose Street, a long road that runs parallel with Princes Street that is now more famous for its almost endless succession of pubs. Despite her lowly beginnings, over the years she learned to affect a very proper Morningside accent and dressed accordingly. She was, it seems, often to be seen sporting a twinset and pearls and to listen to her you might think she was more used to serving crumpets than strumpets and be more at home with a coffee morning than some afternoon delight.

Having bought the house at 17 Danube Street in Stockbridge, Mrs Noyce then set out to make it the premier pleasure centre in the city. She had around fifteen permanent girls in the house at any one time, with another two dozen casual labourers who could be called in when things were busy. American sailors loved the place, for whenever the fleet was in the street it was flooded with bell-bottomed Yanks, many the worse for drink and using language that turned Danube Street blue. On one notable occasion, outraged neighbours were forced to complain because what seemed like the entire ship's company of a US aircraft carrier was queuing up for some rest and recreation. By the time the ship's captain had responded to the protests and declared the house off-limits to navy personnel, Dora's girls had tucked over £4,000 under their mattresses.

Despite that, the house was tolerated for around thirty years, largely because the woman in charge made sure there was seldom any trouble. Trouble was bad for business and that was what she was: a businesswoman, and a successful one at that. After all, the story goes, she did put 'Vote Conservative' posters in her windows at election time. However, for the sake of appearances Dora had to be arrested and charged every six months or so. There were forty-seven such brushes with the law over the years and in 1972, aged seventy-one, Mrs Noyce was actually imprisoned for four months having been found guilty of living off immoral earnings. She dismissed the sentence later, telling reporters 'that was very stupid of the court. I was just a burden on the ratepayers and, goodness knows, they have enough to put up with already.' During her time inside, the house on Danube Street continued to operate.

She loved talking to reporters, perhaps because it gave her the opportunity of free advertising – and she always made sure they got the street number correct. And reporters loved to talk to her, because she always had a ready quip. After each court appearance, she could be found in Deacon Brodie's pub on the High Street, a fitting place for someone who was outwardly respectable to hold court. There she would tell the eager reporters that the busiest time of year for her was the Edinburgh Festival fortnight. However, the sombre men of the cloth who attended the two week General Assembly of the Church of Scotland certainly gave the arty-farty crowd a run for their money. And her place was just like the YMCA, she would say, because gentleman callers were given coffee and sandwiches when they visited. There was, she admitted, 'one little difference . . .'

On 17 July 1977, Dora Noyce died in hospital, aged seventy-six, following a short illness. At her cremation, sixty mourners, mostly women, turned up to pay their last respects. Hundreds of bouquets, the majority from anonymous sources, were donated according to the dead woman's own wishes to the hospital in which she died. Many of the women who arrived at the crematorium had their faces hidden behind thick black veils. One screamed abuse at the waiting press photographers.

Without Dora's steady hand 17 Danube Street did not remain her beloved 'house of leisure and pleasure' for very long. Some neighbours had long complained of the existence of the brothel in their street, arguing that it reduced property values. The council seemed to agree with them and had already reduced their rates. Lawyers had once argued that the property with the 'international reputation' provided 'an essential service'. Within a few years it was just another family home in an increasingly quiet residential street. And Dora's girls moved on to pastures and premises new.

George Pottinger
High-flyer crashed to earth

The trial of architect John Poulson and top civil servant George Pottinger was the longest and most expensive of its kind in British legal history. It lasted fifty-two days and cost the taxpayer an estimated £250,000. More than one hundred witnesses were listed to testify and five hundred items of documentary evidence were lodged but, at the end, it was believed the case merely touched the tip of the iceberg that was corruption in Britain. Eventually, two leaders of English councils were also charged in relation to the case while the scandal threatened to infect the political food chain all the way to the top when it was revealed a former British cabinet member had been implicated.

It all boiled down to whether Yorkshire architect John Poulson had given money and gifts to officials in return for preferential treatment and information regarding council and government contracts. Pottinger was a Scottish Office official when he met Poulson and it was alleged that he had accepted bribes in order to smooth the way for Poulson's firm to obtain further lucrative commissions – and even to realise the Yorkshireman's dream to feel the tap of a royal sword on his shoulder. Pottinger always insisted he was innocent, while friends claimed he was merely a lamb sent for the slaughter to protect those further up the civil-service hierarchy from becoming mincemeat. However, the prosecution contended he was, in fact, 'Poulson's man in the Scottish Office'.

William George Pottinger, the son of an Orkney minister, was educated in Edinburgh's George Watson's College and Glasgow High School before going to Edinburgh University. He also secured a place at Queen's College, Cambridge. He joined the Scottish home department in 1939 but the outbreak of war interrupted his career. He joined the Royal Artillery, seeing action in France, North Africa and Italy, serving with distinction at the battle of Monte Cassino and eventually achieving the rank of lieutenant colonel. At the end of the war, he resumed his career in the civil service and seemed destined for great things, perhaps even a knighthood. He was sharp, efficient and, in the words of a colleague, 'unique in that he had a mind of his own'. A report he penned on the reorganisation of local government in Scotland was said by one peer to be 'one of the best I'd ever read'. Described as a witty and charming man, Pottinger became known as Gorgeous George, or Gentleman George, because of his highly-developed dress sense and love of fine things. However, his high life had its drawbacks, for his bank account was so much in the red Joseph Stalin could have annexed it.

By the time he met Poulson in the 1960s, he was highly placed in the Scottish Office. He was on secondment to the team led by Sir Hugh Fraser of Allander, which was proposing to turn Aviemore into a top-quality ski resort. Pottinger was described as 'a smoother over' and 'an ideas man' in relation to the project. He did his job so well that he became known as 'Mr Aviemore'. As one peer later commented, 'He had to be able to do something of everything and he succeeded.'

Poulson had built up an architectural empire despite never having himself passed the profession's qualifying exams. He had offices in London, Edinburgh, Lagos and Beirut and had personal earnings of over £1 million a year, thanks to his importing the American notion of being involved in a project from consultation to completion. His firm was one of the many deeply involved in the 1960s building boom across the United Kingdom, when the use of grey concrete blocks became the norm for the renovation of rundown town centres and the construction of the many new towns springing to life. Although not a noted architect, his gift lay in spotting talent in others and using them to expand his business. He was also not averse to greasing a few palms where and when necessary. Everyone is corruptible to some extent and Poulson had the uncanny ability of being able to spot who he could buy and how much they would cost. Local councillors and local-government officials were often his targets and many he could buy with a holiday or two, a car, or an envelope filled with crisp fivers delivered regularly to their home. In return, the officials would help him with a nod here and a wink there and Poulson's firm would have another local-government contract to enrich his coffers. In 1963, the gruff businessman wanted to dip his snout into the Aviemore trough – and in Pottinger he recognised a man who could help him.

At the time, Pottinger earned £3,500 a year, a considerable salary for the time. Yet he was not averse to supplementing his official stipend from more questionable sources. Shortly after they met in 1963, he went on an all-expenses-paid holiday, courtesy of Poulson, and over the next six years accepted a number of other gifts, including further vacations, financial assistance to buy his home in East Lothian and a new car. In the end, he received over £30,000.

Poulson also had an overwhelming desire to be named in the honours list, and intimated that perhaps a knighthood would not go amiss. Pottinger made inquiries about how best he could obtain such an honour. As was later noted, there was nothing particularly wrong with a civil servant inquiring about this, unless he was taking cash in return.

Although he admitted that he and the businessman were friends, Pottinger was said to have been dismissive of the brash architect, noting rather disdainfully that he was not 'one of us'. Even when the scandal broke and Pottinger was facing trial for accepting the cash and gifts, which he dismissed as 'baubles', he never lost his savoir faire. He was confident that he would be acquitted, believing that his indiscretions had been far from criminal. Even if he had got off with the criminal charges, he would have faced a Civil Service board of inquiry, but that did not worry him either. 'I don't care about that,' he said. 'I am more concerned about the fact that for the last eighteen months I have been prevented from living in the way I would like to.'

His confidence was misplaced. At the trial, which followed Poulson's highly publicised bankruptcy hearing, Pottinger was described as a man who was 'living in Poulson's house, driving Poulson's car, wearing Poulson's suits, going on Poulson's holidays and even travelling at Poulson's expense'. It was even pointed out that, at the start of their relationship, Pottinger was fitted out in Savile Row suits, courtesy of the architect. It was, claimed the prosecution, 'like fitting out a boy on his way back to school'.

Poulson's approach was a 'general softening-up process, putting Pottinger so much in Poulson's debt, so much under obligation, that any favour needed or asked for might be done'. The defence did what they could to undermine the prosecution case. QCs representing both accused did not mince their words when describing the men's shortcomings. Pottinger, said one, was 'greedy and a sponger' who had lied in court and had, it was claimed, removed documents from the Scottish Office in order to cover up his connection with Poulson. Unfortunately for him, Poulson's own files had been seized before he had the chance to weed anything out.

The defence also admitted that Poulson was perhaps guilty of 'greed, improper professional behaviour and an inability to face up to defects of personality' and had confessed to tax fraud. But what the prosecution had not shown – and could not show – was any real evidence of corruption. The Crown, however, contended that the cash and gifts were given and accepted in the full knowledge that favours were expected in return.

Despite these assertions, the jury believed that both men were corrupt. The judge told Poulson, 'What you did was to corrupt George Pottinger. What he did was perhaps to deceive you.' The civil servant was found guilty on the conspiracy and corruption charges. The two men were each jailed for five years in 1974, although Pottinger's sentence was reduced to four on appeal. One year later, Pottinger tried to fight his dismissal from the Civil Service and the loss of part of his pension. He travelled to the hearings from a Sussex open prison in order to make his case. Once again, he failed.

Even after his conviction, there remained those who believed that he was merely a scapegoat for Establishment figures with much more to hide. His London club allowed him to retain his membership, although his Edinburgh club was far less understanding or magnanimous – they dropped him faster than you can say 'hard luck, old boy'. Once free, he supplemented his depleted pension by writing on a range of topics, including one novel. He died in 1998 while playing tennis.

Johnny Ramensky

The gentleman crook

There is a famous line in the film *The Man Who Shot Liberty Valance*: 'when the facts become legend, print the legend'. And that is what has happened to Johnny Ramensky, the Lanarkshire-born safe-blower whose life has achieved near-mythical status. It is true that he was an active, not to mention agile, criminal. He may not have been the master crook that some sources would have us believe; after all, he was often found to be enjoying the delights of one of Her Majesty's penal establishments. It is true that he was recruited by the War Office to practise his safe-blowing talents on behalf of the Allies, but he may not have won the Military Medal as has often been stated. He was, though, respected and liked by other criminals, the public and even, sometimes grudgingly, by police officers.

For a criminal, he was a man of principle and he detested violence, hence his nickname 'Gentle Johnny'. To quote from another John Wayne film, this time *True Grit*: he 'never stole from no citizens', preferring to target businesses. He also took the risk of being caught and imprisoned philosophically, seeing it as part of the job, although it did not prevent him from doing a runner many times from the so-called escape-proof Peterhead prison.

His name was not even Ramensky. According to one researcher, he was born Yonas Ramanausckas to Lithuanian parents in the Lanarkshire mining village of Glenboig in 1905. His father died before he was ten and his mother, who lost an arm in an accident, moved the family to the Gorbals area of Glasgow. According to some versions of the Ramensky story, he spent some time of his young life down the pits. However, once in Glasgow the young lad, now known as John, began to drift into trouble, having his first brush with the law at eleven. By the age of twenty, he was a fully fledged housebreaker, being found guilty of a variety of break-ins and, curiously given his later reputation, one assault. However, even the court acknowledged that the assault in question was a minor one. He had already spent time in borstal but this time it was the Big House for him and he was sentenced to eighteen months inside.

He married his first wife, Margaret 'Daisy' McManus, in 1931, using the name Ramsay, and for a time he tried to go straight. But the call of the wild life of crime proved too strong and three years later he and his brother-in-law blew a bakery safe in Aberdeen. It has been claimed that Ramensky had gathered a certain expertise with explosives during his mining days and that while inside he met and was further trained in the art of safe-blowing by a prisoner nicknamed Scotch Jimmy, who is not well-known today, but was an extremely active peterman (safe-blower) in his day.

Whatever the truth, the safe was duly blown but the brothers-in-law were nabbed at Perth railway station. A fragment of a ten-bob note was found on Ramensky's person and it matched the other part of the note, which had been left behind in the bakery. His accomplice had also managed to leave a heel print behind. In court Ramensky admitted that he had led his brother-in-law into crime and was given five years. It was during this period of forced lodgings in Peterhead prison that the legend of Johnny Ramensky began to take shape, for this was when he made the first of his many escapes.

According to the myth, he broke out because the authorities refused him leave to attend the funeral of his wife. However, this may not be the case as at least one researcher has claimed that Margaret Ramsay did not actually die until three years after the escape. Whatever the motivation, Ramensky used a wire to pick a lock, climbed a high gate and hung onto a ledge for some time before dropping to freedom. During the course of his flight he swam across a freezing river and hid in a garage for a time. All of this was done while wearing only his underwear. However, he only managed to travel a few miles before he was caught, wet, hungry and almost naked and returned to the jail.

He had promised his wife that, on his release, he would go straight but when she died he went back to his old ways and was blowing safes in Manchester, Glasgow and other cities. However, he was soon banged-up again, this time for a job in an Aberdeen laundry. Forensic scientists matched sawdust found on his clothes to that found in the safe, while a scrap of paper found in a railway timetable on his person married up to an envelope in the laundry. This was the second time such a piece of evidence in an Aberdeen job had helped convict him.

He was back in Peterhead doing five years and now the legend of

Gentle Johnny really took shape. For while he was away, hostilities broke out with Germany and, in 1942, shortly before he was due to be released, the War Office made him an offer. They wanted him to use his peterman skills to help them crack German safes. Johnny agreed but had to complete his jail sentence before being picked up in an army jeep and taken for training. Whether the deal was that he was to train professional soldiers to break into the safes or do it himself is not completely clear, but the legend states that Johnny Ramensky underwent commando training and was parachuted behind enemy lines. Tradition has it that in addition to opening the safes of the Third Reich – including fourteen in one day in Rome – he also used his explosives expertise to destroy bridges and buildings. Again, the story goes that one of the safes he cracked was that of Reichsmarschall Hermann Göring.

At the war's end, it is said that he was awarded the Military Medal, although there seems to be no record of this. Despite having done his patriotic duty, he had no great desire to go straight in peacetime. He was soon back in court, this time in the north of England, and having served his term wound up back in Scotland where he again faced the legal music for safe-blowing and received another five years. In 1952, he made his second break from Peterhead prison, they say with his memoirs tucked under his jacket. The law, then and now, states that convicts cannot cash-in on their crimes by writing an autobiography but Johnny Ramensky thought differently. He managed to remain at liberty for over a day and a half before he was caught at roughly the same spot as before and returned to his cell.

At least his love life was on the up. He met a woman called Lilly Mulholland, and they got married in 1955. No doubt in an effort to raise money for their new home, he and two accomplices blew a bank safe in Oban and got away with £8,000, although his cut was promptly squandered and he began to look around for another score.

Ramensky was, inevitably, soon back in the arms of the law. He had opened a garage safe but had been unfortunate, or careless, enough to be caught by police while still on the roof. He wound up in the High Court where he pleaded for another chance to go straight. However, his judge this time was the notorious Lord Carmont – whose reputation for stiff sentences had spawned the phrase 'copping a Carmont' among Glasgow's crooks – and he deemed the accused a menace to society. By now fifty, John Ramensky was sentenced to ten years. Although a model prisoner in every other respect, the expert peterman took unkindly to the stiff sentence and in 1958 he escaped no less than three times from Peterhead. Each time, though, he was caught and returned within hours.

The public at large began to warm to Ramensky, inspired no doubt by his many jailbreaks. Indeed many people took the view that such a man should not be jailed. Ramensky then became the only criminal to have not one, but two, songs written about him. Actor Roddy McMillan penned 'Set Ramensky Free' while MP Norman Buchan came up with 'The Ballad of Johnny Ramensky'. As the wave of support grew, honest businessmen offered the prisoner employment on his release, and a chance to go straight. However, when he was freed in 1964, the offers had vanished and he took to eking out a living with a pick and shovel as a labourer. For a man like Ramensky this was no way to live and soon he was back to his old tricks.

Within months of his release, he was in Paisley Sheriff Court charged with attempting to blow the safe of the town's Woolworth's. The blast shattered every window in the shop's offices and, naturally, alerted the local law. Ramensky was caught and given two years. After his Carmont-copping in the previous decade, he was taken aback with the lenient sentence and stammered out a thank you. In 1967, the 62-year-old was back in court again, this time after he tried to blow the safe of the National Commercial bank in Rutherglen. He was, by this time, really losing his touch and he used too much gelignite. The resultant explosion was not only heard as far away as Bridgeton Cross, but it also alerted two passing coppers who gave chase, Johnny lugging the only thing he could grab, a bag of half-crowns. When they caught up, the officers claimed that he had assaulted them, punching one on the face. The veteran crook, while admitting the safe-blowing charge, adamantly refuted the police assault allegation, pointing out that his reputation was for always putting his hands up when being arrested. Any violence, he asserted, was done purely in self-defence. The jury, many perhaps brought up on tales of 'Gentle Johnny', believed him and he was acquitted of the charge, although he went down for four years for the safe-blowing.

In 1970 he suffered a bad fall during an attempt to break into the burgh factor's office in Stirling. After being in hospital for fourteen weeks, he was given two years. His final brush with the law came soon after he was released, when he was sentenced to twelve months after being caught on the roof of a shop in Ayr. In 1972, he collapsed in Perth prison and died soon after in hospital. His funeral in the Gorbals saw representatives of both sides of the law rubbing shoulders, all eager to pay their last respects to the man known across Scotland as 'Gentle Johnny'.

His story caught the imagination of many writers and artists, even after his death. In the 1990s, Scottish Television commissioned writer and actor Alex Norton – currently starring in *Taggart* – to script a three-part drama. However, the project was scrapped, reportedly because it had 'no legs': in other words, it could not continue beyond the three parts. Then, in 2005, Aberdeen film maker Lee Hutcheon – hot after winning best feature-length drama at the New York Independent Film Festival – announced he had written a movie script based on Ramensky's life and was in the process of raising finance.

Whether or not the film is ever made, the legend of little Yonas Ramanausckas, aka John Ramsay, aka Gentle Johnny Ramensky will live on.

James Rea

The rewards were astronomical

SCOTLAND'S cities have always been hotbeds of crime. For it is true that wherever there is an honest profit to be made, there is the opportunity to make ten times as much dishonestly. Until the 1970s and into the early 1980s, Scottish underworld figures made their wages through the 'traditional' means: extortion, robbery, money-lending, prostitution. Drug dealing was something of a fringe activity. There was money to be made from it certainly, but few of the old-style gangland bosses dipped little more than a toe into those murky waters. Scotland's addiction problem, although it existed, was not large enough to merit the risks involved.

All that changed in the late 1970s and early 1980s. A new breed of criminal was on the rise and on the make and saw that the road to future riches was through the veins in addicts' arms. The drug trade was about to transform the face of Scottish crime and, according to the authorities, one of the first men to realise it was James Rea.

The son of an Airdrie haulage contractor, Rea was far from penniless when he drifted into the drug trade. At first it was small stuff, buying and selling pills and cannabis before moving to punting – and using – cocaine. It was while he rattled around the Edinburgh drug scene that he first got a whiff of the profits to be had from dealing in heroin. The city was at the forefront of the heroin explosion, with supplies coming in through the docks at Leith. While Glasgow was still a relative smack virgin, Edinburgh already had a full-blown epidemic on its hands. Rea recognised this and resolved to get his share of the cash. He went to Goa in India specifically to find a supply of the drug, which he then successfully smuggled through customs.

However, the stress and risks involved in carrying the stuff past checkpoints was not for him. Basing himself in a top-floor flat in Edinburgh's Newton Street, he set up a network of couriers and runners to bring the junk back from contacts in India, Pakistan and Afghanistan. The potential rewards were astronomical: at the time £2,000 would buy a kilo of heroin worth up to £1 million when cut and packaged for the streets. Rea enjoyed spending his ill-gotten gains. He lived the high life, buying a £9,000 BMW and partying in top nightspots. He made regular trips abroad, ostensibly holidays, but in reality buying expeditions.

Rea, however, make a cardinal error; he grew a touch too fond of sampling his own product. By this time he was separated from his teacher wife but he had found another woman, Maureen Reilly, then twenty-nine. Although she went with him on buying trips to India, she did not like his dependence on heroin. Finally, he agreed to try and kick his habit and checked into an expensive clinic in the subcontinent. His attempts were unsuccessful and he was still burning up £100 per day of his profits feeding his habits. In 1982, Reilly walked out on him for another man. They were not apart for long – three months later they were together again, locked in each other's arms in Edinburgh's Crest Hotel.

Time, though, was running out for the pair. Police and customs officials had been labouring for six months, in an operation code-named 'Dallas', to halt the flood of heroin from India to Scotland. Customs agents Douglas Nish and William Bell followed the drug's track marks through India and Pakistan. They found the names of Rea and Reilly in hotel registers and identified forty-five associates. Cops staked out Rea's Edinburgh flat, which was like a fortress complete with triple-locked reinforced front door to make it harder for any ram-raiding officers to break through. But the real break came when courier Bahawal Quereshi was nabbed at Heathrow airport. Under questioning, he rolled over on his Scottish boss, James Rea, who was himself caught in the Kensington Hilton in the throes of making a £1 million deal. Reilly was arrested back home in Edinburgh.

Also hoovered up were Andrew Wright, himself a heroin addict, and his wife Margaret, old friends of Rea's from his days of smuggling cannabis from Nepal. They were his bookkeepers and sometime couriers, and were involved in the distribution process, passing the cut drug down the line to street dealers for £1,600 an ounce.

Other gang members were apprehended at this time. Robert 'Monkey' McMillan was a hippy who sought out the best deals in India and Pakistan. John McLaughlin arranged the transfer of cash from Edinburgh abroad to buy the product but also acted as a courier. He was caught as he made an attempt to catch a fast plane to take him on the road to Kathmandu. Janus Khan was the London link to Uncle Faisel Mohammed, a jeweller who was the main Pakistan supplier.

In court in July 1984, Rea and Reilly showed that they had genuine feelings for one another. They held hands in the dock and at the end of each day during the six-week hearing, they kissed goodbye. This did not cut any ice with either the jury or the judge at Aylesbury Crown Court. Rea was sentenced to twelve years for drug running. The judge pointed out that the gang was involved in 'a disgraceful and potentially killing operation'. He went on, 'You were killing those who do not have the power to wean themselves away – or the opportunity to do so.'

Reilly – described in court as a 'kept woman' who had lived off the profits of the scheme – got off lightly. The judge said she was 'enthralled' by Rea and sentenced her to eighteen months, half of which was suspended. Andrew Wright, who had assisted Customs officers and had admitted the charges against him, was given five years. His wife, who also admitted to her charges, was given eighteen months. McLaughlin was given eight years and Janus Khan five. Bahawal Quereshi, the courier who had burst under questioning, was rewarded by receiving only two years. He was, however, to be deported back to Pakistan, where he believed he would almost certainly be killed.

At the end of the case, Customs officer Douglas Nish, who was singled out for praise by the judge, said that his 100-hour working week in nailing the gang was worth it. But he knew this was not the end of the drug trade. 'The trouble is that even though Rea has been jailed there will be another dozen like him to take his place.'

Detective chief inspector John Veitch, head of Edinburgh's drug squad, agreed: 'We still have people selling heroin on the streets of Edinburgh, although not on the same scale at the moment. But because of the big profits, other individuals will be ready to step in to take Rea's place.'

As the drug problem mushroomed in Scotland over the next few years, both men were proved correct.

Thomas Restorick

A cruel deception

When 77-year-old Ralph Pride first met Thomas Restorick, he thought he was dealing with a self-employed builder who was offering to carry out repairs to his home in Edinburgh. He had no way of knowing that this six-foot-five-inch young man would bleed him dry financially and leave him with no savings and no home.

Mr Pride was a former civil servant, who had retired as the chief inspector of pollution at the Scottish Office in 1986. On a part-time basis he had then worked on a number of public inquiries, including the probe into the Piper Alpha oil-platform disaster and on a review of the nuclear-power station at Dounreay. His wife of forty-two years died in 1992 and since then he had lived alone in his home in Corstorphine, secure in the knowledge that he was comfortable thanks to his Civil Service pension, his savings and a hefty portfolio of shares left to him by a relative. Even so, he was not a spendthrift, tending to keep himself to himself and was not in the habit of discussing his finances with his children, two daughters and a son. That was about to change, thanks to 25-year-old Thomas Restorick. For if there is one constant in the world it is that if someone has something, there is always someone else who wants to take it away.

Restorick first approached Mr Pride in the summer of 1998. He knocked on his door to point out there were tiles missing from his roof that he could replace. Mr Pride agreed a price and over the next few months the tiles were replaced, the eaves were re-mortared and the garage roof re-felted. Restorick turned up with two other men, who did most of the work, while his duties appeared to be strictly supervisory. During this time, he and Mr Pride would talk and at some point the trusting pensioner mentioned that he had met the Lord Advocate, Lord Hardie, while the lawyer was a QC working at public inquiries. Mr Pride said that he thought Lord Hardie was an honourable man.

This sparked off an idea in Restorick's mind. Towards the end of 1998, he phoned Mr Pride with an unusual proposition. Lord Hardie was conducting a top-secret inquiry into police corruption – and

Restorick was involved. The operation was so hush-hush that funding had to be obtained through unconventional means. Restorick intimated that whatever cash Mr Pride provided would, of course, be returned. Mr Pride was, at first, suspicious but the man's bandying of Lord Hardie's name went some way to convincing him that the story was legitimate. He finally agreed to put up some cash. And so began the systematic fleecing of a trusting old man.

Over the next two years, Mr Pride received numerous phone calls from Restorick looking for more money. The calls were made from a mobile phone and the conman told him how much he wanted. The pick-ups were generally made within hours of the demand. Mr Pride then received another phone call to say that Restorick was outside in his Land Rover Discovery and the old man took the cash out to him. Mr Pride cleaned out his savings account and sold off all his shares in order to help finance this fictional corruption probe. Restorick even convinced Mr Pride to apply for a £30,000 loan.

It was not until the end of October 2000 that the scheme began to fall apart at the seams. Mr Pride's daughter Hilary came to visit him. She noticed that her father was becoming very thin, was having difficulty finding words in conversation and was becoming so forgetful he had missed a doctor's appointment. It later was revealed that he was suffering from Alzheimer's disease and cancer. While in the house, his daughter discovered that he had exceeded his bank-overdraft limit. He told her he had lent her sister Jacqueline some money but she was not to mention it to her. Hilary did not believe that her sister had borrowed money and asked her about it. Jacqueline said she had not received a loan and raised the matter with her father. She discovered that not only was he over his limit, but also that he had no savings left.

When she asked him where the money had gone, he sat her down and made her swear that she was not tell anyone what he was about to tell her. He told her about Lord Hardie's secret probe and Restorick's part in it. Jacqueline knew immediately this was a scam and the police were called. They were not unacquainted with the name Restorick: as was later stated, Thomas Restorick was someone who had the phone number of his solicitor on speed dial. However, he only had two previous convictions, one of which was for credit-card fraud involving a 91-year-old victim. Neither of these convictions had resulted in jail time.

Detectives mounted a sting operation to snare the cunning fraudster. They concealed a video camera in a wastepaper bin in Mr Pride's house just in case Restorick should come by personally. But it was a tap on the old man's phone that produced results. The next cash demand came on 28 November 2000. Restorick phoned five times that day. Prompted by police, Mr Pride asked him when he would be getting some of his money back. Restorick, though, was evasive. He spoke about the money that Mr Pride had loaned him – emphasising the concept of a loan – and that he would, of course, repay it. However, he'd put the money in storage for three weeks as he was not comfortable having cash in his home, but he needed £1,000 'departure tax' to have it released.

As the day progressed it was clear that Restorick was suspicious. He suggested in one call that Mr Pride had loaned him only £230. At one point he said they should call everything off, then he asked, 'Is there somebody there? There seems like there is somebody there.' Finally, his avarice got the better of him and he agreed with his victim that £350 would be put in an envelope in Mr Pride's letterbox and that he would come and collect it.

Outside, police mounted a vigil for their target, or his bagman, to make the pick-up. At about 11.30 p.m., they were rewarded with the sight of the Land Rover nearing the front of Mr Pride's house and a man climbing out to retrieve the envelope from the letterbox. When Restorick saw the flash of officers' torches as they closed in, he pressed hard on the accelerator and sped off, leaving his friend to face the music. The fugitive was spotted by traffic cops, who stopped him in Queensferry Road. Restorick was taken to Wester Hailes police station where he was cautioned and charged with fraud.

By analysing Mr Pride's financial records, and cross-referencing them with Restorick's mobile-phone records and details of his spending, police were able to build up a case. They linked twenty-seven different examples of telephone calls being made from the mobile to Mr Pride, the withdrawal of cash from Mr Pride's accounts and then further calls to arrange the drop. The largest withdrawal was a staggering £39,000 on 11 January 2000. They also drew up a picture of Restorick's spending habits and the spree he had been enjoying for two years. During that time he had bought three plush Land Rover Discovery vehicles, a personalised number plate (W4 TAM) and jewellery. He had also treated himself to expensive foreign holidays and photographs of him smiling with a parrot on his shoulder in Mexico would be produced in court. In all, police reckoned he had swindled Mr Pride out of £454,259. They also discovered that during the period of the fraud, although working as a self-employed builder, Restorick had paid no income tax.

The police organised an identification parade and Restorick was picked out by witnesses from a car dealership, a jewellery store and a travel agency as the man who had spent considerable sums of money with them. Later, the defence would gamely try to suggest that because of his height and ginger hair, he stood out like a sore thumb in the seven-man parade. Police insisted that everything had been fair and above-board and that the accused and the other men had been asked to sit down to disguise any height difference.

In the end, Restorick was trapped by 'the raw power of greed,' said the prosecution. He had used Mr Pride's strong sense of civic duty, not to mention his susceptibility to suggestion, to line his own pockets. Mr Pride had been too ill to appear in court but the case built up by the police was enough for the jury; they took only an hour to return a guilty verdict in March 2002. Temporary judge Roderick Macdonald said Restorick had committed 'a wicked and contemptible crime'.

He said, 'To my knowledge, this is the worst case of the deception of the elderly to come before the courts in Scotland. The nature of this crime calls for the imposition of an exemplary sentence to both punish you for the despicable behaviour and to make it clear to others who may be inclined to prey on the elderly what the consequences are likely to be.'

Restorick was jailed for ten years for his cruel con. He had taken everything Mr Pride had away from him. The man's home had to be sold in order to pay for his ongoing care in a nursing home. His daughter said Restorick had not just taken her father's money; he had stolen his final years.

In March 2004, Restorick was ordered to repay the money he stole to his victim's family. The Crown had been trying to claw back the cash but decided to step back and let the family recoup what they could. However, realistically, it was unlikely they would squeeze much out of the man. It was estimated that the most they might get back was £17,000.

Jacqueline summed the matter up by saying, 'If nothing else, this case should be a warning to elderly people that they should speak to others about their financial affairs and not allow this to happen to them. We still find it difficult to come to terms with the fact that Thomas Restorick could have taken all this cash from our father.'

Clem Robb

'Unworthy of your cloth'

He was a Man of God, supposedly. He was a man young boys should have looked up to, should have respected, should even have admired. Perhaps some did. But others learned to fear him and to loathe him for what he had done to them. One of the young boys who suffered at his hands later turned to drugs to blot out the memories, while another found it almost impossible to sustain any lasting relationships.

He did not coerce the boys into agreeing to his sexual demands. He was, as one of his victims later explained, 'a master at manipulating people into his way of thinking. He even made us feel guilty about what he did.'

They called him Chappie because the former sailor was chaplain to the Sea Cadets in the Lanarkshire town of East Kilbride. And he lured some of his young victims to his manse in Pollokshields, Glasgow by gathering a collection of model planes and ships and even train sets. Once he had them in his home, he played them videos of Nazi concentration camps and pornographic films. He gave them glue to sniff and drugs to smoke. He plied them with alcohol and, finally, drew them into foul and perverted sex acts, sometimes three at a time. He had the young boys who visited him draw straws to see who would be next to satisfy him.

And the following Sunday, he climbed into his pulpit and preached to his flock about love and understanding.

Some of the boys had suspected the Reverend Robb was gay but they had never felt in any danger because they were never alone with him. But still he managed to lure them into his bed. 'He would wait until the boys were buzzing on glue,' said one of his victims years later, 'then do whatever he wanted.'

His crimes came to light when one of the boys – who had been thirteen when Robb abused him – grew tired of the years of nightmares from which he awoke shivering and sweating. He finally went to the police. His claims were taken seriously and he was asked to contact other boys who may have been sexually assaulted. 'It was immediately obvious the pain this was causing,' said the victim. 'It was destroying me and tearing them apart, too.'

When police arrested Robb at his manse in 1994, he told them, 'I think I know what you are talking about.' However, he believed that he had not done anything wrong, except perhaps in law. 'I would describe myself more in tune with the laws of Holland.' A search of his home revealed a collection of books, magazines and videos. He also gave the police photographs of some of his young victims in various poses.

The 54-year-old minister was charged with abusing the boys at his home and at Loch Fyne between 1981 and 1984. In one act of mercy, he pleaded guilty to the charges, sparing the young men the ordeal of having to give evidence. Jailing him for seven years, the judge, Lord Osbourne, said, 'You have shown yourself to be unworthy of your cloth. I cannot ignore the fact that in two cases, the experiences of the young people had lasting and damaging effects.'

Robb's conviction proved to be bad news for another child molester. Robb was also chaplain of the steamship *Waverley* and from his jail cell he implicated the ship's captain in other charges (see **David Neill**). His information – and Neill's subsequent conviction – raised the terrifying spectre of a paedophile ring operating in central and western Scotland.

In 1999, Robb was freed and moved to a family home in the small Ayrshire village of Sorn. However, his presence in this tight-knit community was unwelcome and public pressure forced him to move to another part of Ayrshire, where he died in 2005.

David Santini

From barrow boy to millionaire

Police had been watching the flat on Glasgow's Dumbarton Road for some time before they swooped. They had seen their targets coming and going, carrying certain items in and out of the first-floor flat, including wooden window boxes and a blue plastic bag.

Finally, on 26 June 1997 they decided the time was right to strike. They burst into the flat at about 8.30 p.m. while David Santini, George Faulkner and Christopher McCall were known to be inside. Santini and McCall came running out of the kitchen to see what the noise was. A video of the raid showed Santini was wearing rubber gloves stained with heroin powder. In the kitchen was the gold-and-diamond ring that he had taken off before working on the drugs. Later, in court, Santini claimed he had been in the living room and when Faulkner arrived with the blue plastic bag he went into the kitchen and saw the heroin. He then decided to take some himself. That, however, did not wash with the jury, for it was the prosecution's insistence that he was, in fact, the ringleader of this little gang of drug dealers and that he had made a very substantial amount from the trade.

The drugs found in the Scotstoun flat weighed seven kilograms. It would have been originally purchased for between £105,000 and £126,000 but, once cut and divided, it was worth considerably more. In fact the haul had a street value of over £1 million. However, police believed that the kitchen was just being used for repackaging the drugs into smaller quantities to be passed on and cut into 'score' bags. The police thought the dealers would have made double what they had paid for the drugs in the first place.

Following Santini's arrest, police searched his home in Newarthill, Lanarkshire. There they found £17,000 in cash. Santini insisted this was all above-board; the cash had been legally earned in his second-hand-car business. At his trial, a witness stated that he had sold two cars for him shortly before 26 June and had taken the £7,000 proceeds to Santini's home.

Faulkner and McCall had been 'heavily involved' in drug dealing, it was claimed. Faulkner had even allowed his own home in Drumchapel to be used as a store. Santini, though, insisted that his association with them was purely social. He played snooker with McCall, he said, and attended boxing matches with him, as well as having a common interest in buying and selling cars. In June 1997, one week before the raid, he and McCall went on a trip to Amsterdam together. Santini insisted he was merely visiting the Dutch city on business, but he did admit that it was known as a place to find sex and drugs. When McCall heard he was going, he asked if he could tag along for a short break. The prosecution, however, suggested there was a more sinister reason for visiting Amsterdam – namely the forging of contacts and the buying of drugs wholesale – while the judge said Santini's version of the trip was 'incredible'.

Santini was originally sentenced to thirteen years for being concerned in the supply of diamorphine, a class A drug, contrary to section 4(3)(b) of the Misuse of Drugs Act 1971. This sentence was cut to eleven years on appeal. George Faulkner received twelve years, which was later amended to nine years. Christopher McCall was given thirteen years and his appeal was refused.

After the trial, it emerged that Santini was a multi-millionaire, reputed to be Scotland's second-richest underworld figure. As is always the case, it was claimed he was still controlling his drug empire from behind bars. For his part he insisted he was simply a businessman who had clawed his way up from selling fruit and vegetables in Kirkintilloch to eventually owning a chain of twenty shops, a wholesale operation, restaurants and stalls at Glasgow's world-famous Barras street market. As has already been noted, he moved into the used-car market. Business was good; he had a luxury villa in Newarthill and owned two 7-series BMW cars. However, during his trial he claimed that he had never paid income tax. It was also alleged that he had forged links to gangs in London, Europe and the Middle East.

It was estimated that he had a personal fortune of £5 million hidden away, with almost £400,000 of it directly attributable to his drug interests, it was claimed. However, when it came time for the State to deprive him of some of this booty, the most it could obtain was £57,000. The figure was reached after four years of haggling between his lawyers and the Crown Office. Depreciation, the repossession of cars bought on HP and the fact that his wife owned half the family home all took their toll on the final figure.

However, new legislation was set to make life harder for drug barons by making it easier for the authorities to confiscate their cash. And, perhaps unluckily for the likes of David Santini, it could be wielded retrospectively. Santini was released in 2003 having served less than half of his sentence and took to living quietly.

Vinko Sindicic

The angel of death

British politics can be vicious, with candidates savaging each other verbally whenever they think there might be a few extra votes up for grabs. The so-called 'Irish problem' and sporadic bursts of fervour for an independent Scotland aside, differences of political ideology seldom erupt into violence (religion is another matter). Neither are critics of the United Kingdom government of the day forced to go into exile, no matter how much we might hope, nor do they find themselves all that often at the wrong end of a gun. Other countries are different and in 1988, the often deadly political troubles of the former federal republic of Yugoslavia spilled over into the streets of Scotland.

Until his death in 1980, Yugoslavia, a federation of Serbians, Croatians, Bosnians and other Balkan states, was ruled by former partisan leader Josep Broz, better known as Marshal (and later President) Tito. Although a communist, he parted ways with Stalin in 1948 and as a result was banished from the Comintern, the international association of pro-Soviet communists. Although not part of the Soviet bloc, this popular holiday destination for many Britons was still a repressive country highly dependent on aid from the West.

Some ethnic groups in Yugoslavia criticised, as much as the system would allow, the Serb-dominated status quo. Many were silenced forever by the country's secret service, UBDA. A number of these killings were carried out on foreign soil, and security forces in those countries were ordered to turn a blind eye because their respective governments wanted to keep Tito a happy man in order to use him as a firebreak against the spread of Soviet influence – as a block against the bloc, so to speak. At one stage, Libya's ruling dictator, Colonel Gadaffi, complained that Tito was allowed to carry out acts of extreme prejudice against dissidents while he was not.

The repression continued after Tito's death, even though the Yugoslav federation itself began to crumble. Many Croatians had been unhappy with the merging of their once-independent state into Yugoslavia. Over the years, thousands left the country and dispersed across the globe, particularly in Australia and Canada. Nikola Stedul was a Croatian dissident who became a marked man when he spoke out against the Serbian-controlled government. He had left the land of his birth at the age of eighteen, living first in Austria and Germany before finally travelling to Australia where he met his Scottish wife, Shirley.

In 1974, he moved to Britain where he was to stay for over two decades although never managing to obtain citizenship. Now married and with a family, he first worked in the mines then ran his own taxi firm to put bread on the table. By the early 1980s he was resident in Glen Lyon Road in the Fife town of Kirkcaldy. To his neighbours he was simply Nik Stedul, a man who had worked hard to feed his family and who was now a mature student at Dundee University.

But Stedul was much more than that. He was also president of the Croatian Movement for Statehood and a regular contributor to a Croatian newspaper published in Australia but available underground in his homeland. His writings were hugely critical of the ruling Yugo-slavian regime. He was also seen as a man of influence among his own countrymen and at one point was recruited by the Swedish gov-ernment to dissuade a fellow Croatian found guilty of assassinating a Yugoslav ambassador from continuing his hunger strike. British secur-ity was well aware of his presence and his activities, although sub-sequent events might suggest he was not under constant supervision. In Yugoslavia, Nikola Stedul was viewed as a dangerous man and his death warrant was signed and sealed. All that was needed was for it to be delivered.

On a wet Thursday, 20 October 1988, the 51-year-old was gunned down outside his home in Kirkcaldy as he walked his pet German Shepherd, Pasha. A small black car had slowed down beside him as if the driver was asking directions. Obligingly, Mr Stedul bent down to see if he could help, peering into the vehicle's interior. A gunman, his German-made weapon fitted with a silencer, pumped five bullets into the man's mouth, hip and elbow. But the victim refused to die and tried to drag himself along the path to his house. The killer should have finished him off but Pasha proved too fierce; as the *Daily Mirror* so memorably put it, PET DOG FOILS RED HITMAN'S GUN BID. Had the animal, trained as a guard dog, not been present, the gunman would have been able to take better aim as his victim desperately tried to scramble away.

'We assume that was why the person shot from inside the car rather than pointing the weapon out through the window where Pasha could have grabbed at it,' said Shirley Stedul later. 'Because Pasha was there the man would not get out of the car and couldn't take proper aim while Nikola was lying on the ground.'

Why the killer did not shoot the dog remains a mystery. Perhaps he was an animal lover.

The target survived the murderous attack; two of the bullets had narrowly missed major arteries. The following year, his wife commented, 'If you believe in miracles, he is a miracle. When you shoot someone twice in the head there's no messing about. It wasn't a warning. Nikola is definitely lucky to be alive.'

Meanwhile, the gunman had escaped, although not for long. An alert postman, aware that there had been a series of break-ins in the area, had spotted the parked car the day before. Thinking the man inside was perhaps casing the residential street for likely houses to rob, he jotted down the registration on a spare envelope. The following day – when he saw the hustle and bustle of the investigation into the shooting – he passed the information to the police.

The number belonged to a rented Mini Metro that had been hired by a Swiss businessman named Rudolf Lehotsky a few days before. The car was found parked at Edinburgh airport and Lehotsky himself had boarded a shuttle flight to London. At Heathrow later that day, Customs officers moved in on the suspect.

The man's real name was Vinko Sindicic. He was a Croatian but was now a major in the Yugoslav secret service with, it was claimed, a licence to kill. His background made it easy for him to infiltrate and befriend enemies of the state. To the Croatians he was not only a traitor but also something of an angel of death. Since 1965, they insisted, he had murdered at least ten – and perhaps as many as forty – dissidents in various countries on the orders of his masters. In one case in 1972, Sindicic was said to have befriended Croatian Stjepan Sevo, who was accused of having carried out a guerrilla attack in Yugoslavia. While in Italy, the family, including the 9-year-old daughter, were found dead in their car, each one of them shot in the back of the head.

Sindicic was interviewed by Italian police in relation to the matter but as there was no evidence linking him to the killings he was released.

For the Stedul assassination attempt, Sindicic had flown into Britain on the stolen passport of the Swiss businessman, who had apparently died in Zagreb. Originally, it was to have been a three-man hit team but his two accomplices were halted by Customs and returned home. A decision was taken that Sindicic could handle the assignment alone. A pistol was provided by contacts in London and he travelled by train to Edinburgh. He booked himself into the Old Waverley Hotel, hired the car and spent the following few days driving to Kirkcaldy to carry out surveillance on his potential victim. For four days he sat at a discreet distance from the Glen Lyon Road house, taking note of Mr Stedul's habits in order to identify the best time to move in for the kill. It was during this time that he was spotted by the alert postman. The night before the shooting, he moved his base of operations to a hotel closer to the Forth Road Bridge. The following morning, he retrieved the pistol he had earlier stashed in woods near to Kirkcaldy and settled down in Glen Lyon Road to wait for his target to appear.

Leaving his victim bleeding on his front path, perhaps even believing he had completed his mission, Sindicic sped down the coast road towards Edinburgh, throwing bags containing the pistol, silencer and ammunition out of the window as he drove. He dumped the car, reached Heathrow, and, no doubt to his great surprise was arrested. Firearm residue was subsequently found on his hands.

Sindicic provided a number of stories as to why he was in Scotland, although no explanation of why he was travelling under a stolen passport seemed to have been forthcoming. He was, he said, a simple businessman who knew Mr Stedul of old and was seeking his advice on some personal matters. Mr Stedul said that, although he had heard of the man, he had never met him. Sindicic claimed to have been on the telephone at Edinburgh's Waverley station at the time of the shooting, talking to people back home. He even produced three witnesses who confirmed the conversations. He also claimed that he was not the same Vinko Sindicic who worked for the Yugoslavian secret police. However, his stories were dismissed during the trial as 'fabulous, elaborate lies' to save his own skin. Advocate depute Gordon Jackson

QC argued that the man's story was a case of 'the theory of the big lie'. He explained, 'The bigger the lie is, the more impossible it may seem to disprove it.'

In defence, Mr Edgar Prais QC was critical of what he called 'the big sneer' in the advocate depute's voice. He asked the jury if it was conceivable that a man said to be an international hit man would be so lax as to give himself such a high profile in the days leading up to the shooting.

One of the main witnesses against Sindicic was his intended victim, Nikola Stedul. The dignified, bearded Croatian limped into the court-room and many spectators in the public gallery and in the packed press box rose to their feet in respect.

In May 1989, after a trial lasting eleven days, Sindicic was found guilty by a majority of attempted murder and jailed for fifteen years. The jury, which had retired for three hours to consider its verdict, was unanimous in finding him guilty of other charges, including possession of firearms and a false passport, and he was hit with another sixteen years, to run concurrently.

Throughout the hearing, the smartly-dressed defendant proclaimed his innocence, saying that he had been framed by the authorities, that witnesses against him had lied on the stand, that evidence against him had been faked. For years after his conviction – while Nikola Stedul returned to his native land and began working for the newly formed Croatian government – Sindicic tried to prove he was not guilty of the crime. He insisted that Stedul had never been shot, that the whole thing was a fabrication. That was the story he told his German wife and teenage daughter when they flew to Scotland to support him. Even if Stedul had been shot, Vinko Sindicic swore he had nothing to do with it; he was in Edinburgh at the time.

He appealed against his conviction and, more than a year after the trial, was granted leave to inspect the Metro that the Crown insisted he had rented and used in the shooting. Amazingly, he found a spent cartridge shell that had been missed by the authorities during their 'careful' search two years' before. He lodged a request that he be allowed out on bail on a daily basis to conduct his own investigation into his case in order to uncover new evidence. 'Allow me fifteen days on bail and I will present no problem,' he told the judges of the

Court of Criminal Appeal in his faltering English. 'I will not escape. Out in the morning, in in the evening. I am a category A prisoner. I see only birds flying around, my only contact with anybody. Let me the possibility of fifteen days and I will present it, no problem, everything.'

However, the appeal-court judges refused the request.

After a number of delays, most of them instigated by Sindicic, the appeal was finally heard in May 1992. As for the original proceedings, he was surrounded by the strictest security possible. Sindicic was brought from Perth prison to Edinburgh in a convoy of police cars while armed officers surrounded the court in the city's Parliament Square, searching everyone who entered. The appeal failed.

Sindicic was due for release on 29 October 1998. Once he stepped out of prison a free man he would have vanished. However, the Croatian government wanted him to face charges relating to a murder in Paris in 1978. On 16 October, the twentieth anniversary of the French killing, he was taken to Edinburgh Sheriff Court to face the extradition order. On 29 October, the day Sindicic was due to be released, Henry McLeish, minister of state at the Scottish Office, signed the official order to have him handed over to the Croatian authorities. On 16 November 1998, he was placed in the custody of his new jailers at Heathrow airport. Two years later, after a lengthy trial, he was finally freed when the charges against him were thrown out due to lack of evidence.

Whatever Vinko Sindicic was – an innocent man, a patsy, a hired killer – he appeared to be far from penniless. He was reported to own restaurants, a hotel – said to be a gift from a grateful nation – and fishing boats. By 2003, he was reputed to have amassed a fortune of $5.5 million, and to own a luxury home in the Croatian resort of Rijeka. He had also shown an interest in owning another hotel on the Adriatic island of Vis, although the deal fell apart.

The UVF bombing campaign
When 'The Troubles' came to Glasgow

The source of the bitter rancour between Protestant and Roman Catholic in Scotland dates back centuries. It is an enmity that should have died out years ago but it is still there, eating away at society and exemplified by a divided educational system and football hatreds that take on an Orange or Green tinge.

Historically, the troubles were born even before the Reformation of the sixteenth century, but when the Scottish church finally broke away from Rome, the great split began and soon Protestant Scot hated Catholic Scot and vice versa. When King James the First sent Scottish Protestants to settle the lands of Antrim, and bring the rebellious Catholic lords to heel, he set in motion a chain of events that resonates to this day. Two hundred years later, Catholic and Protestant alike fled the Emerald Isle to escape famine. Some came to Scotland – and brought their religious hatreds back with them. Other Irish workers were transplanted by greedy mine owners who used them as scab labour to break strikes, enflaming passions even further.

The old grudges festered and occasionally erupted into violence, although the country was by and large mercifully free of the large-scale horrors that have marred Irish history. There have been isolated incidents, though. The Fenian Brotherhood, the forerunners of the IRA, conducted a minor bombing campaign in the late nineteenth century, while in the 1920s an attempt to blow up telegraph poles in south-west Scotland and cut off communication failed. In 1921, a band of armed men tried to free an IRA commandant being transported to a Glasgow courtroom. They killed one police officer, wounded another but failed to rescue their target. Following the shoot-out on the Glasgow street, there were riots in the Gallowgate as police made arrests, including a local priest. A cache of arms was found in a tenement during police raids. There have been other arms dumps found in Scotland in the years since, but despite that, the country was spared the bombing terrors visited on England during the 1970s and 1980s.

The divides remained, however. In Glasgow, depending on how

religious your drinking views are, you can drink at a Protestant or Catholic pub; a Rangers or Celtic bar if you are of a footballing bent. During the heyday of the street gangs, mobs could fall on one side or the other: most notably the Protestant Billy Boys and the Catholic Norman Conks. Even today, it is claimed that some of the city's most powerful gang bosses have at one time or another pledged allegiance to terrorist organisations.

In 1979, Glasgow High Court witnessed the most stringent security measures in Scottish criminal history. Twenty men were set to face two separate trials for terrorism charges and the police and security forces were taking no chances on either an escape bid or an attempt to disrupt the proceedings by their supporters. Every person entering the court – be it a member of the public, lawyer, juror or even a judge – was searched. The building on the city's Saltmarket was combed from top to bottom every morning. Tracker dogs sniffed their way around Glasgow Green on the opposite side of the road. Cars were inspected. Frogmen plumbed the depths of sewers beneath the court-house in search of explosives. It was a high-profile operation that left no-one in any doubt that the men on trial were viewed as dangers to the public. The defence objected, saying that the measures were too heavy-handed and designed to poison the minds of the jury against their clients.

Nine of the accused were on trial for raising arms and cash for the UDA in Glasgow and the south of Scotland. But it is the case against the other eleven men that concerns us here. For they were accused of bringing Irish-style bomb terror to the streets.

In February 1979, explosions ripped through two 'Celtic' pubs in the Gorbals area of Glasgow. The most serious damage was caused in the Clelland bar, where a man's drinking preferences had caught the attention of bar staff. He had come in with a bag over his shoulder and ordered a pint of heavy, which was not unusual, but also a glass of sherry, which was decidedly strange for that part of that particular city. While he was there, another stranger was seen in the pub gulping down two pints very quickly. When the first man left he did not have his shoulder bag with him. The other man left soon after – and twenty minutes later a bomb errupted in the bar, injuring a number of people. A subsequent blast at the Old Barns pub in London Road left the ceiling in danger of collapse but when police arrived they found that many customers had elected to remain at the bar and keep on drinking.

A third pub had been targeted in November 1977 but charges relating to this were dropped during the trial because there was no evidence to link any of the accused to it. A bag was left in the doorway of Derry Treanor's pub on the night of a Celtic–Rangers fixture. The lounge bar was packed with about 120 people and a further twenty drinkers were in the public bar. Most were Roman Catholic, but some regulars were Protestants. A number of patrons noticed that there was smoke coming from the sports bag but at the time did not think it was an explosive device. One man kicked the bag outside just before it exploded, and injured five people.

The devices used in the two later incidents were described as 'anti-personnel gelignite bombs containing bullets for maximum effect'. A search of the Clelland Bar after the blast revealed seventy-three rounds and another twenty-three were found at the Old Barns. A bomb expert later stated both devices were wrapped in black carrier bags and hidden in black PVC holdalls. He said that the bullets would increase the 'hazard from high velocity fragments, giving the maximum injury to persons in the vicinity of the explosions'. The gelignite used was of the type commonly found in mining operations and the timers were simple travelling alarm clocks.

Police, naturally, moved fast to trace the culprits and no stone was left unturned. Within hours of the double blasts, a sixty-strong team of detectives were sniffing out the bombers' trail. Informants were tapped, known Loyalist sympathisers were put under pressure and, acting on information received, two houses in Ruchazie were raided with a quantity of weapons, ammunition, explosives and detonators found. One officer was alerted to a pool of blood on a bus and he followed the trail to a house in the East End. He said later that there was so much blood he 'fully expected to find a body at the end of it'. He didn't uncover a corpse, but he did find a man who was later charged in connection with the bombings, washing deep gashes on his legs. The man claimed to have suffered a fall and was taken to the city's Royal Infirmary for treatment. As the investigation progressed, police found members of the UVF who were willing to talk and miners who claimed to have been coerced into stealing explosives for the organisation.

Of the eleven men originally charged, only nine were found guilty. Among them was William Campbell, known as Big Bill. The burly six-footer had already had previous experience with explosives; in 1973 he had been convicted following a blast at the Apprentice Boys of Derry Halls in Bridgeton. Big Bill had been storing his sodium chlorate beside an oven and the unstable substance had gone off when someone decided to heat up some pies. Campbell was originally sentenced to eight years for maliciously causing the explosion but that was quashed on appeal when judges ruled that it was clearly unplanned. However, a five-year stretch for possession of explosives still stood, much of it spent at his own request in a jail in Northern Ireland.

During his time inside he became even more determined to serve the Loyalist cause and when he was released became overseas commandant in Scotland of the Ulster Volunteer Force units in Glasgow. He organised the gathering and storing of weapons in safe houses and was, newspapers claimed, responsible for the tightening up of discipline among the UVF faithful. That did not prevent two of his co-accused in the 1979 trial from assisting police with their inquiries although during and after the court proceedings they had to be kept separate from the others 'for their own protection'. In the end, their co-operation did not help them much; they were still among the nine out of the original eleven who were sentenced to a total of 519 years for a variety of charges.

By the end of the hearing, the charges had been substantially reduced but there was still a hefty thirteen items left on the indictment. The jury members were sequestered for ten hours and forty minutes at the end of the eighteen-day trial in order to decide on guilt or innocence. It was at the time the longest jury deliberation in Scottish legal history. They were given an initial meal of cold meat, salad, fruit juice and coffee but nothing else until they made a decision. When they finally reached their verdict, at nearly eleven that night, the judge, Lord Ross, told them that the reason for their long period of confinement was that the law insisted that once they retired to consider their verdict, they could not come out for any reason until a decision was made. Defence lawyers were critical of this process which, they said, was simply a form of pressure on the fifteen men and women to 'hurry up and reach a verdict'. One said it was 'preposterous' that a modern jury was forced to abide by rules laid down in the sixteenth century. It was also claimed that the strict security measures were also designed to instil in the minds of jurors that the men in the dock were dangerous and, therefore, guilty.

Whatever went on in the minds of the jurors, Campbell himself was given a total of sixty-two years for conspiring to further the aims of the UVF and other charges. All the sentences were to run concurrently so the longest stretch, of sixteen years, would be the absolute limit of time he could serve. As he was led from court, he spotted a Special Branch officer and shouted 'Hard luck, Willie.' Clearly, he believed that the police would have expected him to receive a longer sentence.

Among the other men found guilty of conspiracy was his brother Colin. Sixteen years after the Campbell brothers appeared in the dock together, they were back in the Saltmarket building to see Jason Campbell, Colin's 23-year-old son, being found guilty of murdering a young Celtic fan, Mark Scott, who was just sixteen. He had slashed the young man's throat as he walked through the streets with friends. In 1997, moves were made to have him transferred to the Maze prison near Belfast but these were blocked by the secretary of state for Scotland, Donald Dewar. In 2002, under new rules which dictate that all lifers be informed the minimum period they would have to serve, Campbell was told that he would serve at least fifteen years of his life sentence.

Mark Watt

High-speed chase led to death

It is difficult to believe that road rage is something new. Human nature has changed little in the few thousand years since the invention of the wheel and it is hard to accept that a mixture of arrogance, selfishness and the belief that the road belongs to one person was not present in the days of chariots and wagons. What makes it more lethal now is that cars are more powerful and the roads far busier than ever before. It has often been said that people change when they get behind a wheel of a car. A normally tranquil man can become a snarling, foul-mouthed monster as he sits in his air-conditioned box on wheels, screaming and gesturing at fellow road users who have committed some transgression, whether real or imagined. The danger comes when the driver decides that the transgression merits some kind of punishment. And that way lies madness – and occasionally the road to dusty death for an innocent party.

Mark Watt thought he had evaded justice after one such road-rage incident by fleeing to the Canary Islands. He rented a small apartment on Gran Canaria and, living on money the source of which seems shadowy, began a new, low-profile, life in the sun. But someone was unhappy that he seemed to be getting away with causing the death of a child. And that same someone dropped a peseta to the *Daily Record* to let reporters know that Watt was hiding out on the island. The newspaper sent a team of reporters to the resort of Puerto Rico and tracked him down. And once they knew they had the right man, they tipped off the local law.

Burly Watt, aged forty-five, was wanted in Scotland for forcing a family's car off the M8 in April 2000. He had subjected the innocent Millar family to a six-mile, high-speed ordeal as he continually swerved and braked his Renault in front of their Rover car. It began when Mr Millar tried to move into the inside lane, where Watt was already travelling. Mr Millar sped up to between seventy and eighty miles per hour to get past and then pulled in ahead of the Renault people carrier. For some reason, this incensed Watt, who then stalked the

Rover saloon along the motorway and dodged from lane to lane. As dad Craig Millar tried to get away from the madman – who had been bingeing on wine earlier and was incapacitated in one eye thanks to another accident – both vehicles reached speeds in excess of 100 miles per hour. Finally, Mr Millar's car spun off the motorway near Paisley, severely injuring his six-month-old son Robbie as well as injuring his wife Mary and their other two young sons Sean and Steven.

Watt sped on, later forcing another car to take action to avoid him, before he left his car with a friend and then went out bowling with his girlfriend. As he enjoyed himself that night, little Robbie Millar was fighting for his life in hospital. The baby died the next day.

Police converged on the M8 and in the course of their inquiries they stopped more than 1,300 drivers. Finally, it was a friend of the hunted man who turned him in. However, the manhunt began afresh when Watt, who had previous convictions for dealing in drugs, failed to turn up for his trial. The *Daily Record* quoted an unnamed 'associate' as saying, 'I know he was really laughing when he managed to dodge the courts and the police. He thought he had it made by fleeing [to Gran Canaria] and starting a new life, while the police looked everywhere for him.'

According to the press reports, his plan in the Canary Island resort was to set himself up in the illegal booze and cigarette business. He kept himself as far away from the tourist hotspots as possible, fearful that someone would recognise him and, the newspaper noted, kept his white baseball cap pulled low over his face, just in case. 'He always wears the cap and sunglasses,' someone told reporters. 'He is paranoid about being recognised because the place is always so full of Scots.'

Someone, however, felt it was wrong that he was allowed to walk about in the sunshine while back home a family was still grieving over their dead child thanks to his temper. 'It's about time that he faced up to his responsibilities and went home to face justice,' the newspaper was told.

The *Daily Record* team followed Watt around for a time before they alerted Spanish police. They then watched as armed police took him into custody in the street near his apartment. The stunned fugitive, originally from Uddingston, was led quietly into a police car. Strathclyde Police then began extradition procedures to have him brought home.

In December 2002, he finally faced a Scottish judge and jury. It was claimed by Watt's counsel that witnesses had stated that both men had driven 'like boy racers'. The prosecutor argued that:

> Watt drove in an extremely dangerous manner and, on at least two occasions, he could have driven on. But he chose to intimidate Mr Millar. Mr Millar chose in a very difficult situation to protect his family and drive faster to get out of danger. It may be that it was not the wisest course of action, but it was in a situation which was not of his making and was out of his hands.

The judge told Watt that he had been 'grotesquely irresponsible' and that the offence was 'done deliberately and involved a number of dangerous manoeuvres.' He sentenced him to five years for causing the death of the boy through dangerous driving and a further six months for failing to appear at his original trial. As the family of his tiny victim wept in the public gallery, Watt waved to his own relatives. Outside the courtroom, Craig Millar said that the sentence was of 'little consequence' to his family. 'What happened has changed our lives forever and no sentence was ever going to change that. It will not bring back Robbie; it will not change what happened that day. There is not a day goes by when we don't think about Robbie and the joy he brought us in his short life.'

Anthony Williams
The laird o' Tomintoul

He smiles out from the yellowing newsprint, a cheerful-looking man, clear intelligence shining behind his gold-rimmed spectacles, resplendent in his traditional Highland dress of kilt and green jacket. But the bright smile and prosperous appearance hid a secret; Lord Anthony Williams was not what he appeared. To the residents of Tomintoul, he was the wealthy benefactor who had brought some much-needed cash and employment to their picturesque Highland village. They knew he was something big in London but that his employment was top secret. Both they and his unsuspecting wife believed the source of his seemingly inexhaustible wealth was a bequest from a rich Scandinavian relative.

It was true that Tony Williams was a highly-paid civil servant and that there was an element of secrecy involved in his work. As deputy establishment officer at Scotland Yard he would have been privy to certain classified matters. He was also a Lord, although his nobility was purchased rather than inherited. His title, the Barony of Chirnside in Berwickshire, was bought at auction in London. But the millions he lavished on properties and business in and around Tomintoul most certainly did not come from a family inheritance. For Lord Williams had been systematically siphoning cash out of a secret police account for years.

It all began with a broken marriage and debts that needed to be cleared. Cash was embezzled from a police charity fund and redistributed to his creditors. The larceny seemed easy and Williams was clever enough to pull it off without being detected. The problem with such endeavour, though, is that it can become habit forming and when he was given responsibility for a special fund established to finance an ultra-secret and long-term operation to fight organised crime, the temptation to dip his fingers in the till proved too much. The operation was so confidential that only Williams knew where the cash was being spent and over the next eleven years he scammed over £5 million. A further £2.5 million actually went into the anti-mob operation.

Although Williams was English, he loved the Scottish Highlands.

Any chance he got, he left his £200,000 detached house in Surrey to come north. He owned a timeshare in the exclusive Craigendarroch estate at Ballater and on one trip he and his second wife, Kay, visited the village of Tomintoul. Now perhaps better known for the frequent references made to it by morning radio's top presenter, Terry Wogan – in particular the mythical Mrs McKay and her flying shovel clearing the frequently snow-blocked roads – the village is a quiet, respectable little place.

Like many another English couple before and since, Tony and Kay Williams fell in love with Tomintoul. In 1987, he bought rundown Mallory cottage for £7,000, then spent almost £400,000 renovating it. It was the beginning of a property-buying frenzy that saw a number of sites saved from rubble and also, it has to be said, creating employment for locals. He bought the village's Clockhouse restaurant, lavishing an astonishing half a million pounds on it. When it reopened in 1989, it was as a French-style bistro with its own bakery. He paid well over the odds for the failing Gordon Arms hotel and the Grouse's Nest pub, then pumped almost £2 million into their restoration. He also added a derelict bus station and an adjacent bungalow as well as the disused village fire station to his list of holdings. Finally, he bought the Old Manse of Creggan, a beautiful three-storey stone cottage to which he intended to retire. He used the manse as his headquarters when in Scotland. But Scotland was not the only country to receive attention; he treated himself to a £200,000 villa in Spain in case he felt the need for a bit of sun, sea and sangria.

However, all was not going well with his businesses, although with the seemingly inexhaustible supply of cash at his beck and call, Williams was not overly concerned. However, he did manage to talk David Abdy into leaving his job as restaurant manager at the success-ful Craigendarroch country club to come to Tomintoul and take over the running of the ailing restaurant and hotel. Mr Abdy's expertise helped to reverse the fortunes of the businesses and he was also made a director of Williams's company, Tomintoul Enterprises Ltd (TEL). His father, John, also moved to the village and bought the local post office and shop.

Tony Williams had been very lucky so far but it could not last. Although the Metropolitan Police and the government had no idea their accountant was skimming millions from the fund – and leading a double life as lord of the manor in Scotland – time was running out for the Baron of Chirnside. The end came when the local Clydesdale Bank grew suspicious of some of the cheques going through his account and tipped off the Scotland Yard fraud squad. The whole scheme was then uncovered and officers caught up with Williams at his English home in New Malden.

The news that Lord Williams was an embezzler hit Tomintoul hard. He may have pumped £5 million into the area but his company, TEL, was left with £200,000 of debts to local suppliers. To some, though, he was seen more of a Robin Hood than a Robbing Pseud. 'It was only government money anyway,' one local shopkeeper told *The Herald*. 'It is as well spent in Tomintoul as anywhere else.' The shopkeeper also said that maybe Williams would come back to the village on his release. 'We'll be waiting to welcome him,' he said.

Another local trader also showed support for the disgraced accountant. 'He didn't do anyone any harm,' he said. 'He was quite a quiet fellow and I am certain he was a bit of a romantic. He changed things, and Tomintoul, for the better.'

The local minister also felt that Williams had done good things but conceded it was too early to say for sure what his legacy would be. One villager, though, had no doubt. 'He saved a couple of buildings that were falling down and becoming eyesores,' he told *The Herald*. 'That's the only legacy, apart from giving everyone something to talk about in the pub.' He went on to say that Williams had been like a man playing Monopoly, only with real houses and real money. But now he had landed on the square marked 'go to jail'.

While Williams lay on remand awaiting trial and sentence, David Abdy set about trying to safeguard the businesses he and the staff had worked so hard to turn around. Backed by the National Westminster Bank, he took control of the restaurant and hotel and prepared to keep them in profit.

In May 1995, Williams sat in the dock in London's Old Bailey to hear a judge tell him that the money he stole was 'used for personal advantage in a luxurious lifestyle and the acquisition of properties and business. The aggrandisement was shown in the assumption of a baronial title.'

He sentenced Williams to seven-and-a-half years. The accused had sat in court meekly listening to the comments, a holdall and carrier bag at his feet filled with what he could take with him to jail. He had pled guilty to nineteen charges and asked for an incredible 535 more to be taken into account, so had been expecting jail time, no doubt, but his stunned reaction showed he had not expected quite so much. As he left the court to begin his new life inside, he forgot to pick up his belongings. He was told by his escort that his new life would not include servants to carry his bags.

The fallout from his embezzlement hit the Metropolitan Police. Pertinent questions were asked about the audit systems and the degree of trust placed in one person. 'It is to be hoped,' lectured the judge, 'that never again will any individual, however highly respected, be put in a comparable situation in regard to public money.' The police were quick to point out that, even though the cash had been plundered from the organised-crime crackdown fund, the operation had not been compromised by the scandal. Williams had used the fact that it was a highly confidential project to mask his eleven-year scam. The affair had deeply embarrassed Scotland Yard, which prides itself on catching thieves rather than harbouring them. However, the Metropolitan Police commissioner told the press:

> Confidentiality must never be an excuse for inadequate financial controls. Immediately the fraud came to light, a full audit was launched of all financial procedures and controls in respect of confidential operations. The review had established that there was no evidence of any other theft, corruption or fraud and there were no similar weaknesses in the financial controls of other accounts.

Be that as it may, it was estimated that only about £1 million was likely to be clawed back. The recovery process was no doubt helped by the sale of the Gordon Arms hotel and the Clockhouse restaurant.

John Winning

The great escaper

The acquittal of 'Gypsy' Winning for murder was just one twist in the convoluted tale of violent death that was the Paddy Meehan case. Safe-blower Meehan had been convicted of murdering 72-year-old Rachel Ross in 1969 during a robbery in the Ayr home she shared with her husband, Abraham Ross, a bingo-hall owner. Meehan's partner in this particular crime, it was claimed, was Englishman James Griffiths. Although sentenced to life for the murder of Mrs Ross, Meehan continued to insist he was innocent, that he and Griffiths had been in Stranraer at the time planning a robbery. Griffiths could have provided corroboration had he not gone on a crazed shooting spree in Glasgow, killing one man and injuring others. He was prevented from causing more mayhem when he was shot dead by armed police.

And so Meehan sat in prison, his hopes of being believed alternately raised by various inquiries and then dashed as the establishment fell in line behind the authorised version of the facts. That changed when Glasgow crook William 'Tank' McGuinness was found beaten and unconscious in an East End street in March 1976. There were those who said that he and another man were the real culprits responsible for the Rachel Ross murder and for thirteen days police sat by his bedside hoping he would emerge from his coma and gasp a few words about the Ross murder or his own misfortune.

But McGuinness breathed his last without a dramatic deathbed statement. However, he had earlier confessed his involvement in the crime to his lawyer, Joseph Beltrami, and had stated categorically that Meehan had not been in the house in Ayr seven years before. Mr Beltrami, shackled by the rules of lawyer-client confidentiality, could not repeat this information – until McGuinness died. Then the solicitor could come forward and begin the process that led to Meehan being pardoned for a crime he did not commit. Another man named in McGuinness's confession was subsequently tried but the charges against him were found not proven.

Meanwhile, Glasgow police had another murder on their hands.

Someone had kicked the Tank to death and the finger of suspicion was aimed firmly at his old pal, John 'Gypsy' Winning.

They called him Gypsy because he had Romany blood in his veins and he loved the open air, even though he enjoyed a mere four years in total out of prison from the age of twenty. When free, he lived in a succession of caravans. It was his nature that led him into crime and it was his hatred of being penned up that led to him becoming known as the 'Great Escaper'. In all, he made eight bids for freedom, either from jail or from custody. Each time, though, he was caught.

His first notable escape was in 1954 when, aged twenty-five, he was convicted of assault and robbery. During a transfer of prisoners between Barlinnie in Glasgow and Saughton in Edinburgh, he and another prisoner overpowered the driver and their guards before fleeing. He was at liberty for eleven days before he was caught, literally with his trousers down, when an off-duty cop recognised him in a Turkish baths in Glasgow's East End.

In 1957, he once again made off from a prison bus, this time taking him from Peterhead, near Aberdeen, to Glasgow. When the bus slowed down behind a tram, Winning and another man managed to unshackle their handcuffs, smash a window and leap out. He hid out in a flat Maryhill, in the north-west of Glasgow, until cops were tipped-off. When they raided the tenement flat, they thought it was empty and believed their bird had flown. However, one eagle-eyed officer noticed that a television set and a carpet were out of place and when these were moved, and loose floorboards lifted, they found the Gypsy hiding underneath.

In 1960, he escaped from Barlinnie with Tank McGuinness. Winning was at the time awaiting trial on a housebreaking charge and he and his pal were being housed on the third floor of the jail's remand wing, C hall. Their escape was fairly traditional – they fashioned a rope from bed sheets and lowered themselves to the ground. A rope had been hidden outside and they used it to scale the prison wall and dart into a waiting car. This time, he managed to evade recapture for three months.

One year later, he found himself back in Peterhead and he seized an opportunity to scale a fence and cheekily drive off in an official prison car. He did not get far, though, before he was once again back in custody.

But his greatest escape was in relation to his murder charge – and he didn't even need to file through a single bar. The prosecution contended that he had arrived in Springfield Road by car with Tank and had then proceeded to beat and kick him to death. They backed up their contention by pointing out that traces of the dead man's rare blood type had been found on one of Gypsy's coats. Although they could suggest no motive for the murder, they did point out that McGuinness had felt like a hunted man in the weeks prior to his death. On one occasion, someone had broken into his home and discharged a firearm. There is a gangland tradition that a man marked for death will be led to it by a friend or at least someone he trusts. On occasion, it is that friend who will carry out the hit. This was either such a situation, or there had been a falling out among thieves and Winning had got the better of his former partner-in-crime.

Winning denied killing his old pal and his defence asked why, if their client had kicked a man to death, there was no blood on any of his shoes. There were no eyewitnesses to the alleged attack whereas they could produce a witness to an earlier event which explained the blood on Winning's coat. McGuinness had been involved in a fight with another man and Winning had stepped in to break it up. Tank's nose had been bloodied and some of that could have spattered onto the fabric of the Gypsy's coat.

Despite his strong defence Winning could still have gone down for murder – men have been found guilty on even flimsier evidence – but then the Crown had to admit to a fatal error in its case. The blood sample taken from the dead body had not been recorded properly: the legally required label that forms part of the chain of evidence had not been signed or witnessed by the police present at either the post mortem or the pathologist. Therefore, the Crown could not legally establish that the sample lodged in evidence was, in fact, McGuiness's blood.

In August 1976, Winning's murder trial came to a dramatic end after only two days. He was cleared of the charge and walked from court a free man. On the courtroom steps he spoke to the reporters, saying: 'The Tank was my best friend. In twenty-four years I never had so much as an argument with him.' He had committed crimes with the man, had sat beside him in court and had escaped with him from the jail. 'You can't get closer to a man than that,' he said.

Fourteen years later, aged fifty-one, John Gypsy Winning fought his last fight and this time there was to be no escape. At a drunken party in a cottage in Dunfermline he got into an argument with another man known as 'the Nailer' and died as a result of the subsequent scrap. Witnesses said that although Winning started the fight, what exactly transpired was unclear. Even the accused could not remember how it all happened. The man was sentenced to thirty months for culpable homicide after the judge took into account that the deceased was 'a man of violence'.

The Great Escaper had failed to avoid the Grim Reaper.

Clive Winter

A double life

In eighteenth-century Edinburgh, the city was scandalised by the revelation that a respectable local businessman and town worthy, Deacon William Brodie, had a dark secret. By day he was a successful cabinet-maker, property owner and council official; by night he was a housebreaker and debaucher. The story of Brodie haunted Robert Louis Stevenson and it inspired his celebrated horror tale *Dr Jekyll and Mister Hyde*.

More than two hundred years after Brodie ended his life on the gallows, Edinburgh was once again the scene of a bizarre tale in which a respected public servant seemed to be leading a double life. Although the allegations of violent attacks against complete strangers and intimidation did not shock the hardened public of the twentieth century quite as much as Brodie's adventures had, they still commanded a great deal of headline space. For, according to one witness, Clive Winter believed he would never be caught simply because of who, or what, he was.

Portsmouth-born Winter was forty-five when the scandal reached the High Court in February 1998. He had already been dismissed from his highly-paid job as secretary of Lothian and Borders health board in March the previous year after being charged with a variety of offences, including a number of assaults, which took place between September 1996 and February 1997. Until then, he had been the third highest-ranking manager in the service, earning £47,000 a year. Graham Bell, QC, prosecuting, told the court, 'You may think this is a somewhat extraordinary case and you may think that some of the evidence you have heard beggars belief.' The accused certainly claimed that the evidence against him was unbelievable, for he denied all the charges, claiming alibi and accusing Crown witnesses of lying. In the end, as always, it was up to a jury to decide. But even after that, there were questions.

There were seven charges in total at the start of the trial. The first related to an attack on a man named Tony Chan in his own home. Mr

Chan was a fan of the *Star Wars* movies and he had advertised a variety of memorabilia for sale. In court, the 26-year-old man said Winter and another man, Paul Davidson, arrived at his home with a view to buy the material. As Mr Chan bent to put the items into a bag, he spotted, out of the corner of his eye, the man he identified as Winter pulling a black object from his pocket. At the time he was not sure exactly what the object was but he later said it could have been a handgun that police showed him.

As Winter moved in on him, Mr Chan said he could see 'the hatred, the wickedness, the look of murder in his eyes, like he was possessed by something'. Then he felt two blows to the back of his head and Winter told the younger man to grab him. 'Both of them were pushing me down,' he told the court. 'I was thinking, "They are going to kill me." They were attacking me with full force, with all their might, no wishy-washy stuff, with fists, feet everything.'

His life, he said, flashed before his eyes and he was convinced that these men intended to kill him. But then something happened. 'You might think I am stupid, mad, but I saw a flash of light and I do not know where I got the energy or power from. I shot up and said, "In the name of Lord Jesus Christ, cast you out." ' Amazingly, the two men left. Mr Chan was under no illusion over what happened that day. He had seen demons in these men. 'If it was not for the intervention of something else, I would have died that day.'

Although he had been spared, the victim still felt he had been stripped of his dignity and self-respect. He had not only been damaged physically but also psychologically by the attack. He later felt suicidal.

Another witness against Winter was Leslie Malone, a 23-year-old management-services officer with the health board, who, the prosecution insisted, had been coerced into becoming one of Winter's gang. Malone knew Paul Davidson, another health-board employee, and the man who was also implicated in the attack on Tony Chan. It was Malone's contention that the three of them attacked strangers. He, however, insisted he had been forced into the attacks.

He said that on one occasion Davidson picked him up in a car. The two of them worked part-time at Tynecastle stadium, home to Heart of Midlothian FC, and Malone thought that was where they were headed. But Winter was in the car and instead of Tynecastle they drove to the Dalry area of Edinburgh where Malone waited while the other two men got out. A few minutes later, Malone claimed, they came back with blood smeared on their hands. Winter also had a knife, covered in blood, which he wiped off with a rag before throwing it out of the car window. Someone had 'ripped Paul off', Malone said he was told, and Winter had slashed him on both cheeks.

This charge, however, was dropped midway through the trial because there was no corroborative evidence. No slashing was reported and it later emerged that Winter was prepared to prove he was elsewhere on each of the Saturdays that the alleged incident could have taken place. Had he been able to place that evidence before the jury, he later argued, he could have seriously weakened Malone's credibility over his testimony regarding other charges.

Malone claimed that, through fear, he took part in a number of attacks on complete strangers. These attacks were allegedly committed 'whenever they had the urge'. A man was assaulted in toilets near Edinburgh's North Bridge. A journalist was attacked on Fleshmarket Steps near to the offices of *The Scotsman*. On New Year's Day, a man was picked at random in the streets and attacked by the three of them, according to Malone. Davidson went up to him and shook his hand to wish the compliments of the season, then started hitting him. Malone admitted kicking the victim's legs. Then, he alleged, Winter joined in as the man lay on his side. 'He kicked him in the face. I could hear the thud. It made me feel sick.'

Throughout the alleged spree of violence, the witness stated, Clive Winter insisted that he would never face trial for the crimes. 'Clive came into my office a number of times and said nobody would ever catch him because of who he was,' Malone said. 'Nobody would ever be believed if they ever went to the authorities.'

Finally, Malone and his mother put that claim to the test when they appeared at St Leonard's police station to reveal the incredible tale to police officers. He told them that his tyres had been slashed and the words 'You're next' had been scrawled on a wall near to his home. Malone was given immunity from prosecution in return for his evidence. The defence argued he had implicated his boss to save his own skin, but he strongly denied this.

Paul Davidson also gave evidence against Winter. He had already pleaded guilty to six charges and been sentenced to three-and-a-half years. He underlined the random nature of the assaults by saying that they had targeted Tony Chan for 'no reason'. It was claimed that Winter had some sort of hold over the younger man, which he used to manipulate him. Davidson's rise from kitchen porter to middle manager with the health service may well have been due to his mentor's influence. He was described as 'the clansman' to Winter's 'chieftain'.

Winter denied everything. He lodged special defences of alibi and incrimination to most of the charges. On three of the charges – the one relating to Malone's claim over the bloodstained knife, the assault on the man in the public toilet and a third charge of conspiring to assault a total of nine named persons – the judge upheld a defence submission of no case to answer. The trial proceeded based on the pistol-whipping of Tony Chan, a further two assaults and a conspiracy along with Davidson to break into the home of a colleague. The prosecution contended that they had found copies of keys to the man's house in Winter's office, along with a list of items to be stolen. They also found a replica gun in a cupboard to which only Winter had access. Mr Chan later said this could have been the weapon used in his assault.

In Winter's home in Learmonth Terrace – which the gay man shared with his long-term partner – they found a variety of disturbing videos which police described as 'quite frightening'. On the face of it, possession of a video of the BBC film *The Firm*, which dealt with football violence, and the Australian movie *Romper Stomper*, about gang violence, is nothing sinister. Many people will have such films in their video collection. However, when it was considered that the first told of a seemingly respectable middle-aged man's obsession with violence and the second featured brutal attacks on Orientals, prosecutors drew certain parallels. He also had a video on the right-wing group, Combat 18, which took its name from the numerical position of Adolf Hitler's initials in the alphabet, as well as a documentary on real-life executions. Again, possession of these videos does not necessarily mean Winter was guilty.

It was the evidence of his alleged accomplices Malone and Davidson – along with that of Mr Chan – that brought him down. It was his possession of the replica firearm and the keys that supported their evidence. In February 1998, Winter was found guilty after a five-day trial and sentenced to four-and-a-half years in jail.

After the case, Davidson's mother said, 'I think he just twisted Paul around his little finger and he was definitely the ringleader. He had a stupid, silly, wee boy on his hands. He knew he was easily led and took advantage of it. He was a very strong character who must have got his kicks out of assaulting people.' Davidson's sister went on, 'Justice has been done because we have an evil man off the streets now.'

Police believed that Winter was 'sheer evil'. Officers who dealt with him also believed that his double life extended to deluding himself that he was innocent. 'He would look you straight in the eye and say black was white,' said one. 'He never wavered from his denials. He thought he was untouchable.'

Clive Winter, who continued to proclaim his innocence, was not finished with the legal system. In 2002, by then a free man, he appealed against his conviction, contending that his lawyers had not pressed his alibi defence on Malone's claim over the bloodstained-knife incident. Although that charge had been dismissed, Winter insisted he had cast-iron alibis for any of the dates it was supposed to have taken place. Had Winter's defence pursued Malone over the exact date, then the young man's credibility would have taken a severe knock and the jury would have been bound to have kept that in mind when considering Malone's testimony over the other street assaults. The appeal-court judges agreed and ruled that the failure to adhere to Winter's specific instructions regarding the alibi had resulted in a miscarriage of justice. His convictions for the two assaults were therefore quashed.

However, the convictions for the attack on Mr Chan and the conspiracy to break into the colleague's home still stood. Winter had been identified by Mr Chan, could not properly explain why he had the pistol in his possession and his claim that the duplicate keys in the conspiracy charge had been planted were not accepted.